New in this s

Information on two revived ancient pilgrimage routes! The via
Francigena transverses Italy from the northwest Alps to Rome,
and the Rieti Valley also has it's own sacred path linking the
sanctuaries visited by St. Francis. Read more on page 249.

What others are saying about this book:

"*The Pilgrim's Italy* is a joyous addition to the growing literature of
soulful travel guides. I recommend it to anyone who wants to turn
his or her travels into a sacred journey."

—Phil Cousineau, author of *The Art of Pilgrimage*
and *The Book of Roads*

"A lovely guide for the traveler drawn to the spiritual side of Italy."

—James O'Reilly, editor of *Travelers' Tales Tuscany*

"What an inspiring book! Although there are a few spiritually
oriented travel books, none as clearly address how truthseekers
can attune inwardly to the sacred sites in order to experience them
on the deepest levels."

—Norman Snitkin, East West Bookshop of Seattle

"James and Colleen Heater offer seekers of all faiths a compelling
and comprehensive guide to both the inner and outer realms of
Italy's great spiritual sites."

—Deborah Willoughby, Editor, *Yoga International*

"Saints and mystics through the centuries have been living examples of holiness, yet they were not born saints. They attained a life
of perfection through prayer, meditation and goodwill. *The Pilgrim's
Italy* will help pilgrims learn more about the saints they venerate,
and how to make better use of pilgrimage, by encouraging silence
and meditation on the lives and teachings of the saints."

—Maximilian Mizzi, O.F.M. Conv.
Delegate General for Ecumenism and Interreligious Dialogue

The Pilgrim's

ITALY

A Travel Guide
to the Saints

James & Colleen Heater

The Pilgrim's
ITALY

A Travel Guide
to the Saints

JAMES & COLLEEN HEATER

Foreword by Jyotish Novak

Inner Travel Books
Nevada City, California

Cover Design: Sara Cryer
Interior Design: C. A. Schuppe/Colleen Heater
Maps: James Heater
Photographs by the authors unless otherwise noted
Printed in Canada
ISBN 978-0-9719860-2-2
Inner Travel Books
14618 Tyler Foote Road, Suite 171
Nevada City, CA 95959 USA

Toll free telephone: 866-715-8670
info@innertravelbooks.com
www.innertravelbooks.com

Distributed in North America by SCB Distributors
Distributed in UK & Europe by Deep Books Ltd

Previous edition was catalogued as follows:

Heater, James
    The pilgrim's Italy: a travel guide to the saints /
James and Colleen Heater. – 1st ed.
    p.cm.
    Includes bibliographical references and index.

    1. Christian pilgrims and pilgrimages—Italy—
Guidebooks. 2. Christian shrines—Italy—Guidebooks.
3. Christian saints—Cult—Italy—Guidebooks. 4. Italy
—Guidebooks.   I. Heater, Colleen. II. Title.
BX2320.5.I8H43 2003   263'.04245

Front Cover: Blessed Angela of Foligno, from a fresco in the Convento di San Bartolomeo di Marano, Foligno, titled "Pilgrimage to Assisi" by Ippolitto da Orvieto, eighteenth century, courtesy of Comune di Foligno.

Scripture quotations are taken from *American Standard Version Bible*, unless noted (NIV), in which case they are taken from the *Holy Bible, New International Version*, 1984 by International Bible Society.

Every effort has been made to provide accurate information. The authors and publisher accept no responsibility for loss, injury, or inconvenience sustained by any person using this book. Please reconfirm details before making your trip.

To Paramhansa Yogananda
Our guiding light.

ITALIA

N

Contents

Foreword

Once in a while a book comes along that opens up a whole new way of seeing things. *The Pilgrim's Italy* is one of these rare books. There are numerous travel books covering every aspect of travel, but only a small number of books that direct us to sacred places. Of these few, this book is the only one I have found that gives instruction on how to get the most out of our experience. It offers methods for tuning into the saint's essence, where the living presence of these great souls can lift us into spiritual realms we never dreamed existed. Pilgrimage is so much more than just travel mixed with a little history and a few prayers. It is an inner journey meant to help us explore our own souls.

My own experience with pilgrimage started in Assisi, Italy nearly twenty years ago. My wife and I had recently moved to Italy to help start a meditation center on behalf of Ananda, a spiritual community based on meditation. The transition to a new country and a new language was difficult in the first months. Fortunately, in the midst of our busy schedule we found time to visit Assisi, the spiritual heart of Italy and the home of St. Francis. We arrived feeling a bit frayed but immediately felt a tangible blessing. As the next few days passed we felt more and more uplifted and empowered. Interestingly, my wife and I both had the same inward perception—St. Francis had not only welcomed and blessed us personally, but had welcomed the art and science of meditation, which we were helping to introduce in Italy.

Our experience with St. Francis was so powerful that we knew we had to share it with others. A few months later we organized a pilgrimage for American friends to visit Italy. This was Ananda's first formal pilgrimage, and since that time we have led pilgrimages not just to Italy, but also to numerous holy places around the world. I have personally seen, for many hundreds of people, the powerful benefits of pilgrimage. I have seen it enrich their lives, enhance their spiritual progress and awaken their souls to a new, deeper reality.

While on pilgrimage, the saints become our guides, not just our destination. We can do much more than glimpse the saints through their writings or through the dusty windows of history. If we are quiet enough, we are able to listen to the whispers of their living guidance in the present. When we become calm enough, we discover not only how to meditate on the saints but *with* the saints. Their very thoughts become our thoughts, and their inspiration becomes our own.

This very practical spiritual travel guide provides all the information needed to experience more than twenty of the most important sacred places in Italy, and many lesser known but equally compelling shrines. By learning to visit the shrines *with* the saints, the renowned beauty and spirituality of Italy comes alive in a new and unique way. *The Pilgrim's Italy* is truly a guide for the body, mind and, most importantly, the soul, helping us to rise above the usual frantic pace of an overloaded travel itinerary. It tells us to slow down and teaches us that real pilgrimage only starts once we stop.

Jyotish Novak
Author of *How to Meditate*

Introduction

Why are two American yogis interested in the Catholic saints of Italy? Our spiritual teacher, Paramhansa Yogananda, taught us to read and study the lives of the saints, so that we might be inspired by them, emulate them and strive to become more saint-like ourselves. Following this advice, we decided to make our honeymoon a pilgrimage, and planned our trip around visiting shrines in Italy.

While preparing for our trip, we discovered that most travel guides are not useful for pilgrimage. They describe in great detail the art and architecture of a church or shrine, but rarely mention the saint to whom the church is dedicated. We managed to find a few travel guides on pilgrimage, talked to some friends who made suggestions, and researched on the Internet. We were frustrated with trying to integrate information from so many diverse sources, and realized there was a need for one concise pilgrimage guide for Italy. We wanted a book that contained detailed information about each shrine, great directions and maps, and helpful Italian phrases. Such a guide would make pilgrimage to Italy more rewarding and encourage more people to experience the joys of sacred travel.

While on our honeymoon, we gathered information everywhere we went. The following year we returned to Italy to visit over thirty-five additional shrines. We soon discovered that Italy must be home to more saints than any other country! Though we have not determined exactly how many Italian saints there are, let's just say there are too many to describe in one book. To narrow it down, we decided to include only those saints who experienced direct communion with the Divine, and with whom we felt a special connection. We then continued our research and began writing.

Our descriptions of the saints and their shrines include some of our personal experiences, but remember everyone's experience will be unique. There are tangible blessings to be received at each and every shrine—we only have to be open to the possibility.

We have discovered that we feel a saint's spiritual power and blessings more easily when we create an inner environment that invites them to visit. We do this by stilling our hearts and minds in meditation. When we are receptive, the saints transmit their love of God to us as a taste of what awaits us if we stay centered in God. Many spiritually minded people are seeking profound and transformational experiences to inspire them on their spiritual paths, and we are offering straightforward tools that have helped us to realize this goal. Even without visiting a shrine, we have found inspiration when reading about the life of a saint, and begin to imagine how it would be to live for God alone, as they have done.

Though the saints in this book are Roman Catholic, we have written for people of all faiths. In this age of expanding spiritual awareness and interest in understanding different religions, it becomes apparent that most religions and faiths share basic beliefs. We believe that Truth is universal and transcends religious boundaries. God-realized souls or saints can share that Truth with us, regardless of their, or our, particular faith. To listen for this guidance, our hearts and minds must be still. The techniques we offer will enable you to achieve this stillness.

In this second edition, we have updated email addresses, websites and phone numbers. Additions include the new church of St. Pio of Pietrelcina that seats 8,000, and information on the Via Francigena, the ancient pilgrim road that leads to Rome. New resources have been included on our website for easy reference when making your pilgrimage plans.

Our hope is that this travel guide will provide the inspiration, tools and information you need to create a more meaningful, and possibly profound experience when visiting the saints and their shrines. May the saints of all religions bless you on your spiritual journey.

History of Pilgrimage

In our busy world many people are searching to find balance between their inner spiritual lives and their outer material ones. Pilgrimage is one way to energize our search for deeper meaning and purpose in our lives. Through pilgrimage, the spirit is renewed and our general outlook becomes uplifted, changing the way we look at everyday life. The footsteps of pilgrims have echoed continuously through the halls of time, for by visiting sacred sites we are able to immerse ourselves in their powerful vibrations and have a direct personal experience of divinity. This experience is the power of pilgrimage and why it is a major tenet of most religions.

Pilgrimage has been practiced since the sun first rose on human civilization. Before recorded history, the faithful devotees of the Indus valley, people now known as Hindus, made sacred treks to the revered sites of India. The Hindu spiritual life is a process of reaching complete union or oneness with the Divine, a state of consciousness known as *samadhi*, and pilgrimage has historically been a means of seeking this deep connection. Modern Hindus continue to take pilgrimage very seriously, often traveling to one of the seven sacred rivers, seven liberation-giving cities, or other spiritual sites found throughout their ancient land. For the Hindu, where one "goes" on pilgrimage is not as important as how one follows the "way of the pilgrim." The goal is to have a personal experience of God through a life-changing encounter with the Divine and to experience God as an inner reality.

While pilgrimage in Hinduism relates to universal sacred sites and temples of the deities, the Buddhist tradition of pilgrimage is associated with the specific places important to the life of the Buddha. Following the death of the Buddha in 544 B.C., the sites marking the four sacred events of his life were enshrined. These four primary sites of veneration are the birthplace of the Buddha in Lumbini, Nepal; the site of his enlightenment under the Bo Tree located in Bodh Gaya, India; the locale of his first teaching in Sarnath, India; and the place of his death, or final *nirvana*, in Kushinagar, India. In addition, the ashes from his funeral pyre were distributed to eight stupas, or burial mounds, throughout India, which have also become pilgrimage destinations. A Buddhist pilgrim seeks to abandon the material world and dive into a deeper understanding and assimilation of the teachings of the Buddha. The sacred journey is a means of purification and elimination of karma due to past actions, leading to enlightenment or nirvana, the ultimate goal for every Buddhist. With the blessings of the Buddha and all the great souls that pay homage at these shrines, the holy sites continue to be vibrant spots of power and enlightenment even 2500 years after the Buddha's exit from this world.

Every aspirant in the Islamic tradition is encouraged to make a once-in-a-lifetime pilgrimage to Mecca, if physically and financially feasible. One of the Seven Pillars of Islam is *Hajj*, or pilgrimage to the Haram mosque in the Saudi Arabian holy city of Mecca, in order to pray and commune with God. Muslims descend on Mecca from all over the globe to commune together in peace,

Chiostro del Paradiso, Amalfi

for peace is the dominant theme of their pilgrimage. They seek peace with Allah, with their own souls, with one another, and with all living creatures.

This search for peace actually has its roots in Judaism, as the prophet Abraham and his son Ishmael originally founded the Ka'ba in Mecca two millennia before Christ. They initiated the rituals that are now an integral part of Islam. Following their inception, these rites were practiced in increasingly lower degrees of devotion until the time of the Prophet Mohammed in 622 A.D. Mohammed re-introduced the importance of pilgrimage and specifically the holy significance of Hajj in Islamic life. The Hajj is the peak of religious experience for the Muslim, and over two million pilgrims partake in the rites every year. Jerusalem is also an important pilgrimage destination for followers of Islam, for The Dome of the Rock is the site of Mohammed's ascension into heaven to commune with Allah, Abraham, Moses, Jesus and other prophets, and is said to be the place of Final Judgment.

Pilgrimage in the Jewish tradition also began with Abraham, as he was the earliest to journey into the desert to seek communion with God. Centuries later, Moses led the definitive pilgrimage when he guided the children of Israel out of Egypt and into the Sinai in search of the Promised Land. This pilgrimage was a way of life for forty years, and formed the very basis of the Hebrew nation.

The history of Jerusalem also plays an important and telling role in the life of the Jewish people, for it parallels their history as a people and relates directly to their practice of pilgrimage. The repeated cycle of construction and destruction of the Temple coincided with the acceptance and rejection of the Jewish people: a cycle that has repeated itself throughout history to the present day.

David first conquered the Jebusite city of Jerusalem in the eleventh century B.C. His son Solomon erected the first temple to house the Ark of the Covenant in the tenth century B.C. Jerusalem became a primary pilgrimage destination of the Jewish people, for all devout Jews were expected to visit the holy site yearly. In 586 B.C., Nebuchadnezzar of Babylonia destroyed the temple and the Jews were exiled from the city. But fifty years later, the Persians gained control of Jerusalem and welcomed the Hebrews back, allowing them to rebuild the temple. Thus, the tradition of faith and pilgrimage was

maintained, and even flourished, over the next four centuries, culminating with the rise in prominence of a Roman Jerusalem under the
leadership of Herod the Great at the time of Christ. A new and
lavish temple was constructed during Herod's reign and this was the
site of many visits by Jesus, as he attended holy days in Jerusalem with
his family and later with his disciples.

This temple, too, was destroyed when the Romans attacked the
rebellious city in 70 A.D. and burned the temple to the ground. The
Jews were eventually exiled from Jerusalem in 135 A.D. following
another uprising, and were not allowed to return until the Muslims
captured the city in 638 A.D. The Jews did not rebuild the temple,
but did build an underground synagogue at the West Wall of the old
temple. Their peaceful coexistence with the Muslims lasted another
four centuries, until the crusaders conquered the Holy Land in 1099
and decimated the Jewish population, again exiling them from their
sacred spot of pilgrimage. They were allowed to return after ten years,
and were accepted into the city on a limited basis, but did not regain
control of their homeland until the mid-twentieth century. Even with
the forming of the state of Israel in 1947, the temple has never been
rebuilt, but the West Wall is still an active and revered shrine, a
central focus of Jewish pilgrimage.

The first Christian pilgrims were those early members of the
Christian community who sought out the sites of the martyred apostles

Basilica di San Francesco, Assisi

and their slain followers. This outward veneration was an infrequent occurrence, as it often involved traveling long distances and meeting in great secrecy. With the acceptance of Christianity by the Emperor Constantine in 314 A.D., and the pilgrimage of his mother Helen to the Holy Land, many Christians came out of hiding. Helen traveled to Jerusalem and Galilee, being one of the first to seek out the sacred spots of Jesus' life. She encountered the original cross and many relics of his life and death, and returned to Constantinople with these treasures in tow.

After the fifth century, the Church of Rome began to separate from the patriarchates of Constantinople, Jerusalem, Antioch, and Alexandria. By 1054 A.D., the Church of Rome broke off permanently, dividing into what is known as the Orthodox Church and the Roman Catholic Church. Many of the same pilgrimage destinations are shared by both churches, most notably, Jerusalem, but there are many sites that are unique to Eastern Orthodoxy. These sites include St. Catherine's Monastery on Mount Sinai, Mount Athos in Greece, and Aegina, a Greek island where the relics of St. Nectarios are found. Orthodox pilgrims typically attend religious services, partake of the sacraments of Confession and Communion, and venerate the holy icons and relics of the saints.

The Middle Ages were arguably the golden years for Christian pilgrimage in Europe. Christianity was at the center of the Western world in both political and religious terms. The roads of Western Europe were trod by countless pilgrims traveling to sites such as Rome to visit the relics of Saints Peter and Paul, to Santiago de Compostela to visit the tomb of St. James, to Loreto, Walsingham, Monte Sant' Angelo, and to countless other places. The people were eager for direct contact with holiness and for Divine intercession in their lives. This desire was fulfilled by visiting the holy sites, and by praying for forgiveness, grace and miracles in the presence of the saints' relics. The relics carried back from the Holy Land by the Crusaders enlivened the spiritual ambiance of many churches and created vortices of power and prayer. Many roads were built, and inns and churches erected, to accommodate the multitudes traversing the continent in search of inner peace and a touch of sanctity.

This trend continued until the advent of the Reformation at the end of the fifteenth century. With Martin Luther's separation from the Roman Catholic Church and the beginning of the Protestant movement, many people began to look anew at the practices of the Church. Many Protestants held the act of pilgrimage as useless and felt the worship of saints was misguided. Their misunderstanding of the heart-felt devotion of many true pilgrims dampened the pilgrim spirit for years and placed a negative connotation on sacred travel. The ancient tradition was again bolstered by the Catholic Counter-Reformation of the sixteenth century, although the numbers of pilgrims never again approached those of the Middle Ages.

The beginning of the industrial revolution and the age of scientific thought produced another low ebb in spirituality, and it took Divine intervention to awaken those with spiritual inclinations. Many highly publicized apparitions of the Blessed Virgin Mary occurred in the mid-nineteenth century, raising the spiritual consciousness of the masses and starting a new flood of pilgrims to these "modern" holy sites. Blessed Mary's appearance in France at

Fonte Columbo

Rue de Bac in 1830, La Salette in 1846, at Lourdes in 1858 and Pontmain in 1871, sparked a renewed interest in pilgrimage. After the turn of the twentieth century, the apparitions of the Blessed Virgin Mary spread to other countries, at Fatima, Banneau, Beauraing, and later, Medjugorje, inspiring many people to visit new lands and discover the depths of the pilgrimage experience.

Now, in the twenty-first century, this quest for a personal experience of the Divine continues to magnetically attract people of all religions and beliefs. Pilgrimage was enjoying an all-time high in the latter part of the twentieth century until the terrorist attacks of September 11th, 2001, when the world of travel was abruptly derailed. This created only a temporary barrier for pilgrims traveling to other lands, for pilgrimage will always be a source of inspiration as it has been since the dawn of spiritual aspiration. Whenever world events disrupt the flow of international travel, for a time pilgrimage may be more of the heart than of the body, but the longing for God continues uninterrupted. Whether we travel to a sacred site or stay home and read about a saint, our prayers and focused meditations are the most important aspect of inner pilgrimage. The true essence of pilgrimage is always centered at home in one's own heart.

When God spoke to St. Catherine of Siena as recorded in her *Dialogue*, He said, "The eye cannot see, nor the tongue tell, nor can the heart imagine how many paths and methods I have, solely for love and to lead them back to grace so that my truth may be realized in them!" God, the Father, Mother Divine, offers us many paths to satisfy our inner yearning for spiritual wholeness, but it is up to each of us to seek out that infinite source of love, embrace it as our own, and awaken the saint within.

How to Use this Guidebook

The intention of this book is to provide all the information needed to plan a journey of pilgrimage to the shrines of Italy. Before determining the minute details of your pilgrimage, read about the various saints to discover which ones speak to you personally and call you to visit. Then start planning your personal adventure.

The chapters are organized by region and include the cities that are home to the saints and their shrines. The life of each saint is described in a biography, followed by details about the shrines, points of interest, maps and information on getting there. Finally, there is a guide to basic meditation techniques and how to experience the saints. This guide is essential to making your pilgrimage a deep, personal experience.

This book is not intended to be a complete travel reference with lodging, dining, and other general tourist advice. We suggest you purchase a guide that is published yearly; giving all the pertinent and up-to-date information you will need to plan your trip. There are many excellent guidebooks that cater to different budgets and interests, so visit a bookstore with a large travel section and purchase a book that appeals to your brand of travel.

While researching the lives of the saints, we discovered countless interesting facts and numerous discrepancies. The details of the saints' lives, especially those of antiquity, tend to become "legend" over time. We have attempted to be as true to fact as possible. What is important is the inspiration we receive from their lives.

Below is a short description of some of the information provided in each chapter and how it is best utilized.

English/Italian Names First we list the English name of the saint, shrine, region or city, followed by the Italian name. Some names are the same in Italian and English. This was a hard decision, but we wanted to make the book as user friendly as possible and decided on using English first. Just remember to use the Italian version of the name in Italy, or the natives won't understand you.

Maps We have included regional maps to help you get your bearings, and city maps to get you to the shrines. The regional maps are located at the beginning of each section with the cities mentioned in this book underlined. The city maps follow the shrine information with the name of the shrines underlined. If you are driving, you will need a more detailed map. Refer to "Travel Tips" in the appendix for more information on purchasing maps.

Speaking Italian It is wise to know a little Italian when you travel to Italy, even if it's only "please" and "thank you." Purchase a small English/Italian phrasebook before you go. You will be glad you did, especially in small towns where English is not usually spoken. We have included useful Italian phrases in each chapter to help you navigate the shrines themselves. Italians are always very eager to help, so try speaking Italian. They will love you for it. Then, if you are not getting anywhere, ask if they speak English; "Parla inglese?" When all else fails, show them the questions written in Italian, and say "per favore" (please)!

English Spoken We note under "Shrine Information" if English is spoken at a shrine, using the following scale: rarely=most likely not; occasionally=sometimes; and typically=most likely, yes. We are using these vague terms because we have found that the priests and nuns who caretake these shrines are frequently reassigned, and we cannot be sure if an English-speaking person will be there when you visit. In general, the larger the shrine, the greater the likelihood of finding English-speaking personnel. Usually, you won't need to speak to anyone, but always have your phrase book handy.

Websites There are countless websites that provide plenty of information about anything Italian. They a great resource for pilgrimage planning. The websites listed in each chapter and in the appendix are in English, unless we make a note of them being "Italian." On the

Internet, the British flag or the words "English Version" are used to indicate an English website. Sometimes a website in Italian will have English for portions of the site while the rest is in Italian. At times the English icon is at the bottom of the page, or hiding out in some odd place, so be adventuresome. If you really want the information on an Italian-only site, you can use Google search and click on "translate this page."

Kilometers/Miles and European Time We list both kilometers and miles because you will need kilometers while traveling, while miles give you an idea of how far it is in your own frame of reference. Europeans use a 24-hour clock while Americans use a 12-hour clock. We list American time (AM and PM) but you can easily convert to European time by adding 12 hours to the PM times. For communication purposes, Italy is 9 hours ahead of California, 7 hours ahead of Chicago, 6 hours ahead of New York, and 9 hours behind Tokyo.

Accessibility for Travelers with Disabilities More and more travelers with disabilities are making their way to Europe, so we have tried to give as much information as possible on the accessibility of the shrines. We noticed on our recent trips to Italy that many churches are installing accessible entrances, or are in the process, so this is a moving target. We list, to the best of our knowledge, if a shrine is accessible under "Shrine Information." Always contact the church before visiting so you will not be disappointed. If you do not speak Italian, contact the helpful local tourist agencies. Some of the shrines and cities also offer tours planned especially for accessibility. See Resources for "Travelers with Disabilities" in the appendix.

Update/Correct/Contact Us If you find information in this book that has changed or is incorrect, we would appreciate hearing from you at info@innertravelbooks.com. Websites and email addresses can change; contact us at info@innertravelbooks.com, and we will list the new information on our website. When we first started doing research, few churches had e-mail addresses or websites, but now almost all have them, and many have great sites. Also, if you discover a shrine that you feel should be a part of our book, please let us know so we can try to include it in the next edition or add it to our website. We want to provide the most up-to-date information, and we are grateful for your input and feedback! Grazie mille!

Pilgrims, Città di Castello

Apulia

Puglia

Puglia occupies the southeast area of the Italian peninsula. Its long and narrow profile extends from the very southern tip of the "boot heel," north to the "boot spur" of Gargano, whose mountainous terrain juts out into the Adriatic Sea. The region is mostly agricultural, consisting of continuous waves of gently sloping hills surrounded on three sides by the sea. Bari is the only large city and is known for its medieval atmosphere, active seaport and chemical plants. In the northern area of the region, a round land mass called the Gargano rises out of the hot plains of Tavoliere and extends eastward into the Adriatic Sea. This elevated area has offered a refreshing climate to the people of the lower elevations since pre-Roman times. It is here that the small village of San Giovanni Rotondo is found, and where millions of pilgrims come to experience the blessings of St. Pio of Pietrelcina.

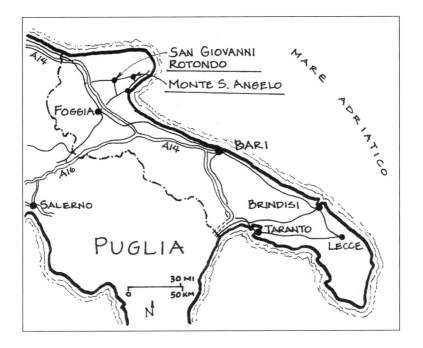

SAN GIOVANNI ROTONDO
St. Pio of Pietrelcina (Padre Pio)
St. Michael the Archangel

San Giovanni Rotondo
Population 25,883

San Giovanni Rotondo rests on the south-facing slope of the Gargano and is primarily known as the resting place of St. Pio. Five to seven million pilgrims make their way to this small, remote town every year to pay homage to the saint at the Church of Saint Pio of Pietrelcina and Our Lady of Grace Shrine. The town revolves around the Shrine and hospital of St. Pio and offers little else of interest. The pilgrimage sites are in the western end of the city, and the district is filled with hotels, restaurants and shops to serve the pilgrims. The Adriatic Sea is a half-hour away, as is the grotto of St. Michael the Archangel, but the powerful presence of the saint from Pietrelcina is what draws people to this sacred place.

SAINT PIO OF PIETRELCINA
San Pio di Pietrelcina 1887–1968

"Through the study of books one seeks God;
by meditation one finds Him."

St. Pio of Pietrelcina

St. Pio is an extraordinary example of a saint who embodied the consciousness of Christ on every level. He lived his life in imitation of Christ to such a degree that he experienced the painful stigmata for fifty-eight years. His mission was one of co-redemption, in that he, as an emissary of Christ, was able to expunge the sins of his spiritual children through his own suffering and his deep connection with God. The importance of his life's mission is emphasized by the interest shown him by

Satan, who physically attacked and tempted him throughout his life. St. Pio's sanctity brought countless souls to God and rescued many from the darkness.

His blessed life began in the southern Italian town of Pietrelcina when Francesco Forgione was born into a family of hard working farmers. His mother initiated him into the spiritual life by introducing him to stories of Jesus, the saints, and the Holy Mother. Even at a young age, Francesco had visions of Mary, whom he called his Celestial Mother. He was a devout child, and would prefer to pray in the local church than play with the other children and risk offending God. At age fifteen, Francesco had a vision of a battle between himself and a dark giant. Assisting at Francesco's side was a being of light, in the form of Jesus. After a tumultuous encounter, the dark force retreated and the brilliant Jesus presented Francesco with a magnificent crown. Christ said to him, "This demon will assault you again, but never doubt my help, I will always be close to you." Thus, Francesco realized that his mission would be a difficult one, but one blessed with the ever-present power of Christ. The following year, Francesco left his home to enter the novitiate at the friary of Morcone, taking the name Fra Pio.

The next years were spent in study and prayer, and Fra Pio dove deep into the teachings of St. Francis. It was during his time as a cleric that he experienced his first bilocation. One night while praying in the choir, he suddenly found himself transported to the distant town of Udine where he witnessed the death of a man, followed by the birth of the man's daughter. Then the Holy Mother appeared to Fra Pio saying he would later meet this girl, and bring her to God. Just as predicted, he met the young girl eighteen years later and became her spiritual mentor, guiding and counseling her for many years.

The year 1910 was a monumental one for Padre Pio, for it was in his twenty-third year that he took his vows as a priest and conducted his first Mass in his hometown of Pietrelcina. It was also the year when he first experienced the stigmata. Initially he felt sharp pains in his feet and hands, and then intense pain in his heart. After their onset, he endured these pains continually. Additionally, once a week he would suffer the crown of thorns and the scourging that Christ received at the hands of Roman soldiers.

These experiences coincided with a mysterious illness that

plagued Padre Pio for many years. Doctors could find nothing wrong, but he was very weak from lung and stomach ailments. In 1916, after several years of alternately living at home and various monasteries, he was assigned to the small Capuchin friary at San Giovanni Rotondo to recover his health. It was here that Padre Pio would spend the remainder of his life fighting for the salvation of souls.

The stigmata were both a blessing and a curse for Padre Pio. Initially, the marks were invisible, and he only felt their presence internally. But, in 1918, he had two visions of a celestial being piercing his body with a blade of light and, following the second vision, he found the stigmata were now manifest on his body, and dripping blood. They would remain this way until his death, fifty years later. The blessing of the stigmata was Padre Pio's ability to take on the sins of his spiritual family through his own suffering, thereby guiding his children more quickly to God. The curse was the response of the Church to his condition, for they treated him with suspicion and mistrust. Padre Pio was the first ordained priest to exhibit the stigmata and this proved to be a bewildering embarrassment to his superiors.

After receiving the stigmata, Padre Pio was examined by doctors and a commission to verify the authenticity of his affliction. Five years later, he was finally allowed to return to serving his congregation—once his wounds were found not to be "supernatural." Padre Pio's sanctity attracted so much attention that the Church again became concerned. For a time, he was banned from giving Mass in public and was not allowed to perform any public ministry. But in 1933, fifteen years after receiving his wounds, Padre Pio was again allowed to fully participate in Mass and hear confessions. Through all these tribulations, Padre Pio was obedient to his superiors, and readily submitted to their authority. His goal was to be a willing servant of Christ, accepting whatever was placed before him.

Padre Pio lived to serve his spiritual children. People would stand in line for days just to confess to him, for he was able to see directly into their souls and guide them on a righteous path. Once a person became his spiritual child, Padre Pio would do anything in his power to help sanctify his or her soul. When not in the confessional, he was most often deep in prayer, working for the salvation of his family. He was very compassionate when dealing with his children, but he would be very stern if the situation called for it. In the course of his duties,

Padre Pio performed many miracles, predicted the future, bi-located, prayed directly with souls in purgatory, and exorcised demons. Many times he had visions of Satan, and battled courageously with him. These brief but terrifying incidents were always followed by joyful experiences of the presence of Christ, angels and the saints. The one constant for Padre Pio was his connection with Christ.

Padre Pio was so united with Christ and his consciousness that many people actually saw Padre Pio as Jesus while he was giving Mass. Many conversions resulted from these miracles, for people had direct experiences of Christ through him. He once said to a spiritual daughter, "You want to see Jesus? Look at me: you will see Jesus." The yearning to imitate Christ was the driving force in Padre Pio's life. He once wrote his confessor, "A most intense desire to possess Jesus entirely inflames my soul ... It is not me ... but He who is in me and above me."

The decades of constant service took their toll on Padre Pio. He ate very little, for food made him nauseous, so he lived solely through the power of God. As he grew physically weaker, he continued to celebrate Mass, but he did so from a seated position, and after his legs became paralyzed, from a wheelchair. On September 23, 1968, at the age of eight-one, Padre Pio died with the words "Jesus, Mary" on his lips. During the three days he laid in state at Our Lady of Grace Church, more than 100,000 of his spiritual children came for a final visit with their guide. His body was placed in a crypt of the church. The plan is to move the body in the near future to the Church of St. Pio of Pietrelcina. Padre Pio was beatified in May 2000 and canonized June 16, 2002.

Because St. Pio of Pietrelcina lived in the twentieth century, we are fortunate to have many contemporary accounts of his life. His story is not based on legend but on facts—there is no doubt about his sanctity or the miracles he performed. The pilgrim needs only to meditate deeply on this great saint to feel his living presence, for St. Pio continues to bless his "spiritual children" at his shrine in San Giovanni Rotondo.

THE CHURCH OF ST. PIO OF PIETRELCINA
Chiesa San Pio da Pietrelcina

The Shrine to St. Pio consists of buildings from three distinct eras: the original church and convent begun in 1538, the church addition completed in 1959, and the new church completed in 2004. This new church accommodates 8,000 pilgrims inside and 30,000 outside in the square, which gives you an idea of the magnetism of this great saint. In the future, St. Pio's body will be moved to a crypt in the Church of St. Pio, under the Liturgical Hall, while many of his relics will remain in Our Lady of Grace Shrine.

The pilgrim office, "Accoglienza Pellegrini," is on the right-hand side at the entrance to the square of the Church of St. Pio. There you can arrange tours in English.

OUR LADY OF GRACE SHRINE
Santuario Santa Maria delle Grazie

Our Lady of Grace Shrine includes the original church and convent, and the addition built in 1959. St. Pio's cell is in the Convent of Capuchin Minors (Convento dei Frati Minori Cappuccini), and the old church (La chiesa antica) contains the choir loft with the crucifix where St. Pio received the stigmata on September 20, 1918.

To take a self-guided tour of Our Lady of Grace Church, enter on the right side, walk toward the back to the information desk, and ask for a English guide. You will first go downstairs to St. Pio's crypt, then upstairs to his cell, and eventually down some long halls to the choir loft where he received the stigmata. If you can get a seat in this small loft, stay

Santuario Santa Maria delle Grazie

awhile for it is a highlight of the tour. Though many people stream through the loft, it is worth lingering to attempt to feel St. Pio's grace, since he spent a good deal of time here. After you leave the loft, there is a crowded bookstore, where you will have to push your way to the front to buy your items. There are also two other bookstores outside on the square.

The English-speaking office is also a good source of books on St. Pio, but it is not easy to find. Start in the main sanctuary of Our Lady of Grace Church, go to the left hand side of the altar and through a doorway, and then turn right. When you see the Sacristy to your right, there will be a door on your left labeled "English Office." Knock and enter. There will be a table of books in English for sale, and English-speaking people to help you. Phone: 088 2417214 Fax: 088 2417241.

Where is the saint's crypt?
Dov'è la cripta del santo?

Where is the English-speaking office?
Dov'è l'ufficio dove parlano l'inglese?

SHRINE INFORMATION

Shrine: Our Lady of Grace Shrine (Santa Maria della Grazie)

Address: Piazza S. Pio 5, 71013 San Giovanni Rotondo (FG) Italia

Phone: 088 2417500 (pilgrim office) **Fax:** 088 2417555

E-mail: accoglienzapellegrini@padrepio.it (pilgrim office)

Website: www.conventopadrepio.it or www.conventopadrepio.com

Quiet areas for meditation: Because there are many crowds of pilgrims there are not many quiet areas. The loft of the stigmata in our Lady of Grace Church is a special place but rarely quiet. However, the Church of St. Pio has the Chapel of the Eucharist, behind the main altar, accessible to the left of the large organ.

English spoken: The Pilgrim Office, "Accoglienza Pellegrini" on the right-hand side of the entrance to the Church of St. Pio and the "English Office" mentioned above.

Hours: 5:30AM–7:15PM.

Visits to the Stigmata Loft and St. Pio's cell: Weekdays: 7:30AM–12 PM; 3:30PM–6:30 (6 winter).

Mass: Main Church: Sun/Hol: 6AM, 7, 8, 9, 10, 11, 12, 4PM, 5:30, 7; Weekdays 8AM, 9, 10, 11, 12, 5:30PM; Crypt 5:45AM, 7:30, 8:15, 4:15PM, 5:15; Ancient Church 6:30AM, 8:30, 9:30, 4PM, 5.

Feasts and festivities: September 23 — St. Pio's Feast day; May 25 — Birthday; June 16 — Canonization.

Accessibility: There are elevators in the new and old churches.

Tours: Tours can be arranged in the English-speaking office, except on Sundays. Phone ahead: 088 2417500 Fax: 088 2417555 Email: accoglienzapellegrini@padrepio.it.

Bookstore: Two bookstores are in the square across from Our Lady of Grace Shrine, where they sell books in English published by The Voice of Padre Pio, the official magazine of the Capuchin Friars. There is also the bookstore next to the Stigmata Choir Loft. You can pick up a brochure at the English-speaking office for your self-guided tour.

Recommended book: *Padre Pio of Pietrelcina: Memories – Experiences – Testimonials*, by Padre Alberto D'Apolito. There are many other excellent books on St. Pio.

Lodging: None. Sixty hotels and seventy private homes provide lodging in the area. See website under "information" & "hotels."

Directions: Viale Cappuccini dead-ends at Our Lady of Grace Church on Piazzale Santa Maria Della Grazie. But it is best to park in the many parking areas as you approach San Giovanni Rotondo. You will see signs for parking, "Sanctuary of Padre Pio" or "Tomb of Padre Pio." The website www.conventopadrepio.com has detailed directions under "Information" and "How to Get There."

OTHER PLACES OF INTEREST

SAN GIOVANNI ROTONDO

The Way of the Cross is to the right of Our Lady of Grace Shrine, behind the large bronze statue of St. Pio, up the flights of stairs.

Casa Sollievo della Sofferenza (Home for the Relief of Suffering) is the large hospital St. Pio was responsible for building. It started out with twenty beds in 1925 and now contains about twelve hundred.

SAN GIOVANNI ROTONDO

Mary Pyle's House can be visited by appointment. Call 088 245667. Mary Pyle (1888–1968) was an American spiritual daughter of St. Pio's who came to San Giovanni Rotondo in 1923. She became a tertiary and dedicated her life to the saint. Mary built her house close the monastery and it became a way station for many tertiaries, monks and pilgrims.

Being an American, Mary Pyle welcomed many travelers from her native country. After World War II, some Americans veterans told her about a miracle that occurred in July of 1943. American bombers were sent to destroy the school building of San Giovanni Rotondo. As they flew towards the town, they saw in the sky a cloud containing the images of a bearded friar, a woman with a child in her arms, and a young man with his sword unsheathed. The planes were miraculously unable to release their bombs, and returned to base. After the war, some of these veterans visited Mary Pyle's house, and she took them to see St. Pio. When they saw him, they recognized him as the friar in the sky, and realized that the women and child were depicted in the picture of Our Lady of Grace. When they visited nearby Monte Sant'Angelo, they saw the final piece of the puzzle in the statue of Michael the Archangel.

After Mary Pyle's passing, St. Pio said, "Now she can finally listen to the Heavenly melodies without having to play the organ."

Her body was laid to rest in the Capuchin Chapel cemetery in San Giovanni Rotondo, where St. Pio's parents are also buried. The cemetery is on the other side of town on the road to Monte San Angelo.

COMING AND GOING

SAN GIOVANNI ROTONDO

Car: Southbound on Autostrade A14, exit at San Severo and follow the signs 20 miles (32 km) east to San Giovanni Rotondo. Northbound from Bari, exit at Foggia, and take S89 toward Manfredonia (see map). After 12 miles (19 km), take S273 north 12 more miles to San Giovanni Rotondo. Once there, follow the signs to "Sanctuary of Padre Pio" or "Tomb of Padre Pio."

Train: Trains arrive at the Foggia railway station. Foggia is accessible from Rome, and all major cities with possible transfers. From Rome's Termini Station to Foggia: 7:30AM, 9AM 1PM, 4PM, 7PM. (Check which ones are direct.) From the station at Foggia, take a SITA bus to San Giovanni Rotondo. Buses depart approximately every hour.

Bus: SITA buses run approximately 14 times a day from Foggia to San Giovanni. The trip takes about one hour. Service from 5AM to 10PM.

Plane: From Rome's Fiumicino airport, regular flights depart at 7:00AM and 9:30AM. The trip to Foggia takes 45 minutes. Airports: Foggia "Gino Lisa" Phone: 088 1617982, Bari "Palese" Phone: 080 538237.

Taxi: From Santa Maria delle Grazie Square Phone: 088 2456670.

TOURIST INFORMATION

❦ I.A.T. Informazioni e di Accoglienza/Piazza Europa 104/71013 San Giovani Rotondo (FG) Italia Phone/Fax: 088 2456240

❦ Puglia Turismo Phone: 083 2230033 Email: crt@pugliaturismo.com www.pugliaturismo.com

WEBSITES

Official Site of St. Pio www.conventopadrepio.com — Official website of Our Lady of Grace Shrine has everything you want to know about St. Pio and his shrine. Directions, maps and hotels are listed under "information."

Capuchin Priests' Communication Center www.padrepio.it — Teleradio & Voce di Padre Pio.

The National Centre for Padre Pio www.padrepio.org — U.S. website authorized by the Friars at Padre Pio's shrine in Italy.

Padre Pio Foundation of America www.padrepio.com — U.S. website with online bookstore.

City of San Giovanni Rotondo www.sangiovannirotondo.com — Tourist information in Italian under "Ospitalità e Ricettività" for lodging.

PLACES OF INTEREST
OUTSIDE OF SAN GIOVANNI ROTONDO

PIETRELCINA

The birthplace of St. Pio is 110 miles (178 km) west of San Giovanni Rotondo near Benevento. In 1909, St. Pio returned to Pietrelcina and lived in a room where he fought many battles with the devil. Jesus, the Virgin Mary, St. Joseph and St. Francis also appeared to him in this room. See the booklet: *Guide to Padre Pio's Pietrelcina*. There is a museum with relics, and you can visit St. Pio's boyhood home. More information is available at Our Lady of Grace Shrine. Pietrelcina Friary www.cappuccinipietrelcina.com
Phone: 082 4991207 Fax: 082 4991099

THE SANCTUARY OF ST. MICHAEL THE ARCHANGEL
Santuario San Michele Arcangelo

Legend tells us that, in 490, Elvio Emanuele, Lord of Monte Gargano, lost his best bull in an inaccessible cave. Elvio tried to shoot an arrow to scare the bull out of the cave, but the arrow returned and hit him. Elvio went to the local Bishop Lorenzo who ordered three days of prayer and fasting. After three days, St. Michael the Archangel appeared to Lorenzo and asked that the sacred cave be dedicated to the Christian God. He said that prayers would be answered and sins pardoned in this sacred grotto. The Bishop ignored St. Michael's request, so the angel appeared to him again two years later. This time St. Michael said he would save the town from attack, and caused a storm to turn back the enemy. St. Michael appeared to Lorenzo a third time to tell him that he did not have to dedicate the grotto since he had already done it himself. In 1656, St. Michael the Archangel appeared a fourth time. This time, he came in response to prayers of the local bishop, and gave instructions for ending the plague in the township. Many saints, including St. Francis of Assisi, have visited this shrine. This is the only Roman Catholic Church that has been consecrated by an angel.

If you are in San Giovanni Rotondo with a car, it is worth the thirty-minute drive. It can be very windy and cold, depending on the time of year, so dress warmly. The large Grotto can hold up to one thousand people and contains two altars, a Chapel of the Relics, the Episcopal Chair, and a Statue of St. Michael behind the altar. At the shrine, you can purchase an English guide, *Tourist Guide of the Shrine*. The shrine is open all year round from 9AM–12:30PM and 2:30PM–5. It is 15 miles (24 km) from San Giovanni Rotondo. The Basilica San Michele Arcangelo has pilgrim lodging, (Phone: 088 462396; Italian speaking only).

Santuario San Michele Arcangelo

St. Michael Shrine on the Gargano www.gargano.it/sanmichele/
— Official site. Describes shrine in detail.

Directions: Monte San Angelo is only 15 miles (24 km) east of San
Giovanni Rotondo on S272. This is the main road heading east out
of the city. There are huge parking areas as you enter Monte San
Angelo, so park here and follow the signs to the Grotto. Most of the
people you see will be walking the same direction!

THE SANCTUARY OF ST. MATTHEW
SANTUARIO DI SAN MATTEO

If you have the time, this sanctuary is in San Marco in Lamis thirty
minutes from Foggia and on the way to San Giovanni Rotondo.
the website has a map and directions in Italian.
Phone: 088 2831151 Fax: 088 2816713 www.santuariosanmatteo.it
Email: pellegrinaggi@santuarisanmatteo.it.

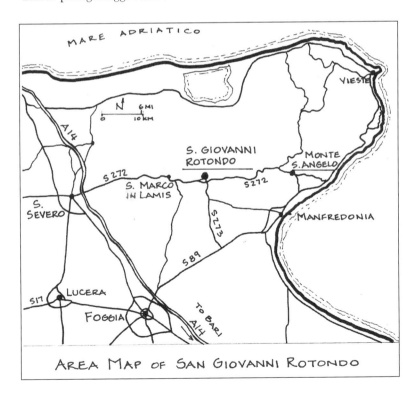

AREA MAP OF SAN GIOVANNI ROTONDO

Campania

This Western region is anchored by the city of Naples and includes some of the most beautiful coastlines of Italy. Campania occupies the west coast of Italy from the plains north of Naples to the Gulf of Policastro in the south. Low mountains make their way to the sea just south of Naples, forming the beautiful Amalfi coast. Towns perched along the rugged shore make for picturesque views and intimate lodging. Campania is also home to the ruins of Pompeii and Paestum, which contain intriguing displays of ancient culture and architecture.

AMALFI
St. Andrew the Apostle

RAVELLO
Blessed Bonaventura of Potenza
St. Pantaleone Martyr

Amalfi

Population 6,000

Amalfi is the largest of a series of small rustic towns along the rugged Amalfi Coast, just 38 miles (61 km) southeast of Naples. The Coast is famous for its scenic grandeur, with local villages built into cliffs overlooking peaceful coves and beautiful beaches. Amalfi was once a great naval power, but was destroyed by the Normans in 1131 and again by earthquakes in 1343. It never regained its prominence in the world of commerce, but it is now one of the most delightful tourist destinations in Italy. The Duomo St. Andrew and its cloister are the focal point of the town's main piazza. Because Amalfi is not known as a pilgrimage destination, few people realize that the first apostle of Jesus is buried within its walls.

ST. ANDREW THE APOSTLE
Sant' Andrea 60 A.D.

"Jesus Christ is the same yesterday, and today, yea and forever."
(Hebrews 13:8)

St. Andrew bust

St. Andrew was a native of Bethsaida in Galilee and a fisherman by trade, as were his father and brother, Simon Peter. Andrew was a disciple of John the Baptist but was drawn to Jesus following His baptism. John said, "Behold the Lamb of God," (John 1:29) and Andrew understood this as a sign of Jesus' sanctity. He approached Jesus, and after speaking with him for several hours, became his first disciple. Andrew went home and returned with his brother Simon, whom Jesus immediately named Peter, and whom he also accepted as a disciple. Andrew and Peter returned to their life as fishermen, but would be with Jesus at every opportunity. Finally, Jesus said, "I will make you fishers of men" (Matthew 4:19) and called them from their fishing boats to be permanent members of his mission. From this moment on, Andrew never left the company of Jesus.

Little more is mentioned in the Bible regarding Andrew, but many stories and legends survive describing his ministry. After the crucifixion, stories tell of Andrew preaching throughout Asia Minor, Greece and Russia. Russian lore tells of Andrew preaching as far north as Kiev, thus Andrew was made the patron saint of Russia. In the end, Andrew was put to death in Patras, Greece for his many conversions of others to Christianity. Legend has it that he was crucified by being bound upside down on a cross in the shape of an X, sometimes called a saltire or decussates. Thus he is often depicted with the sign of an 'X' shaped cross. Once bound to the cross, he preached to his followers for two days before dying a martyr's death.

In 357 A.D., his remains were removed from Patras by Emperor Constantine and brought to the Church of the Holy Apostles in Constantinople (along with St. Luke and St. Timothy). St. Andrew's relics in Constantinople were stolen by the crusaders in 1204 and given to the Duomo in Amalfi, where they reside to this day. Another legend has it that St. Rule received a vision telling him to remove some of Andrew's relics from Patras and take them to safety. After following the guidance of this vision, he traveled to the "ends of the earth" and landed in Scotland, where he consecrated the Church of St. Andrews. Thus Andrew also became the patron saint of Scotland.

On November 29, 1303, it was discovered at the Duomo in Amalfi that St. Andrew's bones secreted a substance called Manna. Since then, the Manna has been collected four times each year, on January 28, June 26, November 29 and December 7. The bishop retrieves the liquid that has collected from the saint's bones, and those present sing a hymn of thanks and give it to the sick. If there isn't any Manna, they sing and pray for forgiveness. The Church does not accept this Manna as a miracle, but the people of Amalfi still celebrate the event. Another miraculous intervention is attributed to the apostle. In the summer of 1544, the town of Amalfi was threatened by invading ships, so the people began to pray to St. Andrew. Suddenly, a terrible storm developed and forced the ships to flee, leaving the city unharmed. The town commemorates this miracle every year on June 26th.

ST. ANDREW'S CATHEDRAL
Cattedrale di Sant' Andrea

The Cathedral of St. Andrew has been restored many times throughout the centuries. Around the year 1000, a larger church was built around the original sixth century sanctuary, with the Arab-Norman style added in the twelfth century. Then, in the eighteenth century, it was embellished with Baroque decorations. A new façade was created in the last century. Downstairs, in the crypt under the altar, are the remains of St. Andrew the Apostle. Take the stairs on the left of the nave down to the crypt. There are pews facing St. Andrew's crypt, and it is not overly crowded, but tourists file past without realizing what is there. Overall, the church feels like a museum, but we felt special blessings here and suggest staying awhile.

The contrasting Cloister of Paradise (Chiostro del Paradiso), with white arches and columns, is connected to the Duomo. It was built in the thirteenth century to bury important people of the times.

During Mass anybody can enter the church for free. At other times the church is closed, but you can enter through the museum or chiostro, which has an entrance fee.

Duomo Sant' Andrea

Relics of St. Andrew: We have read that there are relics of St. Andrew in Scotland, Moscow, Rome, Milan, Nola, and Brescia. A priest from St. Andrew's said that they gave a piece of bone to churches in Totoli, Sardegna and Andria, near Bari. There was a relic of the head in Patrasso, Greece that was given to Pope Pio II and kept in the Vatican, but only the Vatican knows where the relic is now. We also read that pieces of the cross that St. Andrew died on are in Brussels and Marseilles. However, the priest at Duomo St. Andrew's told us that the relic in Marseilles is now in Patrasso, Greece, and he had never heard about the piece in Brussels.

SHRINE INFORMATION

Shrine: St. Andrew's Cathedral (Cattedrale di Sant' Andrea)

Address: Piazza Duomo/84011 Amalfi/Italia

Phone: 089 871324 **Fax:** 089 871340

E-mail: None

Website: www.diocesiamalficava.it Italian

English spoken: Rarely

Hours: Daily 9AM–6PM

Mass: Sun/Hol: 7:30AM, 10, 11:15, 7:30PM Weekdays: 8AM, 7PM; July and August: 6:30PM and 8PM.

Feasts and festivities: Feast day — November 30th.

Accessibility: None at this time.

Quiet areas for meditation: The crypt is relatively quiet, although people are filing through the room, in front of the crypt.

Tours: None

Bookstore: None

Lodging: None

Directions: The Cathedral Sant' Andrea is to the right of the main square as you enter the gates of the town of Amalfi. You will notice a flight of 57 stairs that lead to the main entrance.

COMING AND GOING

AMALFI

Car: From Rome take A1 south to Naples (Napoli), after Napoli take A3 Napoli-Salerno. As you are about to arrive at Salerno, exit at 'Vietri sul Mare" and take S163 west to Amalfi. This is the most direct route—the more scenic route is to make your way to Sorrento on the Gulf of Naples and take the coastal highways along the Amalfi coast, through Positano and other beautiful seaside towns.

Train/Bus: From the Termini station in Rome take the direct train to Salerno. After you have reached Salerno, take a coach of the line "Salerno-Amalfi."

Ferry: Ferries arrive at Amalfi from several nearby ports: Camerota, Capri, Ischia, Naples and Salerno. The schedules are seasonal, so check with the local tourist boards when making your plans.

TOURIST INFORMATION

Azienda Autonoma Soggiorno e Tourismo/Corso delle Repubbliche Marinare 27/Amalfi/Italia Phone/Fax: 089 871107 www.amlfitouristoffice.it

WEBSITES

Amalfi Coast www.amalfi-coast.info/english.htm — History and areas of interest in Amalfi and Ravello.

Costa di Amalfi www.costadiamalfi.it — Tourist info for the Amalfi Coast.

Amalfi Coast On Line www.amalficoast.it — Tourist info for the Amalfi Coast.

Amalfi Coast Web Guide www.divinecoast.com — Tourist info for the Amalfi Coast.

TravelCampania.com www.travel-campania.com — Tourist info for the Campania region.

OTHER PLACES OF INTEREST IN THE AREA

RAVELLO

Ravello is a beautiful hill town about 4.5 miles (7 km) above Amalfi, up the winding "Dragon's Valley." It is well worth a visit. You can spend a wonderful full day walking around this charming town, visiting the gardens and grounds of Villa Rufolo and Villa Cimbrone, feasting on the most picturesque views of the Amalfi Coast. Ravello has attracted artists, writers and composers for centuries and continues to do so with yearly musical festivals and art shows. Like Amalfi, it is not well known for its saintly inheritance, but hidden along a meandering walkway is the resting place of Blessed Bonaventura of Potenza.

BLESSED BONAVENTURA OF POTENZA
Beato Bonaventura da Potenza 1651-1711

"All is lost, but God is never lost."

Blessed Bonaventura's holiness was noticeable from the day he entered the Franciscan order at the age of sixteen. He was granted solitude in a monastery in Lapio at eighteen, and ordained a priest at the young age of twenty-four. For eight years (1672-1680), he lived at the monastery at Amalfi under the tutelage of Father Domenico Giradelli of Muro Lucano, who was considered to be a very holy man. They developed a close and deeply spiritual relationship.

Father Bonaventura's sanctity was much sought after, and he was eventually transferred to St. Anthony's in Porta Madina, Naples. Father Giradelli told him at their parting, "My Son, we must separate. This is the will of God. Let us understand; let us accept this with detachment, with generosity. Go! But remember that you shall return to these paths. Do you see that hill? (pointing to Ravello) Up there we have an old, poor monastery. It is now abandoned. But there you shall end your earthly days. Remember this, your Father, who wanted very much for you to be a saint."

In Naples, Bonaventura attracted crowds by levitating while celebrating Mass. Pilgrims, rich and poor, also wanted to hear his simple sermons. He was sent to Capri for ninety days, then on to the Island of Ishia for ten years, converting thousands and performing miracles for the poor. At the age of forty-eight, his superiors, worried about his health, transferred him back to Naples. From there he was assigned to serve

View of Amalfi Coast, Ravello

Crypt of Blessed Bonaventura

as Novice Master at Nocera Inferiore, where 37 years earlier he had started his religious training. He served there for four years, emphasizing devotion to Our Lady, Saint Francis and St. Anthony, then returned to Naples in 1707. When his left knee was infected with cancer, he remained calm during surgery performed with a hot iron by chanting "Mary, My Mother, Mary."

In 1710, as prophesied by his teacher Father Giradelli, he arrived in Ravello, a small, impoverished community needing his charity and blessings. One day he passed a leper and turned away to avoid him. Then he returned to kiss the leper's face repeatedly and the leper was instantaneously cured. Many more miracles are recorded until the time of his passing, which he predicted, and after his death. On October 26, 1711, he died singing celestial music praising God and Our Lady, and his cell was filled with a beautiful fragrance. After his death, because his face was glowing and seemed still filled with life, the Superior of the monastery commanded him in the name of holy obedience to raise his arm so the doctor could bleed him to prove he was dead. Before he could finish his command, the saint lifted his arm for the doctor. Many miracles were attributed to Bonaventura after his death. His body is in the Convento di San Francesco, a tiny church in Ravello, and is said to be incorrupt.

THE CHURCH OF ST. FRANCIS
Chiesa di San Francesco

Shrine: The Church of St. Francis (Chiesa di San Francesco)

Address: Via San Francesco, 9/84010 Ravello/Italia (SA)

Phone: 089 857146 **Fax:** 089 857145

E-mail: info@ravellofrancescana.it (Write in Italian)

Website: www.ravellofrancescana.it Italian

Quiet areas for meditation: The small church is not crowded.

English spoken: Rarely

Hours: 7AM–8PM If the church is not open, ring the bell at the door of the Convent and ask to see the crypt of Blessed Bonaventure.

Feasts and festivities: October 26th.

Accessibility: Getting around Ravello is difficult because of many stairs.

Bookstore: The church does not have one, but at the entrance of the church is an art gallery. They sell a book in English about Blessed Bonaventure.

Recommended book: *Blessed Bonaventure of Potenza* by Francis Xavier Vassallo published by the Monastery of St. Francis, Ravello and sold in the art gallery in front of the church.

Lodging: None, they have plans in the future to provide lodging. The Monastero S. Chiara in Ravello has lodging Phone: 089 857145 comunichiamo@sorelleclarisseravello.it.

Directions: Chiesa di San Francesco is on Via San Francesco. Just ask where the street is. It is a small town.

May I see the crypt of Blessed Bonaventura?
Posso visitare la cripta del Beato Bonaventura?

ST. PANTALEONE MARTYR
305 A.D.

The stories about St. Pantaleone are suspected to be pure legend, even though some of his blood is claimed to be at Constantinople, Madrid and Ravello. His blood is said to liquefy each year on his feast day, July 27 and also in May. The reason the stories are suspect is because of the differing versions in Latin and Greek, including a story from Syria. The legend has it that Pantaleone was a doctor to the Emperor Galerius Maximian and submitted to all the temptations of his surroundings. A Christian named Hermalaos brought him back to the faith. Some jealous physicians betrayed him when Diocletian's persecution of the Christians started, and he was arrested along with

Hermalaos. The Emperor wanted to spare him, but Pantaleone would not denounce his faith. There were six attempts to kill him—by burning, liquid lead, drowning, wild beasts, the wheel and the sword—all without success. When he finally allowed himself to be beheaded, milk poured from his veins instead of blood.

Shrine: Duomo of St. Pantaleone (Duomo di San Pantaleone) Church of the Holy Mary Ascended to Heaven (Chiesa di Santa Maria Assunta)

Address: Piazza Duomo/84010 Ravello/Italia

Phone: 089 858311 **Fax:** 089 9857160

Directions: The eleventh century Duomo dedicated to St. Pantaleone is in the center of Ravello on Piazza Vescovado. St. Pantaleone's blood is in a chapel on the left hand side.

Hours: Sun/Hol 8AM–1PM, 3PM–7:30; Weekdays 8AM–1PM, 3PM–5.

COMING AND GOING

RAVELLO

Car: Take S163 Amalfitana for Salerno, and 1.24 miles (2 km) after Amalfi, turn left. Park in lots outside the city. If you are staying in the town of Ravello, you can drop your luggage off inside the town, but you have to park outside unless your hotel has parking.

It is connected to the Napoli-Salerno motorway by the provincial road of Valico di Chiunzi (casello di Angri). The state road 373 (Ravello) connects it with the Amalfitan state road (Castiglione).

Train: From Salerno station take a taxi or SITA bus to Ravello. Railway station: Salerno. www.trentiali.

Bus: SITA bus runs from 6AM to 9PM, up very curvy roads from Piazza Flavio Gioia in Amalfi.

Plane: Naples International Airport (65 Km to Ravello) www.gesac.it

TOURIST INFORMATION

Azienda Aut. Soggiorno e Turismo/Via Roma 18 bis/84010 Ravello (SA) Italia Phone: 089 857096 Fax: 089 857977 info@ravellotime.it www.ravellotime.it.

WEBSITES

Amalfi Coast www.amalfi-coast.info — History and areas of interest in Amalfi and Ravello.

Ravello www.ravello.it — Tourist info.

Città di Ravello www.crmpa.it/EPT/ravello/#ferrovia — Tourist info.

Ravello e le sue chiese www.chiesaravello.com Italian Click on "Altre Informazioni" for good map of churches.

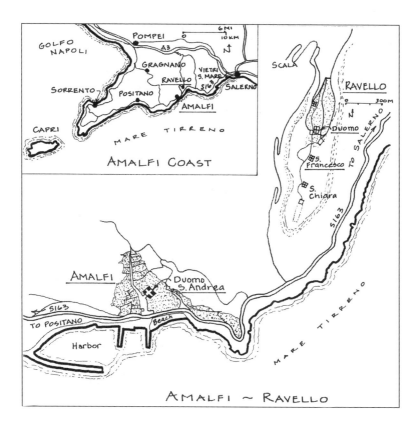

Emilia-Romagna

Emilia-Romagna stretches across a wide area of the northern part of Italy with Veneto and Lombardy to the north, and Tuscany and Marches to the south. The Po River creates the northern border of the region and the Apennine ridge the southern border, with the Adriatic coast to the east. The central plains support farming and industrial development, whereas tourism is predominant on the Adriatic coast with its popular beaches and shallow waters. Bologna, the capital of the region, is recognized as a university town possessing one of the oldest institutions of learning in the world. Other interesting areas are Ravenna, known for the Byzantine mosaics in the Basilica of Sant'Apollinare, and the Republic of San Marino, a tiny European State dating back to 1263. Worthy of note for the pilgrim, the town of Bobbio, south of Piacenza, is famous for the Irish Saint Columban, who established a monastery and a renowned library from the manuscripts he brought from Ireland in around 612.

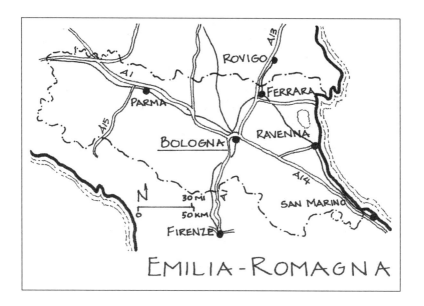

BOLOGNA
St. Catherine of Bologna
St. Dominic of Bologna

Bologna
Population 401,000

Under the rule of the Byzantines, Lombards, and Franks, Bologna became a free municipality in the eleventh century. Around this same time period, the city became the cultural center of Europe with the establishment of the University of Bologna. The center of Bologna is the Piazza Maggiore where students, locals and tourists all gather, taking part in the activities of this bustling city. The "Due Torri" are two towers from the twelfth century, with a view of the city from the top of the Torre degli Asinelli. The churches dedicated to St. Catherine of Bologna and St. Dominic are on the same side of town, south of Piazza Maggiore, and within walking distance from each other. The remains of the patron saint of Bologna, St. Petronio, are in the Basilica di San Petronio, the largest church in Bologna. His bones were moved recently (2000) from the Basilica di Santo Stefano, which is also worth a visit.

ST. CATHERINE OF BOLOGNA
Santa Caterina da Bologna or Caterina de' Vigri 1413-1463

"And His Glory shall be seen in you."

Catherine de' Vigri was born to the family of a lawyer and diplomat in Ferrara, a large city 30 miles north of Bologna. From a young age she spent much time in prayer and devotion. At age eleven she was sent to live with her father's patron, the Marquis of Ferrara, to serve as the maid-of-honor to the Marquis' daughter. Catherine was well educated, and continued her education there, reading and writing in Latin, a skill she would put to great use later in life. After three years, her companion was wed and Catherine returned home, where her father was soon to die. Shortly after his death, Catherine followed her inner calling and left home to join the order of Franciscan tertiaries in Ferrara. At the age of 14, she was one of the youngest nuns, but also one of the most devout, gaining great admiration from her sisters for her sincere striving for perfection.

Catherine was soon beset by many visions; some were of divine origin while others were very disconcerting, induced by satanic powers. When she had visions from God, she would have deep feelings of charity and compassion, with the presence of light. Catherine, in the third person, would later write, "And Jesus would enter her soul like a radiant sunshine and establish there a profound peace." The demonic visions always dealt with issues of doubt and blasphemy, and raised questions of Christ's actual presence in the Eucharist. Ultimately, Catherine had a true vision, which revealed to her the deepest teaching of the Eucharist, and the visions of doubt left Catherine forever.

In art, Catherine is often depicted holding the infant Jesus, a result of another vision. One Christmas Eve at midnight, after praying the Ave Maria for hours, the Blessed Mary appeared to her, holding the baby Christ. Catherine wrote, "This kind mother came to her and gave her Son to her. I leave you to picture the joy of this poor creature when she found herself holding the Son of the Eternal Father in her arms. Trembling with respect, but still more overcome with joy, she took the liberty of caressing Him, of pressing Him against her heart and bringing His face to her lips … He disappeared, leaving her however, filled with joy."

Catherine wrote of her experiences to help train her sisters and inspire others to a holy life. She also wrote a treatise on the Seven Spiritual Weapons, which was published posthumously and became a popular testament in Italy. Her other talents included music, poetry and painting. She played musical instruments and wrote hymns, authored poems on the mystical lives of Christ and Mary, decorated her breviary with beautiful color illustrations and completed several paintings. Her music and breviary are on display at

St. Catherine of Bologna

her shrine in the Corpus Domini, Bologna, and her paintings hang in the Municipal museums of Bologna and Venice.

After twenty-four years at Ferrara, in 1456, the people of Bologna desired to bring Catherine and her sisters to a new cloistered monastery within their city. A huge procession welcomed the sisters and brought them to the site of their new monastery, called Corpus Domini. Here, her fame for healing powers and prophecies continued to spread, attracting more people than the monastery could accommodate.

Catherine's remaining years were spent as superior of the monastery and as a saintly example for the other sisters. Compassion for her fellow sisters was her trademark. When she was brought up for election as abbess, the only fault found with her was her leniency towards the postulants. On occasion, she felt the young sisters were suffering from lack of food, so she would go out and beg for hardboiled eggs. Then, she would peel them and place them secretly in their bags! Her biographer referred to her as the "Mirror of Illumination" for living a life of perfection.

Catherine died on March 9, 1463 at the age of 49. She was initially buried adjacent to the church, in a shallow grave without a casket. There was soon a report of a sweet fragrance filling the area and miraculous cures happening at her grave. Eighteen days after her death, her body was exhumed, and it showed no signs of decay. Eventually, she was laid on a stretcher in her cell, for there were many people wishing to see her and pray to her. When the number of pilgrims became overwhelming for the sisters, the saint was made to sit upright in a chair and rolled to the viewing area. Finally, St. Catherine appeared to one of the nuns in a vision and asked for a special chapel to be built for her body, to make her more accessible to pilgrims. A larger chapel was erected next to the original church, which is where Catherine resides today. In 1953, her body was surrounded in glass for protection, and at some point her hands and feet were covered with wax. Her darkened skin is blamed on soot from the oil lamps used over the centuries, but otherwise she remains untouched and in remarkable condition. Her body was last examined in 1959. Because of her talent as an artist and musician, she is the patron saint of artists. She was canonized in 1712.

SANCTUARY OF CORPUS DOMINI
Santuario del Corpus Domini

The fifteenth century Sanctuary of Corpus Domini (Santuario del Corpus Domini) contains the incorrupt body of St. Catherine of Bologna. The Chapel of the Saint is on the left side of the church. There is a sign that reads, "Alla Cappella Della Santa." Ring the bell during the hours of 10AM–12 and 4PM–6, Tues, Thurs, Sat, & Sun. They will buzz you in. This leads you into several rooms where you ring another bell. Then you enter the shrine of St. Catherine. The incorrupt saint is sitting upright on a throne, and there are many exhibits of her relics. Catherine's breviary, which she copied and illuminated, is on display, along with her "violeta." On this violeta, she played and sang a celestial tune, "And His glory will be seen in you," after she had heard the music during a near death experience with Jesus. You can stay and meditate before the saint as long as you want during the hours they are open. There are a few chairs to sit on if it is not crowded. Picture-taking is not allowed in the Chapel of the Saint.

The Poor Clare nuns are cloistered, so they talk to visitors through a grill covered with a curtain, to the right of the shrine. If you want to visit their bookstore, ring the bell, and they will open the door to the right of the grate. The nuns are very sweet, but do not speak English. During St. Catherine's festival there is an urn displayed that contains her blood.

Santuario del Corpus Domini

Where is the chapel of the Saint?
Dov'è la cappella della Santa?

Where is the bookstore?
Dov'è il negozio con i libri?

SHRINE INFORMATION

Shrine: Sanctuary of Corpus Domini (Santuario del Corpus Domini or Santuario della Santa)

Address: Via Tagliapietre 19/40100 Bologna/Italia

Phone: 051 331274/051 331277 (call up to 6pm) Italian only

Fax: 051 331279/051 330176

E-mail: None

Website: None

Quiet areas for meditation: The chapel of the saint, if it is not crowded.

English spoken: None

Hours: Daily: 9:30AM–12:15; 3:30PM–7

Mass: Sun/Hol: 11:30AM, 6PM; Daily: 6PM;

The chapel of the saint: Tues, Thurs, Sat, Sun: 10AM–12; 4PM–6

Feasts and festivities: March 9 — Feast Day, celebrated from March 8 – 16.

Accessibility: There is a step from the street.

Tours: None

Bookstore: Ring the bell next to the door in the chapel of the Saint.

Recommended book: *The Saint: A short life of St. Catherine of Bologna*, printed by the Corpus Domini Sanctuary and available in their bookstore.

Lodging: None

Directions: From Piazza Maggiore, exit from the southwest on Via Massimo D'Azeglio, turn right on Via Urbana (to the left is Via Marsili and leads to St. Dominic's,) then left on Via Tagliapietre to number 19 on the right side of the street. The Sanctuary is flush with the street and is easy to miss.

OTHER PLACES OF INTEREST

There are other relics of St. Catherine in the Monastero Clarisse in Ferrara, but we do not know if you can visit the Monastery. The oven where St. Catherine baked bread and left it for four hours without burning is here. The story goes that she blessed the bread and went to Mass, saying, "I place you in the hands of Jesus." When she returned the bread had not burned. Every year during the "Festa dell' Ottavario" they bake bread in this oven. There is also the bowl that St. Joseph, disguised as a beggar, left for her at the front door, telling her that Jesus had drunk from it. There is also some cotton with St. Catherine's blood on it.

ST. DOMINIC
San Domenico 1170 – 1221

"Speak only to God or about God."

Dominic Guzman was born in Caleruega in the south of Spain. Little is known of his family history, except that his mother became Blessed Joanna of Aza. At fourteen, he was sent to his uncle in Palencia, who was an archpriest, to receive an education and religious training. Following years of study and duties as a canon at the cathedral at Osma, he was ordained in Osma and lived a communal life there under the Rule of St. Augustine. He spent the next years in seclusion and contemplation, relishing the

St. Dominic bust

life of a renunciate. Dominic gained his strength of character and deep foundation in faith during this time. At age thirty-one, his life of seclusion ended when he became a Prior and began his work in the world.

As Prior, he was sent with the Bishop of Osma to Denmark to negotiate a wedding for the son of the King of Castile. While en route through France, they spent the night at the home of a member of the Albigensian sect. The Albigensians were so extreme in their asceticism that they created a dualist philosophy of life: anything earthly or to do with the flesh is evil, and only the spiritual aspects of man and creation are good. They practiced complete sexual abstinence, minimal eating and drinking, and condoned suicide. Dominic saw this not so much as a threat to the Church itself, but as a direct threat to mankind in general. He was disturbed because the Albigensian heresy was gaining popularity among the people. This was perhaps because the austere Albigensian leaders, known as Perfects, seemed more devout than the priests of the Church, who often led lives of luxury, surrounded by servants and wealth. Aroused to action, Dominic spent the entire night talking with his host, finally persuading him of the evils of Albigensian thought, and converting him back to the Church. From this experience, Dominic knew that God's will for him was to begin preaching and performing missionary work throughout the world.

Dominic and the Bishop went to Rome to gain approval for traveling to Russia to preach to the heretical Cumans, but the Pope requested they preach closer to home, since heresy was gaining momentum there, too. St. Dominic ended up in Languedoc, France where he fought a theological fight against the heretics. His weapons were his own austere life, preaching the Gospel of love, and great compassion for people. He was once asked, following a moving talk, in what book had he studied his sermon? "In no other," he said, "than that of love." When he first began preaching, Dominic was discouraged and prayed to the Virgin Mary for guidance. She told him to "preach my Psalter composed of 150 Angelic Salutations and 15 Our Fathers, and you will obtain an abundant harvest." This is what is believed to be the beginning of the rosary, and Dominic had much success with this teaching.

Dominic was also very concerned for the women under the rule of the Albigensians, for they suffered greatly in the convents and in their homes. In 1206, on the feast day of St. Mary Magdalene,

Dominic founded a refuge for nine nuns who had fled an Albigensian convent. This was the first of many such sanctuaries he would create throughout Europe. Shortly thereafter, following the assassination of the Pope's delegate, civil war erupted between the Albigensians and the people of the Church. Dominic remained non-violent during the conflict and preached the use of righteous living as a weapon: "The enemies of the faith can not be overcome with that. Arm yourself with prayer, rather than a sword; wear humility rather than fine clothes."

After ten years in Languedoc, Dominic refused to be elevated into a position of power. Instead, he gathered around him a small group of preachers, training them in contemplation, austere living and the power of preaching. Thus he began an order of preachers who primarily served the people through example and by preaching the gospel. Dominic applied to the Pope for a new rule for their order, but requests for new orders were being denied at that time. So, he met with his followers who decided to adopt the rule of St. Augustine. The first friary was built in Toulouse, France. In 1216, the Order of Preachers was confirmed in Rome, becoming the first missionary order of the Church.

While in Rome, Dominic had a vision. He saw a world ravaged by sin, but then saved through intercession of the Virgin Mary. Mary then pointed out to her Son two figures; the first Dominic recognized as himself, but the other was a stranger to him. The next day, while in church, Dominic saw a ragged beggar enter, and immediately recognized him as the stranger of his vision. Greeting him with a warm embrace, he discovered this stranger was Francis of Assisi. Since this meeting, seven hundred years ago, the friars of St. Francis and St. Dominic have celebrated their mutual friendship in God twice yearly.

Dominic was not content to have his fellow preachers stay in France, so he sent them all over Europe to preach the gospel. In Rome, his preaching attracted large crowds and brought many to hear the gospel anew. For his ministry, the Pope gave him the church of San Sisto Vecchio, where he founded a new convent for all the nuns of Rome who were living without the benefit of a cloister. Dominic often showed compassion for women, for he was very devoted to the Blessed Virgin.

Leaving Rome, he traveled to Spain, Italy and France, establishing friaries wherever he went, finally ending up at Bologna in 1218.

Although still traveling and preaching, this is where he resided for the rest of his life. By 1221, the Order of Preachers had established monasteries in Italy, France, Spain, Poland, Scandinavia, England, Scotland, and Palestine, and they continue to this day, to preach throughout the world.

Dominic died in Bologna on August 6, 1221 at the age of fifty-one. On his deathbed, he told his friars, "Have charity among you; hold to humility; keep willing poverty." In a fitting eulogy, Father Lacordaire said of him, "Tender as a mother, strong as a diamond."

The vocation of Dominic's friars is "to hand on to others the fruits of contemplation," for deep insight is gained through contemplation, not just strict study of the scriptures. St. Dominic's primary mission was to preach a calm life centered in God: "A man who governs his passions is master of the world. We must either rule them or be ruled by them. It is better to be the hammer than the anvil."

THE BASILICA OF ST. DOMINIC
Basilica di San Domenico

The Basilica and convent were built between 1228 and 1240, and remodeled between 1728 and 1732. St. Dominic's tomb is in a side chapel in the middle of the church, on the right. The beautiful tomb took over three centuries to create and contains the remains of St. Dominic, except his skull, which is behind the tomb in a reliquary made in 1383. You can walk around the tomb if the gates are open.

What is believed to have been St. Dominic's cell is in the convent where it is thought he died. The museum is next to the sacristy, to the right of the main altar.

Basilica di San Domenico

I would like to see St. Dominic's cell.
Vorrei vedere la cella di San Domenico.

SHRINE INFORMATION

Shrine: The Basilica of St. Dominic (Basilica di San Domenico)

Address: Piazza San Domenico, 13/I-40124 Bologna/Italia

Phone: 051 6400411 **Fax:** 051 6400431

E-mail: None

Website: None

Quiet areas for meditation: The basilica is not crowded or noisy.

English spoken: Occasionally

Hours: Daily: 7:30AM–12:30PM; 3:30PM– 7:30; Sun/Hol: 7:30AM–12:30PM; 3:30PM–7:30.

Mass: Sun/Hol: 9AM, 10:30, 12, 6PM, 10; Weekdays: 7:30AM, 12:30PM, 7.

Feasts and festivities: May 24 — Translation of San Domenico; August 4 — Anniversary of San Domenico's death; First Sunday of October — Madonna del Rosario.

Side chapels: The side chapels are open only at these times: Sun/Hol: 3:30PM–5:30; Weekdays 9:30AM–12:15PM; 3:30PM-6:30. It is best to make a reservation if you are with a group.

Museum: The museum is not open during Mass and closed Sunday and Monday mornings. Open 10-12:30AM/3PM-5. It is on the right of the main altar and opens the same time as the side chapels.

Accessibility: There is an entrance on the right side of the church from Piazza San Domenico.

Tours: With a guide you can visit the saint's room, the bell tower, the chiostro and St. Dominic's tomb. Call to arrange and plan to speak Italian. Phone: 051-6400411

Bookstore: Halfway into the church on the right. They have an excellent guidebook in English "The Basilica of Saint Dominic in Bologna." We recommend getting it before looking around.

Recommended book: *The Life of Saint Dominic*, by Augusta Theodosia Drane, Tan Books.

Lodging: None

Directions: From Piazza Maggiore, exit from the southwest on Via Massimo D'Azeglio, turn left on Via Marsili (on the right is Via Urbana which leads to St. Catherine's shrine,) then several blocks to the Basilica of St. Dominic on Piazza di San Domenico.

COMING AND GOING

BOLOGNA

Car: The city is easily accessible from all the major cities for it is at the intersection of A1, A13 and A14. The highways circumscribe the city, so depending on your approach, simply exit at the "Centro" sign, and follow the signs to the city center. If you are staying in the town center, you will need to procure a parking permit from your hotel to leave your car in the street overnight. There are parking lots outside of the town center that have frequent bus service into town.

Train: Bologna is on the major rail lines, connecting to any major city. The Stazione Ferroviaria, Bologna Centrale, is on Piazza Medaglie d'Oro n.2 Phone: Info: 051 257911/051 6303059; Ticket office: 199 166177; Assistance for people with disabilities: 051 6303132/051 6303876.

Bus: The central bus station is located in Piazza XX Settembre 6, next to the train station and city center. City buses also leave from Piazza Maggiore and Piazza Nettuno. Website for the central bus station for online booking in English: www.autostazionebo.it

Plane: Bologna G. Marconi Airport is about 3.5 miles (6 km) north of town. The Forlì Airport is about 37 miles (60 km) southeast of Bologna.

TOURIST INFORMATION

❋ IAT – Informazione e Accoglienza Turistica/Piazza Maggiore 1e/40124 Bologna, Italia. Located in the Podestà Palace. Phone: 051 246541 Fax: 051 6393171 E-mail: touristoffice@ comune.bologna.it www.bolognaturismo.info

WEBSITES

Bologna Turismo www.comune.bologna.it/bolognaturismo IAT — Tourist information in Italian; list of churches in English: At top of page click on IAT, English version, Discover the Area, Art & Culture, Churches.

World Guide to Bologna www.bologna.world-guides.com Tourist information.

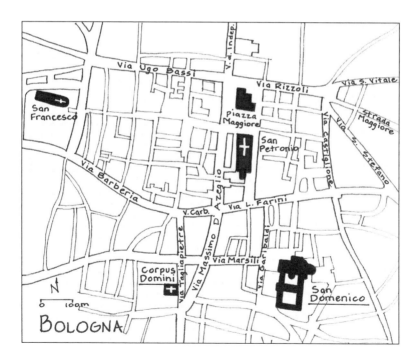

Latium

Lazio

The region of Latium is in central Italy on the western side of the peninsula. The area is best known for the capital city of Rome, but it is very diverse both geographically and culturally. The western border is formed by the Tyrrhenian Sea that gives way to the flat coastal plains. The plains continue past Rome, and are transformed into the rolling topography of Tuscany and Umbria in the north, and the hills and extinct volcanic mountains of Campania in the south. The Apennine Mountains occupy the eastern edge of the region and the Tiber River enters the plains from the northern valleys and flows through Rome to the sea. While Rome is the leader in ancient and modern culture, the other towns and villages of the region offer glimpses into the more typical Italian lifestyle.

RIETI VALLEY
St. Francis of Assisi

ROME
St. Peter the Apostle
St. Paul the Apostle
St. Ignatius of Loyola
St. Philip Neri
St. Catherine of Siena

Rieti Valley

ST. FRANCIS OF ASSISI

St. Francis of Assisi traveled by foot and donkey throughout Italy, spreading his doctrine of love. He visited the Rieti Valley on many occasions and founded several hermitages. It is called the Sacred Valley due to the presence of the saint, and for the deep vibrations of devotion he infused into the area. The Rieti Valley is where the first crèche scene was displayed and where St. Francis's eyes were cauterized near the end of his life. He spent much time here in prayer and seclusion and left a legacy of divine love. There are four hermitages in the valley that are associated with St. Francis: Fonte Colombo, Greccio, Poggio Bustone, and Convento Foresta Giacomo. A welcome addition to the Sacred Valley is a walking route, the Cammino di Francesco, retracing St. Francis's steps between each of these hermitages. For more on this route see page 249. The life of St. Francis is described in the chapter on Assisi, in the region of Umbria.

THE SANCTUARY OF FONTE COLOMBO
Santuario di Fonte Colombo

Fonte Colombo means "Dove Spring" and was named by St. Francis because of the doves that drank from the spring here. In the sacred cave, in 1223, Francis fasted for forty days and wrote the final Rule of his Order, asking for the will of Jesus Christ. A group of superiors in his Order came and indicated to him that they could not follow a certain rule. Francis prayed to the Lord to make them understand that it was Christ who desired the rule. Jesus appeared and spoke to all those present, saying that the rule was God's word and not Francis's, and those who could not follow it should leave the order. The brothers, having heard the word of Jesus, understood.

It was here also, in 1226, in a small house next to the convent, that doctors cauterized Francis's eyes, trying to effect a cure for his glaucoma, and Francis asked "Brother Fire" to be gentle. The brothers ran away at the gruesome sight, but Francis said he felt no pain.

The small chapel of Mary Magdalene (La Maddalena) is where St. Francis and his brothers held Mass. The window has a Tau sign that authorities say was drawn by St. Francis. The letter T is a biblical sign of salvation and, after Christ's death, represented the crucifixion. Follow the steps down to a small cave where Brother Leo spent time.

Beside the cave is the stump of a tree where Jesus appeared to Francis. After more stairs is the cave where Francis fasted for forty days and completed the Rule. (The mountain fissure was caused by an earthquake.) This is the best place to meditate and pray. It can be cold and damp, so bring something to sit on if you plan to stay awhile. There are few pilgrims here, and it is a very quiet place to contemplate the life of St. Francis.

Fonte Columbo

The Sanctuary is 74 miles (119 km) south of Assisi, about 3 miles (5 km) west of Rieti. Fonte Columbo has overnight accommodations, but you must bring your own sheets and towels. English is not spoken so you must communicate in Italian. Phone: 074 671125 Fax: 074 6210157 Email: fontecolombo@santuarivallesanta.it Santuario di Fonte Colombo/02100 Fontecolombo (RI) Italia. A comprehensive brochure in English is available for a donation, inside the courtyard of the convent, in a small room to the right.

SANCTUARY OF SANTA MARIA OF THE FORESTS
Santuario Santa Maria de La Foresta

Former drug addicts now run this community and live off the land. A guided tour in Italian is available by ringing the bell. You can visit a cave St. Francis secluded in, and sit where he sat. St. Francis took refuge here to avoid the crowds of people looking for him for a blessing. When the people found him, they demolished most of a farmer's grapes. When the farmer protested, Francis assured him that his harvest would be successful. There was a small harvest of grapes, but when they were pressed, the wine kept increasing. You can see the wine trough where this miracle occurred. This Sanctuary is 68 miles (109 km) south of Assisi, about 3 miles (5 km) north of Rieti. Phone/Fax: 074 620085 Email: fontecolombo@santuarivallesanta.it Santuariio de la Foresta Comunità "Mondo X" 02100 La Forest/Rieti (RI) Italia.

SANCTUARY OF GRECCIO
Santuario di Greccio

This is where St. Francis recreated the birth of Christ in a stable on Christmas Eve, 1223. There were a group of laymen and women who followed Francis' Rule here during his lifetime, and Francis liked to come and stay here because of their deep piety. St. Francis slept in an alcove in the rock (downstairs). The best place to meditate is upstairs. The cells were built after St. Francis's time. Greccio (pronounced Grechio) is 67 miles (108 km) south of Assisi, about 8 miles (12 km) northwest of Rieti. Phone/Fax: 074 6750127 Santuario di Greccio 02040 Greccio (RI) Italia. Email: greccio@santuarivallesanta.it

SANCTUARY OF POGGIO BUSTONE
Santuario di Poggio Bustone

Francis came here in 1208 for the first time and, according to legend, he received pardon for his sins in the Grotto of Revelations. To the right of the convent are stairs leading to caves used by Francis's brothers. It is a half hour hike up to the caves, starting at a footpath with no marker. The Convent of San Giacomo is about 14 miles (22 km) north of Rieti, just east of Rivodutri. Phone/Fax 074 6688916 Email: poggiobustone@santuarivallesanta.it Santuario di Poggio Bustone 02018 Poggio Bustone (RI) Italia.

COMING AND GOING

RIETI VALLEY

The town of Rieti is about 60 miles (97 km) northeast of Rome, and all the hermitages are located within 15 miles (24 km) of this rural city. You can drive to the hermitages or hike the Cammino di Franceso (see websites). Either way, it is pleasant and picturesque. For directions, refer to the map at right, and look for the signs that say "Santuario" while winding through the valley. The hermitages should be open year round, seven days a week, but they close each day from about 12:30–3 or 4PM. English is rarely spoken, so be prepared to speak in Italian.

WEBSITES

APT Rieti Tourist Board www.apt.rieti.it — Main office for St. Francis walk. Via Cintia, 87 Rieti 02100 Italia Phone: 074 6201146/7 Fax: 074 6270446 Email: colaianni@apt.rieti.it.

Cammino di Francesco www.camminodifrancesco.it — Comprehensive website for walking the trail to all the sanctuaries in the Rieti Valley Email: info@camminodifrancesco.it.

Franciscan Shrines of the Holy Valley of Rieti www.santuarivallesanta.it — Official website with histories of all the sanctuaries listed here with pictures.

Greccio Tour Information Office — Phone/Fax: 074 6750640 Email: greccioturistico@libero.it (write in Italian)

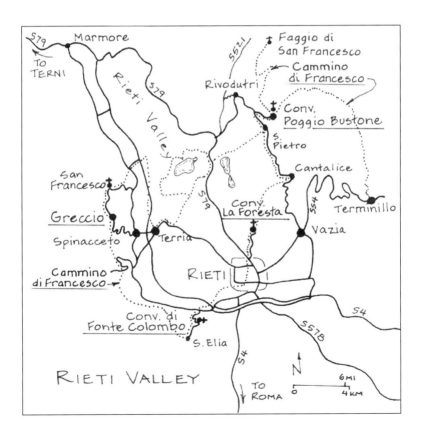

Rome
Roma
Population 2,655,970

Rome is the most heavily populated city in Italy and home to its ancient culture. Now the country's capital, it was once the center of the Roman Empire, ruler of the known world. Its history and culture are still alive throughout the capital, and it continues to be one of the most vibrant cities of Europe. The richness of the city is found in its diverse matrix of ancient ruins and modern shops, historical monuments and contemporary architecture, quaint shrines and monolithic churches. The tourist in Rome can find anything and everything that Western culture has to offer, including some of the most holy pilgrimage sites in the world.

There are countless shrines in Rome and you can visit for several weeks and still not see everything. Plan your itinerary in advance, allowing enough time to see what interests you most, as well as time for relaxation. This will make your visit more enjoyable and your experiences of the shrines more meaningful. When you first arrive, obtain a copy of "This Week in Rome" from your hotel or tourist information office. This magazine contains current hours of operation for all the shrines and sites of Rome.

ST. PETER - PRINCE OF THE APOSTLES
San Pietro 64 A.D.

"Thou art Peter, and upon this rock I will build my church."
(Matthew 16:18)

St. Peter is known as the Prince of the Apostles for his deep faith, strong character and powerful presence among his fellow disciples. He led the early church from obscurity to widespread recognition and laid a solid foundation for the following generations of faithful.

The life of St. Peter is not well documented, but there are several stories in the New Testament detailing episodes in his life. Prior to becoming a disciple, Peter was a fisherman from the Galilean town of Bethsaida, and was called Simon. His brother, St. Andrew, introduced him to Jesus, and at this first meeting Jesus gave him the Aramaic name Kaphas (Cephas), or Peter, meaning rock. Peter and

Andrew soon returned to their trade as fisherman and spent time with Jesus as best they could. Finally Jesus petitioned them to join him permanently saying; "Come ye after me, and I will make you fishers of men." (Matthew 4:19) The brothers enthusiastically followed the Master, becoming his first disciples.

There is no disputing that Peter was the leader of the followers of Jesus for he was often in the forefront of their activities. One incident reveals the depth of Peter's intuitive perception of Jesus. When Jesus asked the disciples if they knew who he was, Peter replied; "Thou art the Christ, the Son of the living God." And Christ responded; "Blessed art thou Simon, because flesh and blood hath not revealed it to thee, but my Father who is in Heaven. And I say to thee, that thou art Peter, and upon this rock I will build my Church." (Matthew 16:18)

The most infamous story concerning Peter is his denial of Christ. After Jesus was forcibly taken from the Garden of Gethsemane, Peter was confronted three different times and asked if he knew Jesus. Just as Jesus had prophesied, Peter denied knowledge of him all three times. While showing his human frailty in this story, Peter would go on to powerfully lead the disciples after the crucifixion. Christ appeared to Peter one last time before his ascension and said to him, "Feed my sheep," (John 21:17) thus inspiring Peter to preach Christ's message throughout Judea and Asia Minor, helping to form the foundations of the Christian church.

Peter led early Christians on many missionary efforts, and was the first of the Apostles to perform a miracle. One day as they approached the temple to pray, a man lame from birth begged Peter and John for alms. Peter said "Silver and gold I have none, but what I have, that give I thee: in the name of Jesus Christ of Nazareth, arise and walk." (Acts 3:6) The man stood and, leaping with joy, went with them into the temple to pray.

As Christianity spread and gained popularity, it began to threaten the entrenched hierarchy of the Roman Empire. In 43 A.D., Herod Agrippa I began to persecute the Christians and killed the Apostle James and imprisoned Peter. Peter was chained between two sleeping soldiers when an angel appeared and led him to freedom. He escaped Herod's wrath and went on to preach for twenty more years.

The remaining years of his life are not documented, but he finally ended up in Rome, once again arrested for his faith. Imprisoned and tried, he was executed, following in the footsteps of his Master and hundreds of other martyred Christians. Sentenced to be crucified, Peter asked to be placed upside down, because he did not feel worthy of facing death in the same manner as Jesus. He was crucified about 64 A.D. on Vatican Hill, and is enshrined there in the Basilica of St. Peter.

ST. PETER'S BASILICA
Basilica di San Pietro or San Pietro in Vaticano

St. Peter's Basilica is in the Vatican City at the end of Via della Conciliazione and fronted by the vast Piazza San Pietro. The site has a long history dating back to the martyrdom of St. Peter, for the first building was an oratory built over St. Peter's tomb immediately after his death. In 324, Constantine began construction of the original Basilica, creating a monumental structure that was in constant use until the papacy left Rome in the early fourteenth century. With the absence of the popes, the church fell into disrepair, and remained in this state until it was finally dismantled in 1506, when work on the current Basilica was begun. After 120 years of design and construction, the new Basilica was inaugurated in 1626. Many great architects and artists were commissioned to perform the work including Bramante, Bernini and Michelangelo.

There is so much to see at St. Peter's and the Vatican that we recommend buying a separate travel guide. Depending upon your

time available, an entire day should be allotted for a fairly complete visit. If you really enjoy museums, plan for additional time. We highlight the more important sites, but use your other guides to plan the details of your visit. You won't want to miss

Basilica di San Pietro or San Pietro in Vaticano

at least some of the Vatican Museums (Musei Vaticani) with Michelangelo's Sistine Chapel (Cappella Sistina), a trip to the top of the dome, and ample time to absorb the wonderful vibrations of St. Peter's tomb.

Your first destination should be the *Vatican City Pilgrim and Tourist Information Office* (outside, on the left, as you face St. Peter's). Strict dress regulations are enforced in the Basilica, so don't wear shorts, or mini-skirts, and be sure your shoulders and midriff are covered.

As you walk into St. Peter's, you will be astonished by the sheer size of the church. Although immense, the proportions are beautiful and the detailing of the interior is well done, if not overdone, in places. On your immediate right is Michelangelo's exquisite *Pietà,* a work of art worthy of its fame. As you walk down the main aisle toward the transept of the church you will approach Bernini's massive bronze canopy with spiral columns, built over the tomb of St. Peter and directly under the dome of Michelangelo. You can visit what is thought to be St. Peter's original tomb below the Basilica by making reservations before you come to Rome through the Excavations Office or "Scavi" (see below). There are four massive pillars support-ing the dome, and each one has significant art or relics associated with it. A piece of the true cross is behind the statue of St. Helena in the pillar at the far right when approaching the tomb. The pillar at the near right with the statue of St. Longinus contains his lance, which pierced the side of Christ. To the right of the main altar you can go downstairs and visit the Sacred Vatican Grottoes (Sacre Grotte Vaticane), which contain the tombs of many popes.

An excursion up into the dome of Michelangelo is time-consuming, but well worth the trip. The elevator is found on the outside of the Basilica on the right as you face it. After going up and viewing the inside of the dome, take the spiral staircase to the cupola for great panoramic views of Rome.

Although the Basilica is extremely large (6 acres) and usually filled with throngs of people, the size seems to absorb the sound, and it is not as noisy as one would think. The area around St. Peter's tomb is very special, although it is not a place to meditate. There is a med-itation chapel, the Chapel of the Holy Sacrament, on the right as you approach the main altar, where silence (silenzio) is enforced—a rare thing in Italy! This chapel is ideal for meditation and prayer after you have made your tour.

Tomb of St. Peter (Fabbrica di San Pietro) and the Pre-Constantinian Necropolis (Necropoli): Reserve your hour-and-a-half guided visit well ahead of time through the Excavations Office (Soperintendenza degli Scavi). Access to the tomb is outside the Basilica on the left, from the Arch of the Bells (Arco della Campane). No one under 15 is admitted and cameras and bags must be checked. It is highly recommended to make reservations before you leave the US. Reservations can be made with the Excavations Office by: E-mail: scavi@fsp.va or Fax: 06-69873017 or by mail: Ufficio Scavi/00120 Città del Vaticano/Roma/Italia. You will need to provide the number of visitors, names, language, contact information and time period of your visit. Full details at www.vatican.va "Info" "Visits to the Vatican Necropolis" Open: Mon–Sat, 9AM–5PM.

Vatican Museum (Musei Vaticani) and Sistine Chapel (Cappella Sistina): Since the Vatican Museum is so large, research beforehand what you want to visit online. Bus service runs continuously from the Tourist Information Office in St. Peter's Square to the Museums and Chapel and back. The schedule is at the bus stop, and you buy your ticket on the bus. The museum is closed Holidays and Sundays, except the last Sunday of the month when admission is free. Check www.vatican.va "Vatican Museums" or mv.vatican.va and click on "Info Museums," "Visitor Services," then "Guided Tours" for detailed information about hours and reservations.

Vatican Gardens: 58 acres of lush gardens. Reserve a guided tour ahead of time online at the same website above. The 2-hour tours are limited to 33 people, and they are partly by bus and partly on foot.

Papal Audience: To participate in the audience of the Pope on Wednesday around 10:30AM, you must reserve tickets distributed free. You have three choices in reserving tickets:

❉ You can reserve tickets from the Vatican at the *Prefecture of the Pontifical Household (Prefettura della Casa Pontifica)*. Reserve in writing, specifying the date and number of tickets, to the Prefettura della Casa Pontificia, 00120 Città del Vaticano, Italia or Fax: 066 9885863. Tickets are also available to the right of St. Peter's Basilica as you face the church through the Bronze doors between 3-6PM on the Tuesday afternoon before the Wednesday audience.

✼ You can also reserve tickets for an audience and a Papal Mass (except Easter and Christmas) by visiting the American Parish in Rome's website at www.santasusanna.org and click on "Pope & Vatican." They have good information on Rome and lodging in religious housing.

✼ You can also obtain tickets for an audience and a Papal Mass from the Bishops' Office for United States Visitors to the Vatican, Attn: Rev. Msgr. Roger C. Roensch/Via dell'Umilita 30/00187 Roma/Italia, Fax: 066 791448, E-mail: nacvisoffrome@pnac.org Check out their website first for all the details at www.pnac.org, click on "Coming to Rome." This website has all the information you will need including lodging in religious housing.

SHRINE INFORMATION

Shrine: St. Peter's Basilica and the Vatican (Basilica di San Pietro & Il Vaticano)

Address: Via del Pellegrino/00120/Cita del Vaticano/Italia

Phone: 066 9884466 **Fax:** 066 9885500 (Vatican Tourist Office)

E-mail: stpetersbasilica@gmail.com

Website: www.stpetersbasilica.org/www.vatican.va/www.vaticanstate.va

Quiet areas for meditation: The meditation chapel, where silence is enforced, is on the right as you face the altar.

English spoken: Typically

Hours: Apr–Sept, 7AM–7PM; Oct–Mar, 7AM–6PM; closed during Papal Audiences in the piazza.

Mass: Inquire at the tourist office or www.vatican.va "information."

Feasts and festivities: June 29 — Feast day; also honored on February 22 and November 18.

Accessibility: Entrance on the left of the Basilica through the Arco delle Campane and follow the signs to the ramp. Wheelchairs can be reserved in advance for the Vatican Museums Fax: 066 9885433 or at the "Special Permits" window in the entrance hall. Visually impaired visitors can reserve a visit at Fax: 066 9881573.

Tours: Tours are given in English beginning at the Tourist Information Office (see below).

Bookstore: The Vatican Bookstore (Libreria Editrice Vaticana) is located on St. Peter's Square to the left of the Basilica as you are facing it.

Lodging: None. www.pnac.org "Coming to Rome" "Where can I stay."

Tourist Office: Vatican City Pilgrim and Tourist Information Office (In the piazza on the left as you face St. Peter's) P. San Pietro/00120 Città del Vaticano/Italia; Phone: 066 9884466 Fax: 066 9885100

Directions: St. Peter's is located in the Vatican at Piazza San Pietro.

Bus: #64 from Rome Termini train station.

Metro: A (Ottaviano stop), 19, 64, 81

BASILICA OF ST. PETER IN VINCOLI
Basilica di San Pietro in Vincoli

This Basilica was built about 442 A.D. as a shrine to preserve the chains believed to have bound the Apostle Peter during his captivity in Jerusalem, and the chains that once bound Peter in Mammertime Prison. When the chains were placed next to each other, they miraculously fused into one link. They are near the main altar in a golden reliquary. Also of note is Michelangelo's *Moses*. The Basilica was restored during the eighth century, and several times during the fifteenth and sixteenth centuries. The Basilica is on Piazza San Pietro in Vincoli # 4A near the Colosseum. Take Metro Line B to Cavour. Hours: Mon–Sat, 7AM–12:30PM; 3:30PM–7:00; Sun, 8:45AM–11:45.

    Other shrines relating to St. Peter: See St. John Lateran (Basilica di San Giovanni in Laterano) and Basilica of St. Sebastian (Basilica di San Sebastiano) following St. Paul.

ST. PAUL - APOSTLE OF THE GENTILES
San Paulo A.D. 64

"I have been crucified with Christ; and it is no longer I that live,
but Christ living in me." (Galatians 2:20)

St. Paul was a tireless missionary, traveling throughout Asia Minor teaching the gospel and living as an example of a faithful disciple. Paul was also fearless. Though many times facing death and imprisonment for his faith, he professed his beliefs and constantly lived in an inner world of Christ's presence. "I have learned the secret of being content in any and every situation …. I can do everything through him who gives me strength." (Philippians 4:12-13 NIV) There is a great deal of information in the New Testament about St. Paul because St. Luke, in the Acts of the Apostles, describes his missionary journeys, and St. Paul wrote numerous letters, or epistles, to members of the church, explaining his spiritual journey.

Paul was born Saul, the son of an upstanding Jewish family, and was sent as a young man to Jerusalem to receive training in Hebrew law, religion and the trade of tent-making. Saul was staunchly conservative and mindful of ancient law, and found the new sect of Christianity to be diametrically opposed to his beliefs. He saw it as his duty to persecute the Jewish converts and rid Jerusalem of their blasphemy. Saul became well known for this activity and was even present at the martyrdom of St. Stephen. He soon set his sights on purging the city of Damascus, and departed Jerusalem with a band of compatriots to assail the converted Jews of the Syrian town.

While on the road to Damascus, Saul's group was surrounded by a brilliant light. From that light Saul heard a voice saying, "Saul, Saul, why do you persecute me?" "Who are you, Lord?" Saul asked. "I am Jesus who you are persecuting. Get up and go into the city and you will be told what to do." (Acts 9:4-6 NIV) Getting up, Saul found he was blinded by the light and was led by hand into the city. Here he fasted and prayed, waiting for his unknown future to unfold. After three days, a local disciple named Ananias came to Saul and restored his sight in the name of Jesus, and baptized him in the Holy Spirit. Thus Paul was converted and immediately began preaching the gospel in Damascus. Soon, he too was persecuted for his beliefs, and had to flee the city in the dark of night to save his life. After preaching in Jerusalem for a short time, he was again threatened and escaped to the desert where he secluded for three years before continuing his mission.

This was a pattern that repeated itself many times throughout Paul's life. A powerful preacher and missionary, he trekked throughout Asia Minor, Greece and Palestine sharing the teachings of the gospel, frequently traveling with other disciples including Saints Barnabus, Mark and Timothy. He often lived for more than a year in a single location, establishing a church and developing a community of believers. Known as the Apostle of the Gentiles, Paul's mission was converting Gentiles to the new sect of Christianity and helping them to remain faithful. As the communities became strong, or when his life was truly threatened, he would move on and help establish a new congregation. His letters of support to his numerous churches eventually became part of the New Testament and form an in-depth look into the early Christian church.

Paul would return to Jerusalem every few years to connect with other disciples of Christ and enliven their mutual bond. On his third such venture to Israel, Paul was arrested by the powerful Jewish Pharisees and imprisoned for two years, continually bound in chains. Paul defended himself before the Roman authorities and convinced them of his innocence, but the Pharisees were threatened by his power and wanted him executed. Paul was a Roman citizen, and demanded to be tried as such, in Rome. Thus began the final chapter of his life.

While on the way to see Nero, the emperor in Rome, Paul was shipwrecked. He survived the ordeal, and eventually was delivered to the capital city. The depiction of his life ends here in the gospels, but there is good evidence that he was tried and initially placed under house arrest. Exiled to his home, he still received many visitors and continued to preach and make converts. He made one final missionary journey but eventually returned to Rome, where he was again arrested and, this time, sentenced to die. His imprisonment was concurrent with St. Peter's, but the exact facts of their demise are not well documented. While Peter was crucified at Vatican hill, Paul had a different fate because he was a Roman citizen. His sentence was carried out through decapitation, which took place on the Appian Way. It is said that after his head was severed, it bounced three times, and three springs miraculously began to flow where there was none before. The shrine, Tre Fonte, was built in his honor.

One of Paul's seemingly simple teachings is still one of the most profound, "If I have a faith that can move mountains, but I have not love, I am nothing…. It always protects, always trusts, always hopes, always preserves. Love never fails." (1 Corinthians 13:2-8 NIV) His feast day, June 29, is shared with St. Peter, and January 25 is celebrated as his conversion date.

BASILICA OF ST. PAUL OUTSIDE THE WALLS
Basilica di San Paolo Fuori le Mura

St. Paul's Basilica was originally built by Constantine in the fourth century, over the tomb of St. Paul. It was destroyed by fire in 1823, and then re-consecrated in 1854. St. Paul's is unusual, having five aisles instead of three. The tomb of St. Paul is under the main altar where a confessional window (fenestrella confessionis) shows the epigraph "Paolo Apostolo Mart." Follow signs to "Altare dell tomba." Chains that bound St. Paul as a prisoner in Rome are in a golden reliquary.

Basilica di San Paolo Fuori le Mura

Basilica di San Paolo Fuori le Mura is located at Via Ostiense, 186, Roma and is open daily from 7:30AM–6:40PM. You will have to take Metro Linea B to San Paulo, since it is on the outskirts of town. www.vatican.va "information." Parish office: 065 410178/065 410341

ST. PAUL AT THE THREE FOUNTAINS
San Paolo alle tre Fontane

This church is said to have been the location of St. Paul's execution, where he was decapitated and where three fountains sprang up where his head landed. The springs are covered over now because the water is polluted. The first church was built in the fifth century and rebuilt in 1599. It takes some time to reach this shrine since it is outside the city, but many pilgrims find this a very blessed site. Take the B line to

Stazione Laurentina which is the end of the line. Go north on Via Laurentina several blocks.

ST. JOHN LATERAN
Basilica di San Giovanni in Laterano

Basilica di San Giovanni in Laterano

Built in the fourth century by Constantine as a classic Roman Basilica, St. John Lateran was frequently plundered, and later destroyed by earthquake and two fires in 1307 and 1361. As a result there have been many restorations through the years, the last being in the seventeenth century by Francesco Borromini, in Baroque style. This church has a long history, as it was the primary residence of the popes until their departure from Rome to Avignon, France. When the pope returned to Rome in 1375, it was no longer used. The main Papal altar contains the heads of Saints Peter and Paul in two silver busts of the saints. This altar also includes the original wooden altar that St. Peter and his successors are thought to have used to celebrate mass. To the left of the altar is the Chapel of the Choir, with a relief panel of the Last Supper above the tabernacle. Behind it rests what is believed to be a piece of the table from the Last Supper. The Basilica is located on Piazza San Giovanni in Laterano #4. Take Metro Linea A to San Giovanni. Open daily 7AM–7PM; in winter closing time is 6PM. www.vatican.va "Information." Phone: 066 9886452.

SANCTUARY OF THE HOLY STAIRS
Santuario della Scala Sancta

Near the Basilica of St. John Lateran on the eastern side of Piazza San Giovanni, the Sanctuary of the Holy Stairs enshrines the stairs that Jesus climbed during his Passion. St. Helena, Constantine's mother, brought them to Rome from Pontius Pilate's palace in Jerusalem. The stairs are covered in wood to protect them. Pilgrims climb the 28 stairs on their knees, ending up at the ancient papal Chapel of San Lorenzo that was transferred from the Lateran Palace.

ST. IGNATIUS OF LOYOLA
San Ignacio de Loyola 1491–1556

"You have given me all that I have, all that I am, and I surrender all to your divine will. Give me only your love and your grace. With this I am rich enough, and I have no more to ask."

St. Ignatius of Loyola was a man of will power, integrity, but most of all, love. As father of the Jesuit order, he may be remembered as an energetic organizer and reformer, but his sole aim was to share the love of God and teach others to experience that divine love for themselves.

Born in the Basque region of Spain, Inigo de Loyola was the youngest of thirteen children of a noble Spanish family. He was raised with expectations of gaining wealth and power for his family, and

St. Ignatius of Loyola

at age sixteen was sent to live in the court of King Ferdinand under the tutelage of the court Treasurer. Caught in the spell of the royal court, Inigo became infatuated with his prospects of a regal future, enflamed by his incessant reading of romance novels. St. Ignatius describes himself at this time: "He did not avoid sin, being particularly without restraint in gaming, affairs with women, dueling, and armed affrays."

Inigo enjoyed life in the King's court for the next ten years, but when his mentor died he was abruptly left with nothing but two horses. So, at the age of twenty-six, he enlisted in the army of the Viceroy of Navarre with visions of adventure, conquest and fame. In 1521, while defending Pamplona from French invaders, Inigo was struck by a cannonball that passed between his legs, shattering one limb and seriously injuring the other. The Spaniards lost the battle, and Inigo was taken prisoner. The French admired his courage and bravery, so they graciously set his broken leg and sent him home to heal.

Time passed slowly for the convalescing soldier. He soon requested romance novels to get through his long inactive days. Because romantic novels were in short supply, Inigo resorted to reading books on the life of Christ and the saints. After reading and re-reading these books, he became increasingly inspired by the courage of the saints and impressed by the high states of consciousness they attained. Inigo began to wonder if he too could accomplish this, and planned upon his recovery to test his new faith by going on pilgrimage to the Holy Land.

This was the turning point for Inigo, as he began to observe and analyze his thoughts. He found that when he thought of worldly things he felt "discontented and dry," but when he thought of pilgrimage to Jerusalem, of Christ and the saints, he felt "joyful and contented." This discovery was the first step in developing his famous "Spiritual Exercises," a systematic process of introspection and prayer that leads to deep contemplation of God. Around this time, Inigo decided to change his name to that of his patron saint, St. Ignatius.

After eight months of recuperating, Ignatius left on pilgrimage to the Holy Land with no specific plans except to visit Montserrat near Barcelona, which is home to the shrine of the Black Virgin. Here he made a commitment to his new life, giving away his fine clothes in exchange for sackcloth, giving up meat and wine, and letting his hair and nails grow. Then, after a year in Manresa, Spain, where he read

"The Imitation of Christ," and received many divine revelations, he eventually realized he could more effectively save souls if he cut his hair, trimmed his nails, and ceased his extreme austerities. His inner training culminated in a profound ecstasy that occurred along the river Cardoner near the Chapel of St. Paul. Seeing this as the end of his "novitiate," Ignatius continued his pilgrimage and began preaching in earnest, sharing his Spiritual Exercises with all who would listen.

Ignatius finally arrived in the Holy Land in 1523 and visited all the sacred sites, preaching wherever he went. His exuberant tirades against the local Muslims were not well received by them, or by the Franciscans who were in charge of the shrines, and Ignatius was asked to leave the country. Without direction, he decided to return to Spain and renew his education.

Ignatius began to attract a small group of students while attending the universities of Spain and Paris. By the time he received his Masters of Arts degree in Paris at age forty-three, Ignatius had six dedicated disciples, including Francis Xavier. After several years of attempting to reach the Holy Land, they all journeyed to Rome and were gratefully welcomed by the pope who granted them permission to become a new order, the Society of Jesus, or Jesuits.

The Society of Jesus was established in 1540, and Ignatius was elected general superior against his wishes. While taking the typical vows of poverty, obedience and chastity, the Jesuits added a fourth vow to accept assignment to any place to spread the teachings of the Gospel. This ultimately led to the Society becoming a worldwide organization in Ignatius's lifetime, with brothers serving throughout Europe, as well as in India and Brazil. For his remaining sixteen years, Ignatius guided the Jesuits through their expansion from ten members to more than a thousand. They established orphanages, houses of refuge for prostitutes, hospitals for famine relief and colleges for both religious and laypersons.

Ignatius was frequently sick, so little attention was given when he again became ill in July of 1556. He passed away quietly on the morning of July 31, at age sixty-six. St. Ignatius was canonized in 1622 and declared the patron saint of spiritual exercises and retreat. At his canonization, the Pope said "Ignatius had a heart bigger than the world."

St. Ignatius was an exceptionally balanced person with tremendous will. He could be tough and take action when needed, and he could be kind and loving when the moment required it. He wisely advised his monks to seek "the presence of God Our Lord in all things and at all times, whether conversing, walking, looking, tasting, listening, thinking, in everything you do."

THE CHURCH OF THE HOLY NAME OF JESUS
La Chiesa del Gesù

The Church of the Holy Name of Jesus is the mother church of the Society of Jesus founded by St. Ignatius of Loyola. It is in Rome on Piazza del Gesù, near Piazza Venezia. The church was built in the Counter-Reformation style twelve years after St. Ignatius' death, and consecrated in 1584. The Chapel and Tomb of St. Ignatius are on the left side of the main altar. The remains of St. Ignatius rest in a gilded bronze urn under the altar. At the level of the altar are seven large bronze bas-reliefs showing scenes from the life and the miracles of St. Ignatius. The chapel of St. Francis Xavier is to the right of the main altar, and contains a reliquary with his arm above its altar.

The rooms where St. Ignatius lived for twelve years, from 1544 until his death in 1556, are open to visitors. The entrance is at Piazza del Gesù, 45. As you face the church, there is a large doorway to the right. Next to the door is a bronze plaque with "IHS" (the first letters of the name of Jesus in Greek), which represents the seal of the Society of Jesus. At the front desk you can ask for a guidebook in

La Chiesa del Gesù

English, and, if you want, ask if anyone is available to lead a tour in English. Follow the long hall to the right, then up a flight of stairs, and at the top take a left. There is a museum and meditation room with chairs. This is an excellent place to sit and meditate on St. Ignatius. It was in this small room (with the window opening on to an enclosed balcony) that Ignatius slept and worked. The larger room (with window on the west opening onto the street), presently the Chapel of the Blessed Virgin, is where Ignatius celebrated Mass, received visitors and died. From these rooms Ignatius governed the Society of Jesus. The museum contains many relics and writings of the saint, all described in the guidebook.

I would like to visit the rooms of St. Ignatius.
Vorrei visitare le stanze di Sant'Ignazio.

Do you have a guidebook in English?
Avete una guida scritta in inglese?

Is there anyone available to give us a tour in English?
C'è qualcuno disponibile per una visita guidata in inglese?

SHRINE INFORMATION

Shrine: The Church of the Holy Name of Jesus (La Chiesa del Gesù)

Address: Santissimo Nome di Gesù all'Argentina/largo di Torre Argentina/Via degli Astalli 16/00186 Roma/Italia

Phone: 066 97001 **Fax:** 066 9700263

E-mail: Both websites below have email, for the Italian site "Contatti."

Website: www.gesuiti.it (Italian) www.sjweb.info "Curia in Rome"

Quiet areas for meditation: The rooms where St. Ignatius lived (le camera di San Ignazio) in the building to the right of the church.

English spoken: Occasionally

Hours: 7AM–12:30PM; 4PM–7:45.

Mass: During the day, every 45 minutes beginning at 6AM; Feast day — every hour beginning at 6AM; Evenings 6:30PM.

St. Ignatius' room: During the week 4PM–6; Sunday 10AM–12.

Feasts and festivities: December 3 — Feast day; December 31 — The Annual Papal Mass and Singing of the "Te Deum" on New Year's Eve.

Accessibility: Plans are being made for the church but access is not possible for St. Ignatius' rooms.

Tours: There is an Italian/Spanish guided tour of the church every Thursday at 4:30PM. To visit St. Ignatius' rooms between 4PM-6, you can ask at the front desk at Piazza del Gesù 45 if anyone is available for a guided tour in English. If not, there is an excellent booklet, "Guide to the rooms of St. Ignatius," for a self-guided tour.

Bookstore: A few English books on the church and the history of the Jesuit Order are on sale in the sacristy. There is a brochure in English on the church called "La Chiesa del Gesù."

Recommended books: *St. Ignatius Loyola*, by F.A. Forbes from Tan Books is small enough to take with you. Written in 1919, it gives you enough information to get a sense of St. Ignatius. *St. Ignatius Loyola: The First Jesuit*, by Mary Purcell, is a much longer version but fascinating reading. It is probably only available from used bookstores, but there are many books written about St. Ignatius on the market.

Lodging: None

Directions: The main entrance to the church is at Piazza del Gesù where V.C. Pebiscito and Corso Vittorio Emanuele meet. It is a couple of blocks away from Piazza Venezia.

From Termini train station to Piazza Venezia: bus 40/64

From Ostiense train station to Piazza Venezia: bus 60/95/175

From Tiburtina train station to Piazza Venezia: bus 492

ST. PHILIP NERI
San Filippo Neri 1515–1595

"He who desires aught else but God deceives himself utterly."

St. Philip Neri was a man of the common people. He taught people to trust their intuition and to follow their heart's guidance in finding God. Philip was known for his big heart and sense of humor, attracting souls through his loving and accepting personality. Born Filippo Romolo in Florence on July 21, 1515, Philip Neri led an uneventful childhood as the son of a not-so-successful notary. Prospects for a successful career led Philip to move at age eighteen to live with his wealthy uncle. Living near the Benedictine abbey of Monte Cassino, Philip began spending more and more time in prayer and contemplation, often going into quiet seclusion amongst the rocky crags that characterize the area. It is here that he experienced a "conversion" and decided to leave the prospect of wealth for a spiritual life in Rome.

Sixteenth century Rome was in material and spiritual decay after being invaded and ransacked by the French Constable of Bourbon. It was a time that called for a vocal reformer to fill the void and help uplift the spirits of the populace. Philip arrived in 1533, just six years after the infamous Sack of Rome, and quietly began his personal mission.

His first four years were spent in rigorous study of philosophy and theology while earning a living by tutoring two young boys. This he did in exchange for a meager amount of corn and residence in a small room. After much prayer, Philip decided to put an end to his studying in order to give himself more completely to God. He began to preach in a very unobtrusive way, engaging people in conversation and gently adding comments about moral behavior and righteous living. He became known for his hearty sense of humor and his acceptance of everyone. During his conversations, Philip would ask people, "when should we begin to do good?" and if he received a positive answer of "now," he would suggest people help in the hospitals and assist the poor and needy.

At night, he would spend his time in prayer, making the rounds of the holy churches of Rome, especially the seven Basilicas. He most relished going to pray at the Basilica of San Sebastiano, where he would go down into the catacombs and enter into silent communion with God. It was here that Philip had a transformative encounter with the Holy Spirit. While praying, a globe of fire entered his mouth and heart, and he experienced such an intense heat that he threw himself to the floor and bared his chest to cool down. When he stood

St. Philip Neri

up, he felt a swelling around his heart and his body shook with an over-whelming joy. For the remainder of his life, he would feel this intense heat in his throat and heart, and his heart would undergo palpitations so strong, that people could feel them transmitted throughout an en-tire room.

After fifteen years in Rome, Philip began meeting with a dozen laymen for prayer and spiritual discussions. Together they formed a benevolent fellowship. Their mission was to help the pilgrims who ar-rived in Rome often ill and without money. They opened pilgrim houses that became very successful, bringing notoriety to Philip and his followers. Philip was advised by his confessor that he could better serve God and his congregation by becoming a priest, so Philip was ordained in 1551.

Philip encouraged everyone to take communion daily, even though this was an uncommon practice at the time. He reveled in the joy he found in the Mass and was often overcome with devotion dur-ing his services, so much so, that he occasionally asked his brothers to read silly books to him prior to starting Mass. This enabled him to focus on the task at hand and not get lost in his ecstasies.

Philip felt a strong calling to minister to the young men of his community, wanting to help them avoid the pitfalls of secular attrac-tions. He would meet with them over lunch to discuss spiritual matters and read inspirational books. His Brothers at Girolamo complained that his young men made too much noise and disturbed the house, but he retorted, "They may chop wood on my back so long as they do not sin." Over time, he attracted many souls to this daily practice, which became known as the Oratory, a Congregation of sec-ular priests and clerics. When someone made trouble for the group after being expelled for unacceptable behavior, Philip realized that his Congregation needed a permanent church, so Santa Maria in Vallicella was given to him for the new home of the Oratory.

Philip saw his congregation as an informal fellowship and did not want to formalize it by becoming an official order of the church. He taught that every individual in his congregation had to discover a personal relationship with the Divine, following his or her own God-given intuition. Thus he avoided giving too many instructions on prayer and contemplation and told his followers, "Be humble and obedient and the Holy Ghost will teach you."

In April 1994, after forty-three years of service in Rome, Philip developed a high fever and became delirious. He beheld a vision of the Virgin Mary and was seen rising about a foot off the floor. He soon descended and then dismissed the doctors saying the Madonna had healed him from his affliction. After a year of good health, he became ill once again in March of 1595. One day, he suddenly collected all his papers and burned them. Then, after a full day of duties, he passed away peacefully on May 25, 1595.

The Romans turned out in throngs to pay their respects to the enigmatic Philip, and filed through the church all day long. When the church was finally closed, the doctors closely examined his body and found that "two ribs over the heart were broken and arched outwards. The heart was unusually large, while the great artery leading from it was twice the normal size." So to say that Philip had a big heart was not an exaggeration! St. Philip Neri was beatified in May 1615 and canonized in March 1622.

St. Philip Neri was a new breed of saint, a saint of the people. He reached out to people where they were and taught them how to find an inner home in God. He recommended reading about the saints because he thought intellectual pride was "more effectively overcome by the examples of the saints." His humor and joy were his trademarks, for he lived by the proverb, "A saint that is sad, is a sad saint indeed!"

THE NEW CHURCH, OR ST. MARY IN VALLICELLA
Chiesa Nuova, or Chiesa di Santa Maria in Vallicella

Chiesa Nuova is part of a complex built in several stages beginning in 1575, comprised of the church, the Secular Oratory, the Vallicella Library and the Convent of the Congregation. Chiesa Nuova contains the tomb of

Chiesa Nuova, or Chiesa di Santa Maria in Vallicella

St. Philip Neri, co-patron of Rome, also known as the "Saint of Joy." St. Philip was given the original church by Pope Gregory XIII as a home for his new congregation. The new church was rebuilt upon the original foundation and completed in 1605, ten years after the saint's death. The other buildings and restorations were made in the following centuries.

On his death in 1595, St. Philip was first laid in a walnut coffin and placed in the church of Santa Maria in Vallicella. Four years later, a new silver casket was made to hold his remains. When the old coffin was opened, the clothing was found to be decayed while the body remained incorrupt. In 1602, the body was transferred to a new chapel built to honor Philip. The casket was opened again in 1922, when St. Philip's body was found to still be incorrupt. Subsequently clothed in new vestments and placed in a crystal casket with a silver mask covering his face, his body now rests at Chiesa Nuova, in the Chapel of St. Philip Neri, to the left of the main altar.

The main altar contains the miraculous image of Santa Maria in Vallicella, behind the painting of Our Lady. The ancient icon is revealed on Sundays and at special times when the painting of Our Lady is slid to the side to display the icon. The story is that a disappointed gambler threw a stone at the image on the outside of the church and drops of blood fell on the cheek of the Virgin. St. Philip requested the painting be transported inside the church, and it became the emblem of the Congregation of the Oratory and a vehicle for many miracles. Once, the Madonna of Vallicella appeared to St. Philip in a dream, warning him of a rotting beam in the church. The beam was subsequently discovered to be rotten and was repaired, saving the congregation from a dangerous situation. Also on the main altar is the "Cor Flammigerum"—the flaming heart, which represents St. Philip and the mystical experience he had while praying in the catacombs of St. Sebastian, when a globe of fire descended and entered his heart.

In the Visitation Chapel (fourth on left), St. Philip's favorite painting is displayed: "The Presentation of the Virgin in the Temple" by Federico Barocci. St. Philip experienced frequent ecstasies and levitations in this chapel. The Assumption Chapel (fifth on right) is known for the painting of the Virgin by Aurelio Lomi di Pisa. The Virgin moved her eyes in 1796 with most of the Oratorians as witnesses. A month-long festival ensued, during which the miracle reoccurred.

The private rooms of the saint are open on Tues., Thurs., & Sun., including the saint's feast day, May 26th. Guided tours can be arranged in advance (see below). The rooms consist of the Red room and Inner chapel on the ground floor and three rooms upstairs.

SHRINE INFORMATION

Shrine: Congregation of the Oratory (Congregazione dell'Oratorio)

Address: Via del Governo Vecchio 134/00186 Roma/Italia

Phone: 066 875289/066 8808448 **Fax:** 066 873124

E-mail: vallicella@tiscali.it

Website: www.chiesanuova.net

Quiet areas for meditation: The Courtyard of the Orange Trees

English spoken: Occasionally

Hours: Summer 8AM–1PM; 4:30pm–7:30; Winter 8AM–1PM; 4PM–7:30.

Mass: Sun/Hol: Summer 8:30am, 10, 11, 12, 7PM; Winter 8:30AM, 10, 11, 12, 12:45PM, 6:30; Weekdays: Summer 8AM, 10, 7PM; Winter 8AM, 9, 10, 6:30PM.

Feasts and festivities: May 26th

Accessibility: There is a ramp to the front door, but there are two low steps at the entrance that you will need assistance with. If you need assistance with the steps, send someone inside to find help. The bathrooms are not accessible. Groups should make arrangements ahead of time.

Tours: Guided thirty minute tours in English for the church and the rooms of St. Philip can be arranged on Tues., Thurs., & Sat between 10AM & 12PM by email mauriziobotta@hotmail.com or calling in advance 066 8804695.

Bookstore: In the Sacristy. No books in English, but a brochure in English is available.

Recommended book: Small pocket book, *Saint Philip Neri*, by Fr. V.J. Matthews, Tan Books, (not available at Shrine).

Lodging: None

Directions: Chiesa Nuova is located at Piazza della Chiesa Nuova on the corso Vittorio Emanuele II, midway between St. Peter's Basilica and Piazza Venezia. Take Bus 40, 46, 62, 64, 190, 571 or 916.

Basilica of St. Sebastian, or St. Sebastian's Outside the Walls
Basilica di San Sebastiano, or San Sebastiano fuori le Mura

Constantine built the original basilica in the fourth century in honor of Saints Peter and Paul who had been buried there for a while during the time of persecution. Excavations in 1916 revealed a secret Christian cemetery under the church, giving credence to this story. In the third century, St. Sebastian was buried in the catacombs and his relics are now under the main altar. Behind this altar there is a reliquary containing the head of St. Fabian; his body lies underneath the floor. In the Chapel of Relics, on the right, are the imprints of Christ's feet from when he appeared to St. Peter and one of the arrows that pierced the side of St. Sebastian. On the left of the altar is the entrance to the catacombs. The Basilica is located outside the city walls on Via Appia Antica 136, before Circus Maxentius and the tomb of Caecilia Metella.

Catacombs of St. Sebastian: There are four levels to these catacombs. On the first level is the chapel where St. Philip Neri would go to pray and where he experienced the globe of fire entering his heart. The catacombs are located next to the Basilica of St. Sebastian, on Via Appia Antica 132. Open 9AM–12; 2PM–5 (closed Sundays). The catacombs are hard to get to. Tours are thirty minutes and occur every ten minutes. Check out ww.catacombe.roma.it for detailed directions. Email: acalo@catacombe.roma.it Phone: 067 887035 Fax: 067 843745. It is suggested that you book a tour ahead of time for groups of ten or more.

St. Catherine of Siena
Santa Caterina di Siena 1347–1380

St. Catherine of Siena spent the last two years of her life in Rome working tirelessly for the unification of the Church. Growing weaker over time, and finally succumbing to intense pain and paralysis of her legs, she died on April 29, 1380, at the age of thirty-three. Her remains are buried under the main altar of the Basilica di Santa Maria Sopra Minerva. Read about her fascinating life in the chapter on Siena, in the region of Tuscany.

BASILICA OF HOLY MARY ABOVE MINERVA
Basilica di Santa Maria Sopra Minerva

The first church, which was destroyed at some point, was built in the 700's over the ancient temple of Minerva (50 B.C.). The current Basilica was started with the help of two Dominican monks, Sisto and Ristoro in 1280 and com-

St. Catherine of Siena

pleted in 1370, with changes made in subsequent periods. The Basilica is known as the only Gothic church in Rome.

A wooden image of St. Catherine, sculpted by Isaia of Pisa in 1430, rests in the glass and stone urn that contains her relics. To the left of the altar and through the sacristy is her chapel, The Room of St. Catherine, constructed in the 1630s from the walls of the rooms where she died at Via Santa Chiara #14. The chapel is open from 9AM–6PM, except Sundays. This is one of the best places to meditate in Rome. There are a few chairs and very few visitors. Be prepared to speak in Italian.

Where is the room of St. Catherine?
Dov'è la stanza di Santa Caterina?

To the left of the main altar is the tomb of Fra Angelico (Fra Giovanni of Fiesole). He is buried inconspicuously in the floor in the Frangipane Chapel. He died in the monastery next door. Blessed Fra Angelico, a Dominican monk, is best known for his beautiful frescoes in the San Marco convent in Florence (see Florence, Tuscany). Santa Maria Sopra Minerva is located near the Pantheon on Piazza della Minerva.

SHRINE INFORMATION

Shrine: Basilica of Holy Mary above Minerva (Basilica di Santa Maria Sopra Minerva)

Address: Piazza della Minerva, 42/00186 Roma, Italia.

Phone: 066 793926 **Fax:** None

E-mail: ballic.op@tiscali.it Rector P. Andrea Ballicu O.P. Write in Italian only.

Website: www.basilicaminerva.it Italian

Quiet areas for meditation: The room of St. Catherine to the left of the main altar and through the sacristy.

English spoken: Rarely

Hours: 8AM–7PM

Mass: Sun/Hol: 11AM, 12, 6PM; Weekdays: 8:15AM, 6PM. Call ahead of time, if you want a special mass for your group Phone: 066 990672.

Feasts and festivities: April 29 — Feast day

Accessibility: There are three stairs to the Basilica.

Tours: None

Bookstore: There is a table set up selling books with some in English.

Recommended book: *Basilica of Santa Maria Sopra Minerva*, sold at the church bookstore.

Lodging: None

Directions: Piazza della Minerva adjacent to the Pantheon.

Basilica di Santa Maria Sopra Minerva

OTHER PLACES OF INTEREST

See the chapter on Siena in Tuscany for information on St. Catherine's shrine and childhood home.

OTHER SHRINES IN ROME

ST. MARY MAJOR
Basilica di Santa Maria Maggiore

The Virgin Mary appeared separately to Pope Liberius and the Roman patrician Giovanni, in 352 A.D., requesting that a church be erected in her honor. The Virgin Mary told them that a miraculous snow would fall indicating where the church was to stand. The next day, on August 4th, during a heat wave, snow fell on the place where the church was to be built. The earliest record of the church's construction is from 432 to 440 by Pope Sixtus III. The original church was replaced in the thirteenth century. A reliquary below the center altar displays a piece of the baby Jesus' crib. You need to check when this relic is displayed as they close it up completely. There is also the crypt of St. Matthias the Apostle who replaced Judas Iscariot. There's a bench on either side of the reliquary to sit on. This church is on Piazza Santa Maria Maggiore Via Liberiana, 27. Take Metro Line B to Cavour or Termini Stazione. The church is between these two stops. Open daily: 7AM–8PM; in winter the church closes at 7PM. Phone: 064 83195 Fax: 064 875521. www.vatican.va under "Information." Email: sagrestiasmm@org.va.

BASILICA OF ST. LAWRENCE OUTSIDE THE WALLS
Basilica di San Lorenzo fuori le Mura

Constantine built the original church dedicated to the martyr St. Lawrence, who was slowly burned to death in 258 A.D. The church was rebuilt in 576 with many remodels through the centuries. The relics of St. Lawrence, St. Justin and St. Stephen are behind the main altar. Located near the Campo Verano cemetery on Piazzale del Verano 3/00185 Roma, Italia. Open Sat–Thurs 7AM–12; 3PM–7. Phone 064 91511. www.basilicadisanlorenzo.org Italian. Email: basilica@basilicadisanlorenzo.org.

BASILICA OF THE HOLY CROSS IN JERUSALEM
Basilica di Santa Croce in Gerusalemme

This Baroque church was first built in the fourth century by St. Helena, Constantine's mother, and houses many relics she brought back from the Holy Land. Many restorations have been made through the years including a complete remodel in the eighteenth century. During one of these restorations, around 1492, a fragment of the cross Jesus died on was found, hidden in an arch. The Chapel of the Relics contains fragments of this cross, St. Thomas's finger, a nail from the crucifixion, two thorns from Jesus' crown of thorns, and a part of the crib of Jesus. The Chapel is on a staircase on the way to the second level and through a doorway to the left of the Sacristy. The remains of Sts. Caesarius and Anastasius are under the main altar. Located on Piazza di Santa Croce in Gerusalemme, take Metro Linea A to San Giovanni. Open daily 6AM–12:30PM; 3:30PM–7:30; in winter it closes at 6:30PM.

COMING AND GOING

ROME

Car: Are you crazy?!!! Pazzo!!! All roads lead to Rome, but don't drive on them! Driving in Rome, really _is_ crazy. We spent time in Rome using public transportation, then rented a car at the airport and drove to other regions of Italy. Arrange your rental before you get to Italy, and it will be cheaper. There are hefty city and airport taxes, so be prepared.

Airports: Leonardo da Vinci, also called Fiumicino, is 16 miles (26 km) southwest of Rome and is the main airport, but there is another airport, Ciampino, that is also used sometimes for international flights, mostly charters. From Leonardo da Vinci Airport, there is a non-stop train that runs hourly and takes about 30 minutes to reach the main train station in Rome, Stazione Termini. It runs between approximately 7:37AM and 10:07PM. There are signs in the airport to the train station, and you buy your tickets from vending machines. If you arrive at Ciampino Airport, hourly COTRAL buses take you to Anagnina Metro station in about 25 minutes, where you connect to Stazione Termini for another 30 minute ride.

Train: Just like the roads, all trains lead to Rome! The Termini Station (Stazione Termini) has connections to the Metro lines A and B and to buses outside the station. Trains to Leonardo da Vinci Airport leave between 6:50AM and 9:20PM. Validate your ticket before boarding using the "obliteratrici" machines. Beware of pickpockets.

Bus: It is well worth the money to buy a good map with the bus and Metro information, even though the free ones from the tourist information centers are adequate. Buses ATAC and Metros use the same ticket. Buy them at newsstands, tobacconists and vending machines. Make sure you stamp your bus ticket on the bus. If you arrive late at night at the airport, there are buses, COTRAL, that will take you to central Rome. www.atac.roma.it Italian. *Roma Christiana* operates pilgrimage bus stops where you can hop on and off yellow and white, double-decker buses for one price starting at Piazza dei Cinquecento every fifty minutes. There are other tour buses that start there too.

Metro: There are two lines, A & B, that serve many of the major tourist destinations.

Taxi: It is advised that you use only the yellow and white licensed taxis with meters. This of course is the more costly way to get around in Rome.

Air: Opera Romana Pellegrinaggi (ORP) www.orpnet.org Italian — The Vatican offers pilgrimage travel packages to holy destinations.

TOURIST INFORMATION

❋ Enjoy Rome/Via Marghera 8a/00185 Roma/Italia; north from the Termini train station. Exit to the north (the Via Marsala exit) keep going straight for three blocks, on the left. A favorite in the tour books and everyone speaks English. Informative website. Phone: 064 451843; Fax: 064 450734. www.enjoyrome.com E-mail:info@enjoyrome.com

❋ IAT – Ufficio Informazioni e di Accoglienza Turistica/Via Parigi 5/00185 Italia; Phone: 064 88991

❋ APT Azienda di Promozione Turistica/Via Parigi, 11/00185/Roma /Italia; Phone: 064 88991 Fax: 064 819316 www.romaturismo.com Great online brochures & info on Rome. E-mail: info@aptroma.com

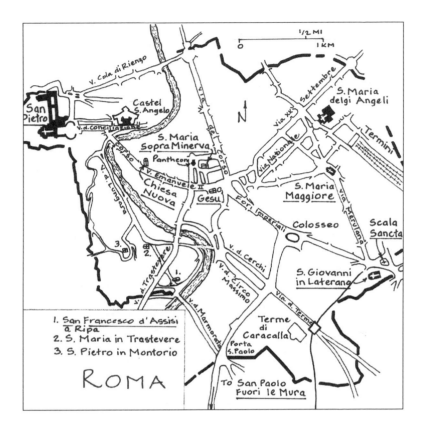

WEBSITES

ActivItaly www.activitaly.com — Tourist information on Rome.

Airports of Rome www.adr.it — Fiumicino and Ciampino airports.

All Roads Lead to Rome www.stuardtclarkesrome.com — Lists churches of Rome and detailed tourist info & maps.

APT www.romaturismo.com — Comprehensive tourist information.

Bishop's Office for US Visitors to the Vatican www.pnac.org click on "Coming to Rome." All you need to visit the Vatican.

CO.IN. www.coinsociale.it/tourism — *Cooperative Integrate ONLUS* is a national non-profit association based in Rome that provides comprehensive services for people with disabilities. *Accessible Tourism* provides tours and info on accessibility for the tourist. Once you are in Rome pick up their free "Roma Accessible" guide at COIN/Via Giglioli 54-a/00169, Roma Phone: 396 23269231 Email: coinsociale@coinsociale.it.

St. Peter's Basilica www.stpetersbasilica.org — Comprehensive information about St. Peter's Basilica, click on "contacts for St. Peter's Basilica."

Enjoy Rome www.enjoyrome.com — Comprehensive tourist information.

In Italy www.initaly.com/regions/latium/church/church.htm — Comprehensive excerpts from June Hager's book on the churches of Rome.

Info Roma www.inforoma.it/romepage.htm — Rome itinerary services.

Opera Romana Pellegrinaggi (ORP) www.orpnet.org — The Vatican offers pilgrimage travel packages to holy destinations.

Parco Via Appia Antica www.parcoappieaantica.it — Guided tours by bicycle or on foot through the Caffarella valley and along the Appian Way.

Roma Termini Railway Station www.fnc.net/termini/fseng.htm — Rome airport & train station info, timetables etc.

The Christian Catacombs of Rome www.catacombe.roma.it

Trambus www.trambus.com — Italian info on transport in Rome.

Vatican www.vatican.va — Comprehensive information on the Vatican.

Vatican City State www.vaticanstate.va — Vatican Government.

Parco Via Appia Antica www.parcoappieaantica.it — Guided tours by bicycle or on foot through the Caffarella valley and along the Appian Way.

The Marches

Le Marche

Located on the east coast of Italy, nestled between Umbria and the Adriatic Sea, this central region is comprised of the Apennine Mountains in the western districts and low rolling hills in the east. The population is distributed among small towns, with Ancona being the only city of note, having a population of 100,000. Most tourists seek the resort towns of the Adriatic and the Frasassi caves, but the real attractions are far subtler. The shrines at Osimo and Loreto are alive with deep treasures, and are very inviting to pilgrims of all faiths.

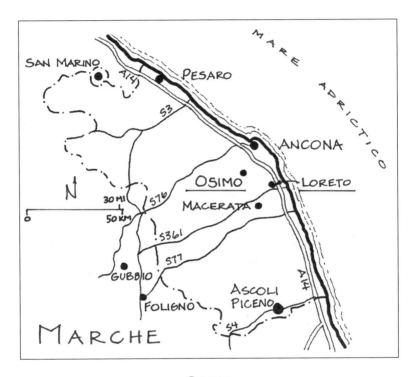

OSIMO
St. Joseph of Copertino

LORETO
Shrine of Loreto

Osimo

Population 29,750

Little remains of the Roman town that is now known as Osimo. Located 11 miles (18 km) west of Ancona, Osimo is comprised of a medieval walled city perched on a ridge between two rivers, surrounded by a modern Italian village. The layout of the town still reflects its Roman heritage but the buildings are all from the sixteenth and seventeenth centuries. The Duomo is worth seeing, as are the "headless" Roman statues in the town hall. In the peaceful town center, cafés and shops are inhabited by locals, for few tourists find their way here. But, for the discerning pilgrim, the Basilica of St. Joseph of Copertino is a worthy destination.

ST. JOSEPH OF COPERTINO
San Giuseppe da Copertino 1603-1663

"True servants of God simply go inside themselves."

St. Joseph of Copertino

St. Joseph sought to emulate St. Francis of Assisi and did so from birth. He was born in a stable, as was St. Francis, in the small town of Copertino on the peninsula of Apulia. His mother was a Franciscan tertiary and raised him in a strict yet loving environment. Together they attended Mass daily, and she often treated him to stories of Jesus, Mary and the saints. He later said of his childhood, "I didn't need a novitiate, I received one at the hands of my mother!"

Joseph was fortunate to attend school, but at age seven he developed painful ulcers and had to remain home in bed for the next four years. He lagged far behind his peers in education and was often thought to be a dullard due to his slow and deliberate speech. He would also stare off into space for long periods of time, seemingly dazed. At these times he was experiencing the ecstatic joy of God's presence, caused by deep feelings of devotion or hearing inspired music. His mother continued to take him to Mass during his illness, carrying him to the services. Prayers for Joseph's healing were ever on her lips. They were answered when, one day, a priest came to her with some oil from a lamp blessed at a nearby Marian shrine. Joseph was healed instantly by the power of the Virgin Mary, and he henceforth held a special place in his heart for her.

Joseph attempted to join the Franciscan order when he was seventeen. After only a short stay at the local friary, he was expelled due to his inattentiveness and his inability to perform even menial tasks. Unknown to his brothers, his lack of attention was due to his frequent ecstasies. Fortunately, his uncle was a Franciscan priest in nearby Grotella, who accepted Joseph there as a tertiary after much arm-twisting from Joseph's mother. Joseph was well received in his new home. By age twenty-three, he was accepted as a cleric and began studying intensely for his ordination examinations. Learning was always difficult for Joseph and only divine intervention would allow him to pass the tests. Joseph miraculously passed each exam with help from his Holy Mother, and was ordained a priest in 1628, at the age of twenty-five.

October 4th is the annual feast day for St. Francis. In 1630, Joseph was invited to his hometown of Copertino to join in their celebration of this holy day. The town turned out for the yearly parade and festivities. As Joseph walked through the familiar streets, chanting to his beloved St. Francis, he was suddenly overtaken with a joyous rapture, and rose high off the ground and hovered over the crowd. For several minutes he remained there in deep ecstasy, holding his arms outstretched to receive his inward blessing.

This was the first of countless flights of ecstasy experienced by Joseph. He continued to levitate nearly as often as he celebrated Mass, and was soon dubbed the "Flying Friar," attracting great attention. While devoted pilgrims came from all over the country to witness his feats of flight, he also attracted the attention of the powerful Inquisition.

Joseph was called to Naples, and then Rome, to answer charges of heresy and impropriety. After four years of harassment, he was found innocent of all charges. Still, the Church was uncomfortable with one of their own inexplicably flying about their sanctuaries, and decided to exile the saintly friar to the Basilica of St. Francis in Assisi. Here, Joseph spent the next fourteen years dutifully living in the home of his mentor, leading a life of guarded seclusion.

Although not free to leave, Joseph was able to spend many of his nights communing with St. Francis at his very crypt. On one such occasion, Joseph was alone at the crypt in the Lower Basilica. (Author's note: At this time, the body of St. Francis was entombed beneath the altar of the Lower Basilica, as the current subterranean tomb was not constructed until 1932.) The sanctuary was lit by a few candles along the aisles and at the altar. While Joseph was deep in prayer, he heard someone enter the Basilica and tread heavily towards him. As the sinister figure advanced down the central aisle, one by one the candles were extinguished by the dark presence. Joseph turned to face the approaching menace, when he was attacked, gripped by the throat, and thrown to the floor. Gasping for air, he hoarsely called to St. Francis for help. Immediately, the crypt began glowing with ethereal light and the blazing figure of St. Francis appeared. The candles relit, and the dark figure fled from the light.

Although Joseph was confined to three small rooms in the bowels of the Basilica, he was often allowed to see visitors and to occasionally give Mass. He continued to have frequent levitations and was well known to pilgrims throughout Europe. Nobles and paupers alike would travel long distances to see him and witness his ecstatic states. As his fame grew, the humble friar was so overwhelmed with the attention that he begged his confessor to stop the onslaught of visitors. He wanted time for personal prayer and meditation, and he disliked being seen as a spiritual sideshow.

The Inquisition again caught wind of Joseph's notoriety and ruled that he should be moved to a new location. Joseph sadly left the home of St. Francis, and was taken to Capuchin monasteries, first in Pietraurubbia, then in Fossombrone. Here Joseph lived among the Capuchin brothers, but longed to be reunited with his Franciscan family. After three years, his desire was fulfilled, and he was secretly sent to the St. Francis Church in Osimo, in the region of Marche.

Traveling by night and hiding by day, Joseph and his keepers made their way slowly to his new refuge. The day before they entered the city, Joseph gazed at a monumental church on the horizon and went into a blissful stillness. He saw the distant town of Loreto, with many angels descending on the Holy House of Mary and instantly went into rapture, flying off the balcony and landing safely on the ground. The men then continued the final leg of their journey and delivered Joseph to his new and final home.

Joseph's new residence consisted of only three small rooms, but he was very content to have sanctuary with his fellow Franciscans. During his last six years, he never left the monastery, living a life of prayer, contemplation and service to his brothers. One day, sometime after his sixtieth birthday, he developed a serious fever. Joseph requested the last rites and was heard whispering, "Oh what light! Oh, what splendor...Oh, what beautiful words...Oh, what fragrance…Oh, what beautiful voices…Oh, what sweetness…Oh, what taste of paradise!" After saying the "Ave Maris Stella," he gave up his body on September 18, 1663. He was laid to rest in the chapel of the Immaculate Conception at the Church of St. Francis in Osimo (renamed the Basilica of St. Joseph of Copertino in 1781).

During his thirty-five years as a priest, St. Joseph performed many healings, prophesied the future, bi-located, materialized food, professed infused wisdom, exuded sweet perfume, and levitated nearly as often as he performed Mass. But there is more to learn from St. Joseph than to be impressed by his miraculous outward demonstrations. St. Joseph plainly stated, "True servants of God simply go inside themselves." Like St. Joseph of Copertino, we may not be in control of our outward circumstances, but we do have the ability to look inside ourselves, to experience divine love within our hearts and to share that love with all.

THE SANCTUARY OF ST. JOSEPH OF COPERTINO
Santuario San Giuseppe da Copertino

The old Romanesque church of San Francesco has been refurbished, inside and out, in High Baroque to celebrate its later reincarnation as

Santuario San Giuseppe da Copertino

the Sanctuary dedicated to St. Joseph of Copertino. It is now an important center of pilgrimage.

St. Joseph is enshrined downstairs under the altar, in a crypt that was built in 1962. You reach the stairs to the crypt on either side of the main altar. The beautiful urn, held aloft by gilded angels, displays the saint's skeleton clothed in a Franciscan habit. St. Joseph's head is covered with a clear plastic facemask, fashioned from his death mask. Gilded sculptured hands and feet have plastic openings that allow you to view his remains. You may walk behind the urn and stand right next to the reliquary, and there are many benches in the crypt. We have never found the church to be crowded. Just a few local people come to pray, so there is much opportunity for quiet meditation.

The rooms where St. Joseph of Copertino lived the last six years of his life are located to the left of the altar as you face it. There is a sign that says, "To the rooms." Walk through the sacristy to a lobby with a small counter where books and religious materials are sold. You will need to find a priest and ask the following:

Where are the rooms of St. Joseph?
Dove sono le stanze di San Giuseppe?

Do you have a description of the rooms in English?
**Avete una descrizione delle stanze del Santo in inglese,
per poterle visitare da soli?**

Do you have books in English?
Avete libri in inglese?

If you would like to meditate in St. Joseph's rooms, it is good to let the priest know.

Is it possible to meditate for a while upstairs?
E'possibile meditare per un po' nelle stanze al piano di sopra?

Do you have any chairs we could use?
Avete delle sedie che potremmo usare?

The self-guided tour begins on the main floor at the chapel where St. Joseph said daily Mass from July 25, 1657 to August 15, 1663. The chapel contains his vestments and other relics.

Up the stairs are his three rooms, each containing relics of the saint. Everything is described in detail in the self-guided tour. The first room is where St. Joseph slept, and where he died on September 18, 1663. Not to be missed is the plaster cast of his death mask, which gives you an opportunity to see how he actually looked. The second room is where St. Joseph spent his time during the day in prayer and contemplation. This room also contains the urn that held the saint's remains from 1781 to 1963. If there are no chairs, the windowsill is a great place to sit and commune with St. Joseph. The third room is where St. Joseph wrote, and received visitors. The trap door in the floor was used by the saint to enter the chapel below. Because the monks leave you alone in the shrine, it is a prime place for meditation and prayer. Give yourself enough time to sit and experience the beautiful vibration of St. Joseph.

SHRINE INFORMATION

Shrine: Sanctuary of St. Joseph of Copertino (Santuario San Giuseppe da Copertino)

Address: Santuario San Giuseppe da Copertino/Piazza Gallo, 10/60027/Osimo (AN)/Italia

Phone: 071 714523 **Fax:** 071 7230162

E-mail: ufficio.basilica@virgilio.it Write in Italian.

Website: www.sgiusecoperosimo.it Italian

Quiet areas for meditation: The Basilica, the crypt and the rooms where St. Joseph lived are all quiet and suitable for meditation.

However, there are no chairs in St. Joseph's rooms. You can ask and see if they can provide chairs (see questions in Italian above).

English spoken: Sometimes, but there is an excellent self-guided tour written in English.

Hours: 6:30AM–12:30 and 3:00PM–8:00.

Mass: Sun/Hol: 7:30AM, 9, 10:15, 11:30, Summer 7:30PM; Winter 7PM. Weekdays: Winter 7AM, 7:45, 8:30, 9:15; Summer 7PM;

Feasts and festivities: September 18 — Feast day; October 4 — Feast of St. Francis of Assisi.

Accessibility: The shrine has a wheelchair lift that goes to the downstairs crypt. The rooms where St. Joseph lived are accessible by an elevator. There are a few stairs at the entrance of the church which they will help you with.

Tours: None. The self-guided tour for St. Joseph's rooms is excellent.

Bookstore: After you go through the sacristy, there is a small counter in the lobby you should visit before starting the self-guided tour to St. Joseph's rooms. You need to request books in English, they don't always have them on display. (See the questions in Italian above.)

Recommended books: *St. Joseph of Copertino*, by the Rev. Angelo Pastrovicchi, O.M.C. Tan Books; *Ecstasy, Jail and Sanctity: The Flying Saint*, by Gustavo Parisciani, O.F.M. is available at the church bookstore.

Lodging: The Friary provides lodging only for groups of up to 70 young people, ages 10 to 25 years old. Loreto, 14 km away, is the best place for lodging.

Directions: The Basilica of San Giuseppe da Copertino is located on Piazza Gallo in the center of Osimo.

MORE ST. JOSEPH OF COPERTINO SHRINES OUTSIDE OF OSIMO

ASSISI

Another special place to visit are the five rooms St. Joseph of Copertino lived in for fourteen years at the Basilica of St. Francis (Basilica San Francesco) in Assisi. However, getting to see them might be a problem, since they are not officially open to the public.

One of the priests will have to escort you there. Ask at the information office (See Assisi chapter, under the Basilica of St. Francis).

St. Joseph had a favorite spot for meditation in the Lower Basilica of St. Francis in the "Cappella dell'Immacolata" (next to Cappella San Martino di Tours). He used to go there at night when no one was around. The saint would pray to the same statue of the Virgin Mary (La Statua della Vergine), which is there today. Because it is a small side chapel, it is one of the only quiet spots for meditation in the Basilica.

COPERTINO

CHURCH OF ST. JOSEPH OF COPERTINO
Santuario San Giuseppe da Copertino

Copertino, the birthplace of St. Joseph, is located in the very southern tip of the heel of Italy, southwest of Lecce. The little shed (la stalletta) where he was born and a relic of his heart are in the Santuario. Santuario San Giuseppe da Copertino/73043/Copertino (LE)/Italia; Phone: 083 2947011. Joseph's cell is located in the convent, near the "Santuario di Santa Maria della Grottella."

Loreto
Population 11,000

Loreto rests atop a high hill, surrounded by beautiful rolling landscape that reaches to the Adriatic Sea on the east side, and to the Apennine Mountains on the west. Sixteenth century walls built as protection for the Holy House surround the city. The town grew up around the Sanctuary and serves thousands of pilgrims every year.

THE SANCTUARY OF LORETO
Santuario di Loreto

The Holy House is said to be the same house in which the Virgin Mary was born and raised in Nazareth. This is where she received the visitation of the angel announcing that she was to be the mother of Jesus. The legend goes that in 1291, the stone house was transported by angels to Croatia, and then to Loreto in 1294. From archeological excavations and documents uncovered recently, it is now believed that the stones were actually transported by humans to the site, but the stones do indeed match ones found in Nazareth. Millions of pilgrims have visited this holy site for centuries, and their faith and devotion can be felt inside the small Holy House of the Blessed Virgin Mary.

The Basilica of the Holy House was built in 1469 to house The Holy House, and has been remodeled in many architectural styles, ending up with a predominately Renaissance exterior and a Gothic interior. The interior is in the form of a Latin cross, with 13 chapels surrounding the Holy House. The Museum and Art Gallery are located on the upper floor of the West wing of the Apostolic Palace (closed on Mondays).

St. Joseph of Copertino was not able to visit the Holy House because of all the attention he received around his levitations. On his journey to Osimo, seeing the Holy House from afar with angels surrounding the dome, he flew from an upper balcony to the ground in ecstasy and stayed enraptured for hours.

The Basilica is located on Madonna Square (Piazza della Madonna) at the end of Via C. Boccalini. Loreto is 18.5 miles (30 km) from Ancona and 8.5 miles (14 km) from Osimo. Because of the close prox-

imity between Osimo and Loreto, both of these shrines should be on your itinerary. There is much more lodging in Loreto, since it is a town built for pilgrims and many monasteries are available for lodging.

Santuario di Loreto

SHRINE INFORMATION

Shrine: Sanctuary of Loreto (Santuario di Loreto)

Address: Palazzo Apostolico, Piazza della Madonna 1/60025 Loreto (AN)/Italia

Phone: 071 970104 **Fax:** 071 9747176

E-mail: santuarioloreto@tin.it

Website: www.santuarioloreto.it

Quiet areas for meditation: There are many crowds of pilgrims, but people remain silent inside the Holy House. It is standing room only, but you can lean up against a wall and feel the vibration of the ancient and holy stones.

English spoken: Sometimes in the information office, before you enter the Basilica, to the left as you face it.

Hours: Basilica: Summer 6:15AM–8PM; Winter 6:45AM–7PM; Holy House closed from 12:30PM–2:30.

Mass: Sun/Hol: see website. Weekdays: Summer 6:30; Holy House 7AM,7:30;Winter 8AM, 9, 10, 11, 4:30PM, 6 , 5PM.

Feasts and festivities: September 8 — Birthday of the Virgin Mary; December 10 — Celebrate the arrival of the Holy House in Loreto; Holy Friday — Miracle play "La Morte del Giusto."

Accessibility: The Shrine has an Italian organization, UNITALSI, that welcomes and transports people with disabilities to the shrine. They also provide free lodging at the Casa del Clero. Contact the shrine for more information.

Tours: To book a tour guide phone: 071 970104.

Bookstore: The information office and bookstore are on the left as you face the Basilica.

Recommended book: In the bookstore, a small book, *The Tradition of Loreto*, with detailed information about the Holy House.

Lodging: The only lodging provided by the Shrine is for people with disabilities at Casa del Clero. There are many religious lodgings available, for a list in Italian check out : www.marcheaccessibili.it/cerca_strutture_ricettive.aspx?id=11&provincia=AN&comune=042022.

Directions: As you approach Loreto, you will see the Shrine atop the hill, which defines the city. You can visually make your way directly to the Shrine. There are large parking areas all around the shrine and arrows directing you to Piazza Madonna.

OTHER PLACES OF INTEREST OUTSIDE OF OSIMO/LORETO

SANCTUARY OF CAMPOCAVALLO
Santuario Beata Vergine Addolorata di Campocavallo

In 1892, in the Sanctuary of Campocavallo, many people witnessed a painting of the Virgin Mary weeping. Ever since, many pilgrims have venerated the painting, and it has wept on several other occasions. The impressive Lombard Neo-Gothic church is located in Campocavallo, a few kilometers south of Osimo, on the way to Loreto. Via Jesi, 75 60027 Osimo (AN) Marche/Italia. Phone: 071 7133003 www.comune.osimo.an.it/campocavallo.

COMING AND GOING

OSIMO/LORETO

Car: Osimo and Loreto are both just west of Autostrada A14, which runs along the Adriatic coast. Osimo is 12 miles (20 km) southwest of Ancona. Loreto is just 7 miles (11 km) west of Porto Recanati and the Adriatic Sea.

Train: The closest train station to Osimo is in Ancona. Loreto and Porto Recanati each have rail stops. There are two main rail lines in the Marches—the coastal Milan-Bari line that links up most of the seaside resorts, and the trans-Italy Ancona-Rome line that joins up a few of the larger towns in the central part of the region. Buses run about every hour from Ancona to Osimo.

Bus: Ancona is on major bus lines, and local buses run every hour from Ancona to Osimo. Buses also connect the Loreto and Porto Recanati stations to Loreto.

TOURIST INFORMATION

❈ Ufficio Informazioni, Municipio/V. Fontemagna 12/60027 Osimo/ Italia; Phone: 071 7249247 Fax: 071 7231554.

❈ IAT – Loreto/Via Solari 3/60025/Loreto (AN)/Italia; Phone: 071 970276 Fax: 071 970020 E-mail: iat.loreto@regione.marche.it

❈ IAT – Ancona/Via Thaon de Revel 4/60124/Ancona/Italia; Phone: 071 358991 Fax: 071 3589929 E-mail: iat.ancona@regione.marche.it

WEBSITES

Marche Voyager www.le-marche.com — Good tourist info. Check out Itineraries then go to "Tour Five." Offers free brochures, a road map, and free phone service <u>within</u> Italy with English-speaking operators 800-222111. E-mail: questions@regione.marche.it

Marche Worldwide www.marcheworldwide.org — Tourist info on the region of the Marches.

Santuario di Loreto www.santuarioloreto.it — Comprehensive info about the Holy House of Loreto.

Santuario San Giuseppe da Copertino www.sgiusecoperosimo.it — Italian website for the Sanctuary of St. Joseph of Copertino.

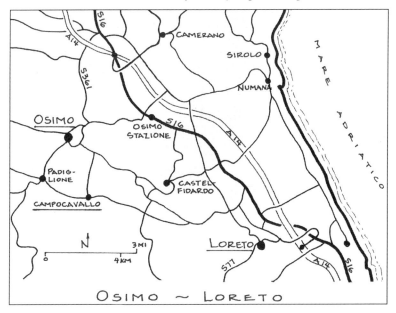

OSIMO ~ LORETO

Tuscany

Toscana

Tuscany is as diverse as it is beautiful. Bounded in the west by the Mediterranean Sea, the rolling countryside expands eastward to the Apennine Mountains. The emerald Tuscan hills are dotted with towered medieval cities and encased with plush vineyards and olive groves. Florence is the artistic and architectural jewel of the region, but the hill towns of San Gimignano, Siena, and Cortona also sparkle with a beauty all their own. Along with its rustic ambiance, Tuscany includes a wealth of historical sites and breathtaking art, making it the most popular tourist area of Italy. Also hidden within the region are many profoundly sacred shrines, awaiting discovery by the sincere seeker.

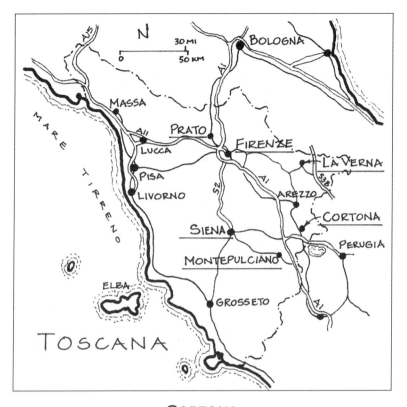

CORTONA
St. Margaret of Cortona

FLORENCE
Museum of San Marco
Blessed Fra Angelico
St. Antoninus

LA VERNA
St. Francis

MONTEPULCIANO
St. Agnes of Montepulciano

PRATO
St. Catherine de' Ricci

SIENA
St. Catherine of Siena

Cortona

Population 22,500

Cortona's old Etruscan walls intertwine with its "newer" medieval ones to form a rich historic fabric of Renaissance buildings, cobbled streets and intimate piazzas. The town is cozy and friendly with plenty of good food, shops and art. Resting atop tall rolling hills and over-looking the Valley of Chiana, Cortona is located on the eastern edge of Tuscany and is a close neighbor to Florence, Siena and Montepulciano. It is an easy and pleasant stop on any itinerary. The town also has a long spiritual history, being the home to the Basilica of St. Margaret of Cortona and "Le Celle," a hermitage founded by St. Francis.

ST. MARGARET OF CORTONA
Santa Margherita 1247-1297

"I neither seek nor wish for aught but Thee, my Lord Jesus."

"No one is perfect" is the common expression used to excuse mistakes and shortcomings. Margaret of Cortona was certainly not perfect, but she was wise enough to use her mistakes to her own advantage, learn-ing from them and changing herself from a "sinner" to a saint.

Born in the small Tuscan village of Laviano, Margaret did not have the blessing of growing up in a loving home. Her mother died when she was only seven and, two years later, her father married a woman who was unkind and demeaning. Margaret was young and spirited, seeking love and acceptance from her new stepmother, but none was found. So Margaret sought love elsewhere, looking for affection and approval from whomever would grant it to her. At the age of sixteen this outward life led her to a young aristocrat named Arsenio, who convinced her to elope and live with him in his castle near Montepulciano. But, life for Margaret was still void of true love. Though she lived in Arsenio's castle, loved him faithfully and bore him a son, he never legitimized their relationship with marriage vows. Margaret lived amongst royalty and riches, and frequently flaunted her situation, defiantly riding through town showing off her finery. Because of her prideful demeanor, she was never accepted by her own family, Arsenio's family or the local people of Montepulciano.

After nine years, Margaret's life of luxury took an unexpected turn. One day, after Arsenio had been unexpectedly absent for the night, the family dog returned to Margaret and entreated her to follow him. Scurrying through the woods, the dog began to dig at the foot of an old tree and uncovered the body of their master. Margaret was deeply distressed by the brutality of Arsenio's murder, but even more distraught by the life that had led her to this point of despair. With the death of her lover, Margaret saw the death of her former life and decided to search for love in the arms of God.

Margaret left all the accoutrements of her previous life with Arsenio's family, gave alms to the poor, and departed Montepulciano with her son and a few belongings. In quest of forgiveness, she returned to her father's home to make amends and begin a new life, but her stepmother shunned Margaret's attempt at reconciliation and convinced her father to reject his daughter once again. Now God was Margaret's only family, for He was the only one who accepted her as she was.

Margaret had heard that the Franciscan Friars in nearby Cortona were open to receive all faithful people, so she headed there to begin life anew. Arriving in the town, Margaret and her son had no place to go, but were immediately adopted by two women of the community, Mariana and Raneria. They offered the vagabonds shelter in their home and introduced Margaret to the Friars of San Francesco.

St. Margaret of Cortona

For three years following her conversion, Margaret fought an inner battle between her new soulful life and her old worldly life. Margaret understood the deep importance of winning this conflict and told her confessor, "Between me and my body there must needs be a struggle till death." Margaret was able to overcome all interior doubts and gained new energy from her victories. Her commitment and sincerity were rewarded by acceptance into the third order of St. Francis as a tertiary.

In this new role, Margaret lived in a small cottage and tended to the sick and poor of Cortona, living only on alms and grace. Her son was sent to school in Arezzo, ultimately taking vows as a Franciscan monk. Margaret's work slowly expanded, and as other women joined her, they developed a small facility to nurse the unfortunate of the city. Eventually the city of Cortona sanctioned their activities and assisted them in starting a hospital. Margaret and her fellow tertiaries staffed the hospital, and the women became known as "Poverelle," or poor ones. She also founded the Confraternity of Our Lady of Mercy, an organization dedicated to sustaining the work of the hospital financially and serving the poor.

When Margaret took the cloak of the Franciscans at age twenty-eight, she also took on the austerities of the order. She spent many hours a day in prayer and contemplation, quickly advancing spiritually. Soon she began having visions and ecstasies, communing directly with Christ. In one episode He asked her, "What is thy wish, poverella?" and she replied: "I neither seek nor wish for aught but Thee, my Lord Jesus." She began to operate in both worlds, continuing to serve the poor, but also working on her inner life, making great strides towards perfection.

Though leading a saintly life, Margaret's challenges were not diminished. At age forty-two, eight years before her death, the people of Cortona began spreading rumors of an illicit relationship between her and her confessor, Fra Giunta. Though Margaret had proven herself to the townspeople for many years, the unfounded rumors still caused turmoil in the small community, and Fra Giunta was transferred to Siena. Margaret withstood the criticism in silence, knowing the truth of her relationship with her confessor and God, and dove deeper into prayer and solitude.

Margaret soon had another vision, one of Christ telling her to "call others to repentance...The graces I have bestowed on thee are not meant for thee alone." She took the vision seriously and began preaching in earnest, calling for all her congregants to seek forgiveness in God and live a righteous life. Margaret was the perfect instrument for this message, for she had turned her own life around. She was also compassionate and forgiving with people, understanding their struggles and giving them support to change their lives for the better. Margaret was so successful in her mission that people came from all over Italy, France, and Spain just to hear her speak and to be in her blessed presence. The people of Cortona were also accepting of Margaret and sought her counsel in many affairs.

Many things were revealed to Margaret in vision, one being the occasion of her death. In preparation, Fra Giunta returned from Siena and performed the last rites for his saintly friend, and Margaret passed on February 22, 1297 at the age of fifty. After twenty-three years in service to the Franciscans and the people of Cortona, the town unofficially proclaimed her a saint and started to build a church in her honor that same year. She was canonized as St. Margaret of Cortona in 1728.

Margaret is a good example of how a misguided life can be turned around and be fulfilled in God's will. Many of us have made mistakes in our life, especially in our youth. We chose the path of pleasure only to eventually find its emptiness and pain. St. Margaret reminds us that it is never too late to change and make a fresh start.

SANCTUARY OF ST. MARGARET OF CORTONA
Santuario di Santa Margherita

In 1297, the year of St. Margaret's death, Giovanni Pisano started building a simple church for her relics. Her body was moved there after construction was completed in 1330. The present Basilica eventually replaced this modest church because the people of Cortona vowed to build a shrine deserving of a saint. The current Basilica was completed in

Santuario di Santa Margherita

1897 built in the Gothic Lombardic style. All that remains of the original church is a stained glass rose window by Giovanni Pisano, located over the front door.

The incorrupt body of St. Margaret of Cortona is in a reliquary on the main altar of the Basilica. A mausoleum was built for her in 1362, but she was never interred there after her body was found to be incorrupt. The current reliquary was constructed in 1580 so her body could be viewed through the glass. The reliquary was once decorated with many precious gems, but over the years they have all been stolen. St. Margaret's first burial casket is in the chapel of St. Basilio (Chiesetta di San Basilio) and her second casket is displayed to the left of the main altar.

The cell of St. Margaret is through the sacristy on the left of the altar. The Basilica was actually built over the site of her original cell. To the right of the main altar is the wooden crucifix that St. Margaret would kneel before while speaking with Jesus. Behind the altar is the

Interior of Santuario di Santa Margherita

choir (Coro) where, starting in the 1800s, people placed heart-shaped medallions as a sign that a miracle was performed from the saint's intercession. In modern times, grateful people place candles, flowers or money there to signify miraculous events.

The Friars Minor have been in charge of the church since 1392 when they were appointed caretakers by the City of Cortona. The Franciscan Missionary Sisters of the Infant Jesus have been serving in the church since 1997.

SHRINE INFORMATION

Shrine: Basilica of St. Margaret of Cortona (Basilica di S. Margherita)

Address: Convento "Santa Margherita"/Via Santa Margherita 1/52044 Cortona (AR) Italia

Phone & Fax: 057 5631113

E-mail: smargheritacortona@interfree.it

Website: www.santamargheritadacortona.org Italian

Quiet areas for meditation: The church is not crowded and is usually quiet. You can sit anywhere inside the church to meditate.

English spoken: Occasionally

Hours: Summer 8AM–12, 3PM–7; Winter 8:30AM–12, 3PM–6.

Mass: Sun/Hol: Summer 8AM, 10, 5PM; Winter 8AM, 10, 4:30PM; Weekdays: Summer 8AM, 5:30PM; Winter 8AM, 4:30PM.

Feasts and festivities: February 22 — Feast day

Accessibility: The lodging has two rooms with an elevator for people with disabilities. The church has a few steps.

Tours: None

Bookstore: There are some postcards for sale and a brochure in English available to the right of the front door as you walk in. To purchase something, you must ring the bell to the convent on the right of the main altar for assistance.

I would like to buy some books. **Vorrei comprare dei libri.**

Recommended books: We did not find any books in English on St. Margaret of Cortona, only small biographies on the web and in *Butler's Lives of Saints.*

Lodging: Hotel — The Franciscan Welcome House of St. Margaret (La Casa Francescana d'Accoglienza S. Margherita) The lodging is connected to the Basilica and is for pilgrims interested in being on retreat. Use the same phone/fax as the Basilica. Plan on speaking in Italian.

Directions: Drive outside the old city walls on the west side of town, following signs to Santuario Margherita, which is on the north side of the city. From inside the city of Cortona, there is a street called

Via Santa Margherita that leads from Piazza Garibaldi up to the Basilica, with 15 Stations of the Cross by Gino Severini along the way. It is a steep walk, about 20 minutes.

COMING AND GOING

CORTONA

Car: Cortona is 9 km north of S75, which runs east-west between Perugia and Autostrada A1. Coming from Perugia, exit at S71 and drive north. From A1 take S75 toward Perugia and exit at Appalto.

Train: There is a direct train: Milano-Bologna-Firenze-Roma. The Rome-Florence trains stop about 7 miles (11 km) south of Cortona at Station Terontola-Cortona. Local trains stop at Camucia station about 3 miles (5 km) from Cortona. There is bus service to Cortona from both stations.

Bus: There is a bus departing for Cortona after each train arrives. The last bus is at 8:00PM.

TOURIST INFORMATION

✣ APT — Arezzo/Ufficio Informazioni/Via Nazionale 42/52044 Cortona (AR) Italia Phone: 057 5630353 Fax: 057 5630656 infocortona@apt.arrezzo.it www.apt.arrezzo.it

✣ Tuscanmagic/Via Guelfa 24-26/52044 Cortona (AR) Italia Phone: 057 5605235 Fax: 057 5605295 E-mail: tuscanmagic@technet.it www.tuscanmagic.com

WEBSITES

Cortona Web www.cortonaweb.net — Tourist Information.

TuscanTreasures.com www.tuscantreasures.com — Books about Cortona.

OTHER PLACES OF INTEREST

CHURCH OF ST. FRANCIS
Chiesa di San Francesco

This church is inside the walls of Cortona at the cross streets of Via G. Maffei and Via Berrettini. Brother Elias, St. Francis's companion,

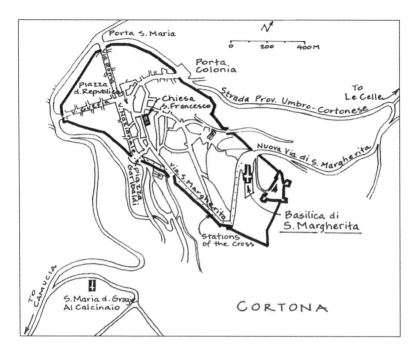

built the church in 1245. It is said that St. Margaret visited here many times, and there is a fresco of her on the left, at the rear of the church. There are relics of St. Francis, a habit and pillow, in the room to the left of the altar. Behind the altar is another room where Brother Elias's bones are buried in the floor. You will need to find a monk to gain access to these rooms. Behind the altar is a piece of the Holy Cross carried from Jerusalem by Brother Elias. It is opened for viewing only on special occasions.

THE MUSEO DIOCESANO

The famous "Annunciazione" and "Adorazione dei Magi" by Fra Angelico are in this museum in Cortona. Piazza del Duomo, Cortona, Italia. Phone: 057 562830. Closed Monday.

HERMITAGE OF THE CELLS
L'Eremo delle Celle — Le Celle

Le Celle is located two miles outside of Cortona, on the same road you take to the Basilica of Santa Margherita. St. Francis founded Le Celle in about 1211 as a small monastic community. St. Francis

L'Eremo delle Celle — Le Celle

was looking for a remote place to seclude, and this land was eventually given to him. There are references to St. Francis being at Le Celle at different times. A few months before his death, it is recorded that he stayed for a "period of time," and it is thought that he wrote his Testament here. After many years of neglect, the Capuchins brought Le Celle back from ruin, and they have been in charge of it since 1537.

To reach Le Celle by car, take the road outside the walls of Cortona to the Basilica of St. Margaret. As you are heading east on the north side of the city, there will be a hairpin turn to the right towards the Basilica, and on the left a dirt road, with a small sign that says "Celle." Turn left and follow the road for about 2 miles (3 km) until you reach the Hermitage. Park on the left, outside the gates. Enter the gates and walk downhill to the monastery. This path takes you over a bridge to the entrance of a lobby, where books and holy cards are for sale, including a good book in English, *"Le Celle" of Cortona*. You pay by the honor system; there is no one around to help. To the right of the front door as you enter the lobby is a chapel which was the dormitory for St. Francis' companions. Beyond the altar is a small room used by St. Francis.

This is a delightful place to meditate and take in the vibrations of St. Francis, as it is very isolated and still. You may see monks around the facility, but they are mostly in quiet seclusion. There is no public transportation from Cortona, and it is a fairly long walk. Car recommended. English spoken rarely. Hours: 8AM–12 and 4PM–6. Convento dei Frati Capuccini/Eremo "Le Celle"/52044 Cortona (AR) Italia. Phone: 057 5603362. Email: eremo@lecell.it www.lecelle.it Italian.

Florence
Firenze
Population 461,000

One of the most picturesque cities of the world, Florence straddles the winding Arno River, and is bordered by the Fiesole Hills on the north and Chianti Hills on the south. The city is best known for its art and architecture, housing works by Michelangelo, Brunelleschi, Donatello and Fra Angelico. Walking down any street is a treat for the senses with striking buildings, glamorous shops and bustling markets. Being a major tourist town, Florence can be noisy and crowded, so you may consider staying on the outskirts of town, or even in Siena, making day trips to the city by bus or car. Monasteries and convents are available for lodging throughout the area and can be a peaceful retreat from a busy day of sightseeing.

BLESSED FRA ANGELICO
Beato Fra Angelico Giovanni da Fiesole around 1400-1455

"He who does works of Christ must always live with Christ."

Anyone who has seen the sublime fresco of the Annunciation by Fra Angelico knows of his artistic merit. The grace and subtle beauty of his art is a reflection of his inner life, for he was a very quiet and humble man, and had a deep connection with Christ. Before painting, he would always pray and commune with the spirit of Christ, and try to maintain that consciousness while he worked.

Very little is known about the personal life of Fra Angelico for he lived very modestly, working primarily as a painter of religious frescoes. Born Guido di Pietro in the province of Mugello near Florence, Fra Angelico and his brother Benedetto entered the Dominican monastery in Fiesole around 1420. It is thought that both brothers were apprentices to master artists before entering the priesthood, for they were recognized as fine artists in illuminating missals and choir books. Due to papal and political upheaval of the times, they left Fiesole after two years and took refuge in the monastery at Foligno. After some time, they moved once again because of the plague, and went to Cortona for four years before returning to Fiesole for sixteen years. Now forty-eight years old, Fra Angelico was invited to paint the new convent at San Marco in Florence.

Fra Angelico's work at San Marco was a labor of love. He spent many years painting the cells of the convent with vivid pictures of the life of Christ. Each cell was painted in fresco style on fresh plaster, requiring the artist to be truly in the moment. Fra Angelico was a master at channeling the grace of God through his work and produced pieces with great depth. The cells of the convent are now open to the public, so we are able to experience the art and also the deep spiritual vibrations Fra Angelico poured into his painting.

After fourteen years at the convent of San Marco, Fra Angelico was appointed prior, at the age of sixty-three. Three years later, he was asked to take the position of prior at San Domenico in Fiesole, the site of his initial entry into the Dominican family. After two short years, he was once again called to move to Rome to paint the chapel of Pope Nicholas V at the Vatican. It is said Fra Angelico was offered the position of Archbishop of Florence, but he humbly refused, suggesting that his friend Antoninus be appointed instead. Fra Angelico completed his mission in Rome, then died on March 18, 1455 at the age of sixty-eight. He was buried in Rome in the church of Santa Maria Sopra Minerva to the left of St. Catherine of Siena's tomb, which is on the main altar. He was very well respected by his peers and often called "Beato Angelico" long before his beatification in 1982.

St. Antoninus said of Fra Angelico, "No one could paint like that without first having been to heaven." Surely Fra Angelico had a taste of heaven in his lifetime for his work reflects such an enlightened view of the spiritual realms. As a channel for God's grace there was no room for ego in his artwork. His paintings are meditations in themselves — serene, peaceful and reverent. We can learn from Fra Angelico how to channel Divine grace into all our creative efforts.

MUSEUM OF SAN MARCO
Museo di San Marco

The Basilica, museum and convent of San Marco are located on Piazza San Marco in Florence. The convent was founded in the thirteenth century and enlarged in 1437, financed by Cosimo the Elder. Fra Angelico began his frescoes here around 1438 and completed the project in 1446. He completed the first ten cells by himself, while the other 32 were completed with help from assistants. Each room is like the cell of a battery, vitalized by the energy and painting of Fra Angelico and the three hundred years of prayer and contemplation performed thereafter. Angelico never retouched his paintings because he felt that was how

Museo di San Marco

God wanted them. He painted on wet plaster with clay colors, not knowing how the colors would blend until they were dry. This is remarkable when you see how the colors blend perfectly. Each day he began his work with prayer, because he felt that to paint the perfect Christ, he must be Christ-like himself.

After the religious suppression and the unification of Italy, the convent was re-opened in 1869. The museum was opened in the 1920s and devoted to Fra Angelico. The frescoes are located upstairs in the convent, above the museum. Restorations were finished in 1983, making the colors more vibrant. They appear as if they were just completed.

Upstairs you can also visit the rooms of Savonarola (cells 12-14) who was the Father Superior at San Marco until his death in 1498, when he was burned at the stake after being falsely accused of heresy. He spoke out against the decadence of the day and created enemies in high places, including the Pope. Take notice of Fra Bartolomeo's (1472-1517) famous portrait of Savonarola.

The first floor houses more art by Fra Angelico and other artists. There is also a library with over one hundred illuminated choir manuscripts.

MUSEUM INFORMATION

Museum: Museum of St. Mark (Museo di San Marco)

Address: Piazza San Marco 3/50121 Firenze, Italia

Phone: 055 2388608 / 055 2388704 **Fax:** 055 2388704

E-mail: museosanmarco@polomuseale.firenze.it

Website: www.polomuseale.firenze.it/musei/sanmarco Italian

Quiet areas for meditation: It is a busy museum with many tourists.

English spoken: Rarely

Hours: Weekdays: 8:15AM–1:50PM; Weekends: 8:15AM–7PM; Closed December 25, January 1, May 1; Closed 1st, 3rd, 5th Sundays of the month and 2nd & 4th Mondays of the month.

Accessibility: After a couple of stairs, the main floor is accessible to wheelchairs. The upstairs is accessible by an outside staircase that mechanically facilitates wheelchairs. It is not usable when it is raining.

Tours: You can buy an English guide to the museum, *San Marco Guide to the Museum*, in the bookstore. The book is also available in other bookstores in Florence.

Bookstore: Same hours as above. No credit cards accepted.

Directions: See "Coming and Going" below.

ST. ANTONINUS
1389-1459

"To serve God is to reign."

Fifteenth century Florence was a place of wealth, power and decadence. Many lived this lifestyle, including church clergy and members. Some fought against such wasteful living and tried to bring compassion to the people of Florence. One of these fearless souls was St. Antoninus.

Antonius Pierozzi was born March 1, 1389 in Florence. He signed his name Antonius, but his faithful followers in Florence affectionately called him Antoninus. Raised in a devout religious family, Antoninus was known as a serious child, praying more than he played. By the age of fifteen he was ready to begin a life of dedication to God and asked to be accepted into the Dominican order. His request was denied, and he was told facetiously to return only after he had memorized the "Decretum of Gratian," a large work of Canon law. He took the request seriously and studied the doctrines for a year. He was ultimately accepted after reciting the Decretum and answering questions to demonstrate his understanding of the principles of the text.

Antoninus was assigned to Cortona and here he met the artist/monk Fra Angelico, with whom he became lifelong friends.

Antoninus was a serious scholar and was concerned with the self-indulgence of his day, spending much of his time studying and writing about moral theology. He was appointed prior of Cortona in 1418 at the age of thirty, and went on to serve in many other cities as prior. Although Antoninus was not known for his eloquence as a preacher, he was a popular confessor, valued for his wisdom and often called the "angel of counsel." He also took on the task of reforming his order, bringing the current practice of spirituality in line with the moral tenets of St. Dominic. Antoninus was well respected and considered by many to be a saint in his own lifetime.

When Antoninus was informed that he was to be appointed Archbishop of Florence, he humbly refused, not wishing to be a part of the extravagant hierarchy. The Pope threatened him with excommunication if he did not accept, so Antoninus took the position, vowing to reform the station. Antoninus refused the luxury of his new post and gave one third of his salary to God, one-third to the poor, and used the rest for his personal sustenance. Though he lived in the appointed palace, he had little furniture, owned no horses, worked with only six servants and had one mule that was on loan. Antoninus was a tireless worker, sleeping and eating little, but praying constantly. His coworkers tried to keep up with his energetic pace, and when his secretary complained of all the work, Antoninus suggested that he

Crypt of St. Antoninus

create an inner space where he could retreat to find calm and peace in the midst of his responsibilities. Wise counsel indeed.

One of Antoninus's goals was to use his position to help the poor and needy. When plagues, earthquakes and famines struck the community, he would be seen with his mule delivering needed supplies to the people of the city. He also had the formal gardens around his palace removed—feeling they were wasteful in hard times—and replaced them with wheat to feed the poor. He worked diligently to reform his order and once, to demonstrate to his priests the severity of excommunication, he said the words of excommunication over a piece of bread. To the priests' amazement, the bread turned black! But after Antoninus blessed the bread, it returned to its original color.

Antoninus died May 2, 1459 among his Dominican brothers, with his last words being "To serve God is to reign." He was canonized in 1523.

St. Antoninus is a strong example of integrity. He practiced his beliefs and principles even when powers greater than himself were against him. He withstood anger and condemnation in order to speak the truth against the morality of his day. In the end, he was beloved by popes, clergy, and his people for his wisdom and holiness.

THE BASILICA OF SAN MARCO
Basilica di San Marco

The Basilica of San Marco, to the left of the museum and convent, was restored around 1420 with its original structure dating from the twelfth century. It contains the incorrupt remains of St. Antoninus, Archbishop of Florence. St. Antoninus founded the neighboring convent in 1436 and hired his friend Fra Angelico to paint the frescoes. The remains of St. Antoninus are in an urn located to the left of the main altar. He is dressed in the clothes of a Cardinal with a wax mask over his face. Two monks who died in 1494, Pico della Mirandola and Agnolo Poliziano, are also buried here, on the left near the second altar.

SHRINE INFORMATION
Shrine: Basilica of St. Mark (Basilica di San Marco)

Address: PP Domenicani 56/Firenze/Italia

English spoken: Rarely

Hours: 7:30AM–12; 4PM–8.

Mass: 6:30PM

Feasts and festivities: May 24 — Feast of St. Dominic.

Directions: See "Coming and Going" below.

COMING AND GOING

FLORENCE

Car: It is easy to drive *to* Florence, but don't drive *in* Florence! Drive to your lodging, then use the convenient public transportation. The city is accessed by Autostrada A1 from the north and south, and by A11 from the west. Four-lane freeways also make connections to Siena and Livorno. There is no parking around the Museum.

Train: Frequent connections to all major cities. Stazione Santa Maria Novella is closest to the central tourist area.

Bus: Located next to the train station, buses connect to all major cities. Convenient buses to Siena depart hourly. Local bus stops are located all around the train station and these buses travel throughout the city. Take local bus 1,6,11,or 17, from the train station to Piazza San Marco. From Piazza San Marco buses 1, 6, 7, 10, 11, 17, 20, 25, 31, 32, 33.

Directions to Museum and Basilica: San Marco and the Basilica of San Marco are connected and on Piazza San Marco #3, between Via G. La Pira and Via Cavour. It is a block north from the Galleria dell'Accademia; if you want to combine your visit with Michelangelo's *David* (highly recommended). Be aware that the *David* has long lines, and you might want to buy your ticket ahead of time.

TOURIST INFORMATION

✸ APT — Azienda Provinciale per il Turismo/Via A. Manzoni 16/Firenze/50121 Italia Phone: 055 23320 Fax: 055 2346286 Email: apt@firenzeturismo.it www.firenzeturismo.it

✸ APT— Via Cavour 1r/Firenze/50129 Italia Phone: 055 290832 / 055 290833 Email: infoturismo@provincia.fi.it www.firenzeturismo.it

✤ City of Florence Tourist Office/Borgo S. Croce/29r/Firenze/Italia
Phone: 055 2340444 Fax: 055 2264524
Email: Turismo2@comune.fi.it www.comune.fi.it/inglese

WEBSITES

ATAF www.ataf.net — Bus timetables in Florence.

Firenzi Musei www.firenzmusei.it — Thirteen state museums in Florence.

Firenze by Net www.mega.it/eng/enot/mess.htm — Lists churches of all religions in Florence, including a good description of San Marco in English.

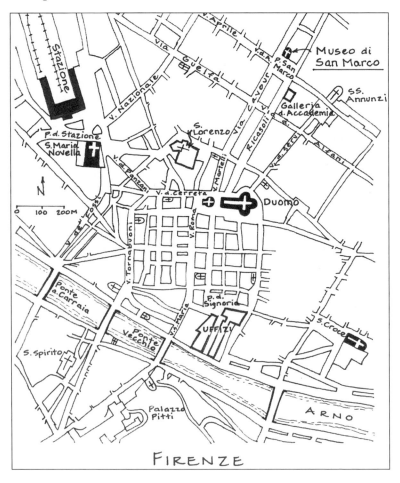

FIRENZE

LA VERNA
Santuario della Verna

La Verna is a small monastery in the mountains in the region of Tuscany about 72 miles (116 km) northwest of Assisi, and 37 miles (60 km) north of Arezzo. This is where St. Francis received the stigmata and is one of the most inspirational places in all of Italy. If at all possible, give yourself at least two days here. It is very quiet and peaceful, a perfect place for meditation and contemplation. The monastery is still run by monks and nuns of the Franciscan order, and the vibration of St. Francis is particularly tangible.

La Verna was given to St. Francis by Count Orlando of Chiusi in May 1213. This most holy mountain has many significant spots to visit related to St. Francis. There is a guidebook in the bookstore, entitled *The Sanctuary of La Verna*, by Rodolfo Cetoloni, describing all these special sites. We recommend you purchase this book before walking around. The most important place to experience is the Chapel of the Blessed Stigmata, which was built around the rock that St. Francis was sitting on when he received the stigmata. The rock is on the floor, in front of the altar, covered in glass. There are places to sit and meditate in this chapel, so take your time here.

The Chapel of Santa Maria degli Angeli was built from 1216-18 and was dedicated, by the wish of St. Francis, to Our Lady of the Angels who had appeared to him and indicated the site and measurements for the first church of La Verna. Below the floor rest the bones of Count Orlando, who donated La Verna to Francis. The Basilica, begun in 1348 and finished in 1509, contains the Chapel of the Relics. In a cabinet backed with deep red material above the altar, *The Relic of the Blood* from St. Francis's stigmata

Santuario della Verna

wound is preserved in a cloth. His drinking cup, a tablecloth, wooden bowl, a girdle, iron scourge and part of a stick used by St. Francis are also displayed.

Oratories of St. Bonaventura and St. Anthony of Padua are to the left of the Chapel of the Blessed Stigmata and down some steep steps. These are tiny chapels that offer quiet places to meditate and very deep stillness. It's easy to feel like a monk or nun of old while praying there.

St. Francis' first cell (Chapel of St. Mary Magdalen) contains the stone, now used as the altar, that Jesus sat on in conversations with St. Francis. As you leave the Chapel of the Blessed Stigmata, in the middle of the long hall, there is a door on the right leading outside, then, on the left of a small stone structure, stairs that lead down to the Chapel. This chapel is also very quiet, but can be very cold.

Little Chapel of La Penna is at the end of a long walk through the forest. You will have as your reward a beautiful vista of the surrounding mountains and valleys. Along the way you will see the Rock of Brother Lupo. The walk will take a half hour to 45 minutes each way, depending on your physical condition.

SHRINE INFORMATION

Shrine: Sanctuary of La Verna (Santuario della Verna)

Address: Santuario Francescano, Via del Santuario, 45/52010 Chiusi della Verna (AR) Italia

Phone: 057 55341 / 534211 **Fax:** 057 5599320

E-mail: la.verna@libero.it

Website: www.santuariodellaverna.com / www.santuariolaverna.org

Quiet areas for meditation: La Verna is remote, and is one of the best places for meditation. There are many small, secluded chapels.

English spoken: Rarely

Hours: Closed: Nov. 15–30 & Jan15–Feb15. Lodging: 8AM–8:30PM.

Feasts and festivities: October 4 — Feast of St. Francis.

Accessibility: Most of the shrine is accessible, but you'll need to inquire about lodging.

Bookstore: There is a bookstore on site where you can purchase the guidebook, *The Sanctuary of La Verna*, by Rodolfo Cetoloni.

Lodging: It is highly recommended to make reservations ahead of time for pilgrim's lodging. They do not speak English, so try to have your fax translated when making reservations. If lodging in the monastery is full, there are facilities in the town of Chiusi della Verna, at the base of the mountain, see website under "Useful Information."

COMING AND GOING

LA VERNA

Car: There are three roads leading to La Verna: 1) from Rassina, through Chitignano and Chiusi; 2) from Bibbiena through Dama; and 3) from Pieve San Stefano in the valley of the Tiber.

Train: Take a train to the nearby towns of Bibbiena, Rassina, which are located on the Arezzo-Pratovecchio-Stia line. Bus service is available from the station.

Bus: Bus service is available from Bibbiena, Rassina (in connection with train service from Arezzo-Pratovecchio-Stia) and from Pieve San Stefano.

On Foot: There is a pedestrian path starting from Beccia, at the foot of the cliff of La Verna, that climbs up to the Monastery (1/3 m).

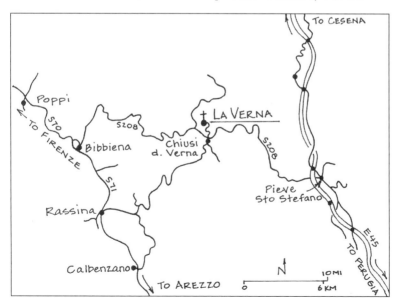

Montepulciano
Population 14,000

Montepulciano is called the "Pearl of the 1500s" because of its abundant Renaissance art and architecture. It is a charming medieval town perched on a hill above the valleys of the Chiana and the Orcia. Driving is not permitted inside the city walls, allowing the pedestrian to quietly wander the old streets that gently climb towards La Fortezza at the top of the hill. On a clear day, you can see the Tempio di San Biagio (built over a chapel where a Madonna was said to have performed miracles) and climb the tower of the Palazzo Comunale for other great views of Tuscany.

ST. AGNES OF MONTEPULCIANO
Sant' Agnese Segni di Montepulciano 1268-1317

"I have been useful in my life, but I will be more so after my death."

Purity of heart. That is the feeling we receive when contemplating the life of St. Agnes. When visiting her shrine in Montepulciano, her pure love of God is evident, for one can feel her calm, still presence.

St. Agnes' life was one of quiet, cloistered service to her fellow nuns. Her deep dedication and devotion were unhindered by outward circumstances, so she remained inwardly focused on deep prayer and inner communion. St. Agnes said, "I have been useful in my life, but I will be more so after my death." This is true, for it is easy to tune into the blessings of her peaceful spirit, even though it's been almost 700 years since her death.

St. Agnes's love for God was manifest, for when only nine years old she felt the calling to be a cloistered nun, and left her middle class family to enter the convent at Montepulciano. As a novice, she quickly impressed the sisters of the Augustinian order with her heartfelt austerities and deep dedication. She displayed an amazing spiritual maturity despite her young age, and as an adolescent of fourteen, was asked to go to the convent at Procena. After only a year at her new post, her peers elected her abbess! A special dispensation was required due to her age, but this was granted, and she continued as the abbess for the next 22 years. During her tenure, she served her sisters faithfully, but also lived austerely, sleeping on the ground with a stone pillow, and taking only bread and water for sustenance. After a serious illness, she consented to lessen her severe self-discipline, but continued to guide her order as a living example of one dedicated only to God.

After 23 years in Procena, she was asked by the townspeople to return to Montepulciano to start a new convent. To make room for the new church, houses of prostitution were leveled, and a new sanctuary was constructed in their place to welcome home the highly respected Agnes. While contemplating the move back to Montepulciano, Agnes had a vision of St. Dominic, who invited her into his order. Although she had been an Augustinian nun for 30 years, she felt the vision was based on truth, and initiated her new order under the rule of the Dominicans. Her holiness increased over the years, and many miracles began to happen around her. She was often seen in ecstasy, levitating above the ground in bliss, and receiving Holy Communion from an angel. In another vision, she was allowed to hold the infant Jesus, and she frequently experienced blissful communion with her Lord. Her inspired life was that of a living saint, and she brought many souls to God. She served as prioress of the order until her death on April 20, 1317, at the age of 49. She was canonized on May 12, 1726, becoming the first female Dominican saint.

St. Agnes's life was punctuated with many miracles, and these continued after her death. St. Catherine of Siena went to Montepulciano to pay her respects 30 years after the passing of St. Agnes. As she approached the incorrupt body of the saint to kiss her foot, the foot raised itself to meet her lips. On St. Catherine's second visit to the shrine, manna, in the form of small white-shaped crosses, fell upon the visitors. This was an encore to many instances in which manna fell upon St. Agnes when she was alive. Another

Crypt of St. Agnes

miracle happened in 1354, when Emperor Charles IV of Luxembourg paid tribute to the saint. As he approached the body, the saint opened her eyes to greet him!

SHRINE OF ST. AGNES OF MONTEPULCIANO
Santuario di Sant'Agnese di Montepulciano

The Sanctuary of St. Agnes was built in 1306, with additions made in 1500 and 1700. The church's façade, completed in 1926, retained its original Gothic door and there is a delightful mosaic of the saint above it. The exterior of the church is reflective of the simple austerities of St. Agnes, and the more ornamental interior is likewise reflective of her vibrant inner life. The interior highlight is the large statue of St. Agnes, which dominates the main altar. The pure white marble of the work and the small band of white lights illuminating the statue are a just symbol for the saint's purity and simplicity.

Santuario di Sant'Agnese di Montepulciano

After Agnes's death, plans were made to embalm her, but when her hands and feet began to exude large quantities of a sweet-smelling liquid, the plans were abandoned. This miraculous oil cured many people, and a sample is still kept in her cell. Fifty years after her death, Blessed Raymond of Capua (confessor to St. Catherine of Siena) found the saint's body completely intact. In 1510, the saint perspired blood, which saturated her shroud, and a silver mask was then laid over her face. The current papier-mâché mask eventually replaced this mask.

In 1539, St. Agnes's body was moved from her cell to the high altar. Until that time, the body was incorrupt. But after being moved inside the damp walls of the high altar it succumbed to the elements, with only her arms, hands, legs, feet and brain remaining intact. In 1949, the saint was placed in a new metal and glass urn on the high altar, and today you can view her body, including her incorrupt hands and feet. Every fifty years there is a medical exam and her clothing is changed. During Mass, the doors to her crypt are closed and the body of St. Agnes is not visible.

The church is a quiet place to meditate as it is outside the primary tourist area of the walled city. Locals often frequent the shrine, and their devoted presence adds to the still ambience of the sanctuary. On the right side of the church, near the altar, is a door to St. Agnes's cell (Cella della Santa) in which she lived for the last 11 years of her life. This is also where her incorrupt body was enshrined for 222 years, until 1539. There are many relics here, including the cross-shaped manna that fell like snow around St. Agnes on occasion, the mother of pearl necklace she removed from the baby Jesus in a vision, the liquid that her body secreted in 1510, and the saint's garments. Access to the private rooms must be requested by ringing the bell, and waiting to see if a priest is available to guide you. This cannot be done during Mass. You are not allowed to remain in the rooms unattended, but they are beautifully decorated and St. Agnes's essence is distinctly felt in her relics.

May I see the cell of St. Agnes?
Posso visitare la cella di Sant'Agnese?

Is there a guidebook in English?
C'è una guida scritta in inglese?

SHRINE INFORMATION

Shrine: Sanctuary of St. Agnes (Santuario di Sant'Agnese)

Address: Piazza Sant'Agnese 1/53045 Montepulciano (SI) Italia

Phone: 057 8757205 **Fax:** 057 8715621

E-mail: info@santaagnesesegni.it

Website: www.santaagnese.it — Official site of St. Agnes Segni.

Quiet areas for meditation: The Sanctuary is small with locals and tourists coming in and out. When there is a lull you can enjoy some peaceful moments.

English spoken: Occasionally

Hours: 7:30AM–12:15PM; 2:30PM–7:30

Mass: Weekdays: summer 6:30PM; winter 8AM, 6PM; Sun/Hol: summer 8AM, 11, 6:30PM; winter 6PM.

Feasts and festivities: A popular fair is held in St. Agnes's honor on her feast day of April 20th and lasting till May 1st; January 28 — St. Agnes's birthday.

Accessibility: A ramp is under construction and will be accessed from the right of the cloister. Inquire to see if it is completed.

Tours: None, but visiting the cell of St. Agnes requires special admittance. On the right side of the church, near the altar, there is a door with a bell to ring for entry to the cell (Cella della Santa). If someone is available, they can show you her cell with relics. Ask for a handout in English that is a brief guide to the Sanctuary. Please do not ring the bell during Mass.

Bookstore: If you get a tour of her cell, there are a few books there, but none in English. There is a guide to the sanctuary in Italian *Guida al Santuario di Santa Agnese Segni*. Donations are requested for the books and pamphlets.

Recommended books: We could not find any books in English on St. Agnes.

Lodging: None

Directions: The Santuario di Sant'Agnese Di Montepulciano is on the north side of Montepulciano, just outside the walled city at Porta al Prato. The church faces Porta al Prato and the Giardino di Poggiofanti at the corner of Viale Calamandrei and Via Bernarei. The façade has gray and white horizontal stripes and is fronted by a parking lot.

COMING AND GOING

MONTEPULCIANO

Car: Coming from the south, take Autostrada A1 and exit at Chianciano Terme. Follow route 166 for 11 miles (18 km) north through Chianciano to Montepulciano. From the north, take A1 to the Val di Chiana exit and follow the signs.

Train: To Chiusi-Chianciano Terme F.S. Station N on the main Rome-Florence line. There are connecting buses to Montepulciano coinciding with all train arrivals from 6:00AM–9:40PM June to August and from 6AM–9PM Sept to May.

Bus: There are buses to Siena Via Pienza eight times per day, leaving Montepulciano from 5AM–5PM; and from Siena to Montepulciano from 6AM–5:40PM Siena is 41 miles (66 km) from Montepulciano.

TOURIST INFORMATION

✤ La Rondine/Servizi Turistici/Piazza Don Minzoni n.1/ 53045 Montepulciano (SI) Italia Phone/Fax: 057 8757341 E-mail:info@prolocomontepulciano.it www.prolocomontepulciano.it.

WEBSITE

Shrine of St. Agnes Segni www.santaagnese.it — Official site.

Prato

Population 171,000

The town center still lies within ancient Etruscan walls, where modern buildings mingle with structures from the past to create a lively atmosphere. Although not a tourist destination, the old city center has many museums and is fun to walk around while enjoying some typical Italian food and shopping along the way. Prato is primarily a large modern industrial city known for its textiles. If you have extra time, Prato is a short day trip via car or bus from Florence (11 miles west). The Basilica of Saints Vincent and Catherine de' Ricci is small and not well known, but a visit to this shrine can reap many spiritual blessings.

ST. CATHERINE DE' RICCI

Santa Caterina de' Ricci 1522 - 1590

"I pray that I may be His and that He will never abandon me and let whatever He wills come of it, for I abandon myself always into His arms."

Some saints live mostly in the spiritual realms, while others appear more grounded in their earthly responsibilities. Catherine de' Ricci seemed to have had her feet in both worlds, experiencing deep ecstatic states in the passion of Christ while being the prioress of her convent and dealing with all the problems of the physical world.

Catherine was born Sandrina Lucrezia Romola on April 23, 1522 in Florence. Her father, Francesco de' Ricci and her mother, Caterina di Ridolfo da Panzano were nobility from old and prominent families in Florence. When Catherine was four, her mother died. Two years later, the young girl was sent to a Benedictine monastery on the outskirts of Florence to receive a full education. This was the convent of her aunt, Louisa, and Catherine enjoyed the quiet, contemplative life of the nuns. Even at this early age, the child was devout, often found lost in prayer and offering great devotion to Christ. Catherine was serious about her faith and became dismayed when two nuns of the convent argued over the possession of a religious book. She returned, disillusioned, to the home of her father.

After some time, she realized again that family life did not suit her, for she was still called inwardly to lead a life of devotion and service. Catherine petitioned her father to allow her to enter a convent and follow her aspirations. After many heartfelt pleas, he reluctantly agreed and, at the age of thirteen, Catherine took her vows and received the veil of the Dominican order, entering the monastery at Prato where her uncle was the confessor of the nuns.

Religious life did not go as Catherine had hoped. She became very sickly during the first two years, suffering from intense internal pains and high fevers. She also was very distracted, unable to focus on and perform her assigned duties. Her fellow sisters were not sympa-thetic to her trials and would have expelled her from the convent if not for their respect for her uncle. Though seemingly ill, Catherine still spent many hours in devoted prayer, fasting two days a week and deeply con-templating the passion of Christ. After two years of suffering, Catherine was miraculously healed fol-lowing fervent prayers by the nuns and her father to St. Vincent, the patron saint of the convent, and Savonarola, the deceased mentor of Catherine.

St. Catherine de' Ricci

After the healing, it was apparent that

Catherine's distracted behavior was a result of frequent ecstasies, for she would often become transfixed on her inner visions of Christ. The visions became increasingly real to Catherine, and she began to fast every Thursday and Friday, coinciding with the times of Christ's passion. In February 1542, Catherine first experienced the "Ecstasy of the Passion." This experience continued every week after that for the next twelve years. Every Thursday at noon until Friday at 4 p.m., she would visualize and enact the life of Christ, including the scourging, receiving the crown of thorns and being crucified. The wounds of the stigmata would appear on Catherine's body, and often an indent in her shoulder would be observed where the she bore the weight of the cross.

Another of Catherine's visions was of her espousal to Christ. He gave her a wedding band to symbolize their union, and Catherine was able to see the band of gold and the brilliant diamond as it encircled her finger. Three of Catherine's fellow nuns witnessed the event, and were able to perceive the ring as a red impression on her finger. One sister saw the ring and diamond as a dazzling light. Many tried to see the ring over the years, but only Catherine had the ability to fully sense the presence of the blessed band.

Catherine also had the ability to see suffering souls who were far away from her. On Wednesdays, the eve of the passion, Catherine would bi-locate, traveling the world and witnessing the lives of many pious and sinful people, actually experiencing

Crypt of St. Catherine de' Ricci

their lives. Catherine would return from her worldly wanderings feeling the great pain of their sins and praying earnestly for their redemption. She said of her travels, "There is no place in the world I have not been to." Philip Neri of Rome documented her bilocation. Catherine and Neri had great admiration for one another and often corresponded by letter. One evening, Catherine visited Neri in Rome, and they held a lengthy conversation regarding the grace and love of God. This event was witnessed by five of Neri's peers and recorded in Neri's writings. Though Catherine appeared to Neri in Rome, she was also present at her cloister in Prato.

The news of Catherine's episodes spread throughout the countryside and people flocked to the convent to witness the holy sight. Catherine was very reluctant to become a public figure and desired only to be left alone to commune with Christ. At times, she was ordered by her superiors to display her gifts, but this was difficult for her. She described it as "putting things of God in a shop-window."

Over time, the Dominican sisters also grew weary of the public attention, and they all prayed for the outward signs of the passion to cease. This occurred in 1554, twelve years after the visions began. Although Catherine still witnessed the passion, she did not display visible signs of the events or the stigmata. Catherine continued to have ecstatic episodes at various times, usually becoming immobile with her gaze fixed upwards. One time, as she was picking violets in the garden, she exclaimed, "How I love these violets! They signify the blood of Jesus." She immediately went into an ecstasy, smiling for two hours until the prioress pulled her from the rapture in order to attend supper.

Catherine often lived in ecstatic realms, but she also lived in the world of a sixteenth century monastery. Her pious, wise and humble nature greatly impressed her Dominican sisters. She was appointed novice mistress, then several times sub-prioress, and at the age of twenty-five, prioress of the convent. All this was accomplished while she was undergoing the weekly visions of Christ, so it is clear Catherine was able to live on the highest levels of consciousness and still complete her more mundane responsibilities.

Cardinals and popes sought her wise counsel, and she was interviewed by many famous pundits of her time. But Catherine was happiest when serving the poor and needy of Prato. She was well known for her compassion, and many would come to the convent seeking help, knowing that their beloved Catherine would not turn them away. Up to three hundred people a day came to her door, and she would take her meager stores and feed them all by multiplying the bread into sufficient quantities. She also received a dispensation from her vow of poverty to gain dowries for underprivileged girls. The dowries allowed the impoverished girls to leave their desperate situations and begin families of their own, with hope for the future.

Catherine continued her life of service as the prioress of the convent until her passing on February 3rd, 1590 at the age of sixty-seven. As the great spiritual patroness of Prato, she was canonized in 1746.

St. Catherine de' Ricci shows us that you can offer your life to God and continue to have an effect in the world. St. Catherine was cloistered, yet she attracted people who needed her help and grace. She lived her life for God as an offering to alleviate the suffering of others and help them find their way back to God.

THE BASILICA OF SAINTS VINCENT AND CATHERINE DE' RICCI
Basilica dei Santi Vincenzo Ferreri e Caterina de' Ricci

The Basilica is located on Piazza San Domenico. The exterior façade is unadorned from the outside, but the interior of the small Basilica is lavishly decorated and very sweet. The incorrupt body of St. Catherine de' Ricci is in an urn on the main altar. Episodes of her life are depicted in marble relief behind the altar. The church has limited hours, and is quite often empty, so it is a very quiet place to retreat from the city. The front entrance to the church is on Via San Vincenzo, but if you arrive when the church is not open, enter from the side of the church, on Corso Savonorola.

If you can't make a visit during

Basilica dei Santi Vincenzo Ferreri e Caterina de' Ricci

the church's normal open hours, you can call and let them know you would like to visit. If you do not speak Italian, you can ask the tourist office to call for you. After ringing the bell on the side of the church, enter to the left to talk with the nuns (in Italian). Ask for the small booklet in English on the life of St. Catherine. Then return to where you entered and access the church through the right of the entrance (they will buzz you in). You will be next to the main altar. This is an excellent place to meditate and pray since there are not many visitors.

Do you have a book in English?
Avete un libro in inglese?

May I visit the saint?
Posso vedere le reliquie della santa?

SHRINE INFORMATION

Shrine: The Basilica of Saints Vincent and Catherine de' Ricci (Basilica dei Santi Vincenzo e Caterina de' Ricci)

Address: Piazza San Domenico 15/59100 Prato/Italia

Phone: 057 424706 **Fax:** 057 4930527

E-mail: monastero.s.vincenzo@pioistitutoscaterina.191.it

Website: In process.

English spoken: Rarely

Hours: Daily 7AM–11, 4PM–7.

Mass: Daily: Summer 5:30PM; Winter 5PM.

Feasts and festivities: February 4 — Feast day; June 29 — On this day it is possible to visit the monastery; October 23 — Anniversary of the translation of her body to the altar.

Accessibility: One step from Piazza San Domenico.

Bookstore: The nuns speak only in Italian through a partition and offer postcards and a small booklet in English on the life of St. Catherine de' Ricci.

Recommended books: Booklet, *Catherine de' Ricci: A Profile*, D. Di Agresti, G. Zaninelli available at the shrine bookstore; *St. Catherine de' Ricci: Selected Letters*, Dominican Sources, (used on the Internet).

Lodging: None

Directions: Prato is a big city and driving there can be stressful, so be prepared. We suggest getting a map of the city from the tourist office before you go, to study before you arrive. Park in any of the public parking areas around the city. Basilica San Vincenzo e Santa Caterina de' Ricci is on Piazza San Domenico on Corso Savonarola across from St. Dominic's Church (Chiesa di San Domenico). It doesn't look like a church from the piazza side, but that is the door you enter to gain access to the sisters who buzz you into the church. The front of the church is on Via San Vincenzo.

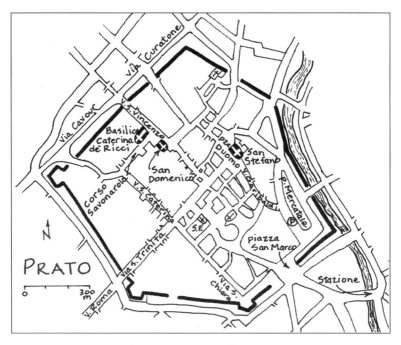

COMING AND GOING

PRATO

Car: Autostrada A1: Exit at Prato Est or Prato Ovest; follow signs to Centro.

Train: On the Firenze-Bologna line to Prato Stazione Centrale. On the Firenze-Viareggio line to Prato Porta al Serraglio or Prato Stazione Centrale.

Bus: SAP and LAZZI bus lines from Florence.

Tourist Information

❋ Ufficio Informazioni/Piazza Santa Maria delle Carceri 15/Prato/Italia Phone/Fax: 057 424112 Email: info@prato.turismo.toscana.it.

❋ Azienda di Promozione Turistica di Prato/Via L. Muzzi 38/59100 Prato/Italia Phone: 057 435141 Fax: 057 4607925 E-mail: apt@prato.turismo.toscana.it www.prato.turismo.toscana.it.

Siena
Population 59,200

Siena is one of our favorite cities. It is the perfect size, not too big or small, with something for everyone. The heart of Siena contains the large semi-circular Piazza del Campo with its striking medieval towers and wonderfully detailed façades. It's a delightful place to relax and watch people stroll the Piazza. The undulating cobblestone streets of the town center are off limits to cars (unless you are going to your hotel), so the pedestrian is free to roam. The Duomo and affiliated museums are noteworthy, and offer great panoramic views of the surrounding countryside. Good restaurants and shopping abound, and Siena has one of the few laundromats in Italy! The deeper side of this Etruscan city is discovered in the original residence of St. Catherine of Siena, her Basilica, and Siena's own Eucharistic miracle. Siena is located in the plush Tuscan hills south of Florence, and is an easy day trip to or from Florence.

St. Catherine of Siena
Santa Caterina di Siena 1347-1380

"Oh love, grant me the consolation to see all hearts forced open by the strength of your love! I want to enlighten my beloved children; Lord, tear down the wall that divides you from them, so that they may love you totally!"

The impact of saints on the spiritual world is usually significant but their impact on the secular-political world is often minimal. St. Catherine was an exception to this rule for she had great influence in both worlds, bringing many souls to God through her writing and preaching, while changing the face of the Church by being instrumental in returning the pope to Rome after seventy years' residence in France. She is one of only two women recognized as Doctors of the Church for the significant theological doctrines expounded in her *Dialogue.*

Catherine was born in Siena as the youngest of twenty-five children of a middle class dyer and his wife. At the tender age of six, she had a vision of Christ that would set her entire life's work in motion. While returning home with her brother from a visit to her married sister's home, Catherine was halted mid-stride by a glorious vision of Jesus, and Saints Peter, Paul and John appearing over the church of San Domenico. She stood rooted in place with her gaze fixed skyward, taking in the exalted vista. Christ raised his hand in blessing, and Catherine inwardly accepted him as her only bridegroom. When her brother returned and abruptly pulled her from her vision, she said, "If you had seen what I saw you would not have done that."

As Catherine grew older, she remained a merry and energetic child, but also displayed a profoundly devotional nature. At times, she was seen to kneel while going up stairs, stopping to say a Hail Mary at each step. By age twelve, her parents were eager to groom her as a potential bride for one of the local gentry. Catherine rebelled and defiantly cut off her beautiful golden-brown hair. Shocked by the insolence of their daughter, her parents, Giacomo and Lapa, punished Catherine by treating her as their servant and housemaid, causing her to serve the family as if lowly hired help. Catherine took this treatment as a blessing and chose to remain happy and cheerful by acting as if they were the Holy Family. The turning point came when Catherine's father witnessed a dove of light hovering over her head while she was in deep prayer. Taking this as a sign of Catherine's sanctity, he accepted her choice of lifestyles and supported her pious practices and austerities.

Shortly thereafter, at age sixteen, Catherine took the vows of a Dominican tertiary and retired to her small room in the lower level of the house. She withdrew from the world, coming out only to attend mass and receive Holy Communion. She spent her days in prayer, often fasting on water and herbs, sleeping little, but also learning to read. Not only did she experience visions of Christ, Mary and the saints, but also witnessed the temptations of the world. One day, after three years of seclusion, she was praying for her townspeople, who were celebrating the town carnival. Suddenly she beheld a flash of light accompanied by celestial music and sweet perfume. Jesus Christ appeared flanked by the Virgin Mary, St. John, St. Paul, St. Dominic and David playing the harp with a legion of angels. To her great astonishment, Jesus approached and slipped a ring on her finger saying, "I will betroth you in faithfulness." Jesus also told Catherine that she must now serve God through her neighbors. Though in awe of the vision, the usually obedient Catherine responded, "I cannot help my neighbor without losing my peace of mind!" Jesus explained to her, "Your neighbors are the channel through which all your virtues come to birth, go, it is dinner time. Go and join them." Thus, Catherine reluctantly left her secluded cell and began serving the poor, sick and needy. True to the words of Jesus, Catherine developed the doctrine of neighborly love as the theme of her work, selflessly serving and loving all with the universal love of Christ.

Soon Catherine's world expanded into political and social realms, and she became embroiled in the upheaval of her day. The many city-states of the Italian peninsula were in constant battle with one another, with the Papal states and with the other powers of Europe. On another front, the Black Plague struck Siena in 1348, killing 70,000 of the 100,000 citizens, devastating the town along with many other areas of Italy. The twenty-year-old Catherine was a stalwart soldier on both battlefields, working as a peacemaker between various warring factions and serving as a tireless nurse to the sick and dying.

Through all the turmoil, Catherine continued to experience ecstatic visions, particularly when in

St. Catherine of Siena

Santuario-Casa di S. Caterina

deep prayer after receiving the sacrament of Holy Communion. She was often seen to rise off the floor in rapture, completely enveloped in ecstatic union. Her magnetism and spiritual depth began to attract a family of disciples who were dedicated to supporting her work and who followed her wherever she went.

While many people considered her a saint, others thought she was a fanatic and hypocrite, calling for her censure. To resolve the charges, Catherine was called to Florence to be interviewed by the chapter general of the Dominicans. All charges were summarily dismissed, and Catherine was recognized as a righteous soul and was allowed to return to Siena. At this meeting, Raymond of Capua was assigned as her confessor and guide, and they quickly became great friends and constant companions. Raymond eventually became her biographer and, later in his life, the master general of the Dominican order.

Peace was in short supply in fourteenth-century Italy, so Catherine's reputation as a peacemaker caused her to be called to many cities to resolve disputes. In 1374, she was summoned to Pisa to reconcile differences between that city-state and the Pope. While she was there, she went into a deep ecstasy after receiving communion, and fell prostrate on the floor of the chapel. While entranced, Catherine beheld a vision of Jesus surrounded by a vast light. Five bloodstained rays descended from him and pierced Catherine's hands, feet and heart, leaving on her the marks of the stigmata. Catherine accepted the blessing from Jesus, but asked that the marks be invisible, which they were until after her death. This encounter fortified Catherine with renewed strength and vigor, and she went on to preach tirelessly for peace, brotherly love and redemption.

Forty-two years before Catherine's birth, the papacy was stripped from Rome and re-established in the French town of Avignon. This relocation of power, in connection with the ascent of French and Spanish emperors, caused constant mayhem among the independent city-states of Italy. As Catherine became increasingly involved in politics, she became determined to return the Pope to his original home in Rome and to unite the diverse factions of the church. Her chance came in 1376 when Florence was placed under a papal interdict and Catherine was asked by the Florentines to travel to Avignon to mediate with Pope Gregory XI. Catherine's services were requested because of her ability to negotiate, but her true gift was her power of righteous persuasion. After arriving in Avignon, Catherine was very firm with the weak-willed Pope, and directly told him to "act like a man" and return to Rome. The pope heeded her counsel and departed for Rome in September of that year. Catherine returned to Siena, and then Florence, continuing to work for peace between the Pope and the defiant cities.

At this time in her life Catherine wished to record some of her deep communications with God, so she asked her disciples to write down whatever came out of her mouth when she was in ecstasy. Thus began her renowned *Dialogue* with God. Over the next ten months, Catherine communed with God and asked four questions of Him. She petitioned for knowledge of her self, the church, the world and about the influence of His presence in all things. Although there are numerous topics covered in the *Dialogue*, the constant theme is to love God by loving your neighbor.

"For I (God) could well have supplied each of you with all your needs, both spiritual and material. But I wanted to make you dependent on one another so that each of you would be my minister, dispensing the graces and gifts you have received from me. So you see, I have made you my ministers, setting you in different positions and in different ranks to exercise the virtue of charity."

After Pope Gregory XI died in 1378, and Urban VI was elected in his stead, a deep schism formed in the church. Cardinals opposed to the new appointment elected another Pope in Avignon, and the two sides fought bitterly for the papal throne. Catherine was once again called to Rome to work for peace and spent the remaining two years of her life in that city working tirelessly for the unification of the church. Growing weaker over time, and finally succumbing to intense pain and paralysis of her legs, she died on April 29, 1380, at the age of thirty-three.

St. Catherine of Siena was recognized as a major force of her time. She worked for God on all levels, in the larger world of politics and in the individual lives of those who sought her counsel. Her urgent advice was to not waste time but to live for God, constantly reminding her devotees about the "shortness of life." Catherine shows us that God desires to see us tasting the "food of angels, for [we] have been created for nothing else." As a soldier of God she tirelessly fought for each soul's divine right to taste this most precious food.

St. Catherine of Siena was canonized in 1461, named the Patron Saint of Italy in 1939, and made a Doctor of the Church in 1970. Clearly, her wisdom is timeless.

CATHERINE'S BASILICA OF ST. DOMINIC
Basilica Cateriniana di San Domenico

The Gothic Basilica of St. Dominic built from the thirteenth through fifteenth centuries contains the incorrupt head of St. Catherine of Siena. When she died in Rome in 1380, she was buried there in a cypress coffin in the cemetery of Santa Maria Sopra Minerva. In 1383, Catherine's confessor and biographer, Blessed Raymond of Capua, had her head separated from her body and enclosed in a gilded copper reliquary. On May 5, 1384 the town of Siena received the sacred relic and a huge procession led by St. Catherine's mother, Lapa, delivered it to San Domenico. The chapel of St. Catherine (Cappella di Santa Caterina) now houses her head, which can be seen to be in incredible condition considering she died more than five hundred years ago. In 1619, the remains of St. Catherine's family were placed in this same chapel, under the marble altar.

As you enter the Basilica, turn left, and face the main altar. The chapel of St. Catherine is on the right. Beyond the chapel on the right is the sacristy, and through that, a bookstore. In the far right side of the transept is the reliquary that held St. Catherine's head from

Chapel of St. Catherine

1383-84. A sign in Italian reads: "Teca reliquaria in bronzo dorato."

As you enter the church, to the right is a large column and a few stairs. Up the stairs is the Chapel of the Vaults (Cappella delle Volte) where St. Catherine and the other Mantellates met for meetings and prayer. This chapel and the column are said to be the site of many of Catherine's ecstasies. Also displayed is a lifelike portrait of Catherine created ten years after her death by one of her disciples, Andrea Vanni. It was originally part of a larger fresco but was detached in 1667 and placed here.

St. Catherine may have more relics disseminated throughout Italy than any other saint we researched. She was very popular in her own time, and everyone literally wanted a piece of her. After many centuries of St. Catherine's relics being distributed, on August 3, 1855, her remains were finally sealed in a sarcophagus and placed in the high altar of Santa Maria Sopra Minerva in Rome, where they can be viewed today. (See Rome)

SHRINE INFORMATION

Shrine: Catherine's Basilica of St. Dominic (Basilica Cateriniana di San Domenico)

Address: Piazza San Domenico, 53100 Siena, Italia

Phone: 057 7286848 **Fax:** 057 7280540

E-mail: basilica@si.technet.it

Website: www.basilicacateriniana.com — Official website.

Quiet areas for meditation: It is a large basilica with many tourists.

English spoken: Rarely

Hours: 7AM–6:30PM.

Mass: Sun/Hol: 7:30AM, 9, 10:30, 12NOON, 6PM; Weekdays: 7:30AM, 9, 6PM.

Feasts and festivities: April 29 — Feast day.

Other Events: July 2 and August 16: The Palio horse race is a very crowded time in Siena. The town is very noisy then, and it would be good to avoid if you don't like noise and crowds.

Accessibility: There is a ramp.

Tours: None

Bookstore: To the left of the chapel of St. Catherine (Cappella di Santa Caterina) and through the Sacristy, you will find many books in English.

Recommended books: *Catherine of Siena: Passion for the Truth, Compassion for Humanity*, Selected spiritual writings by O'Driscoll, Mary, O.P.; *Catherine of Siena: The Dialogue*, The Classics of Western Spirituality, translation by Suzanne Noffke, O.P. O'Driscoll's book is a nice small book introducing you to some of St. Catherine's writings. Noffke's book is a complete compilation of the *Dialogue* that is inspiring reading, too large to take traveling, but excellent to read before you go.

Lodging: See lodging under House of St. Catherine, Hotel Alma Domus.

Directions: Piazza San Domenico is across from Stadio Comunale and is a major transportation hub at the end of viale dei Mille.

HOUSE OF ST. CATHERINE
La Casa di Santa Caterina

The house where St. Catherine grew up is one of the most sacred places in Siena. It is an easy walk from San Domenico and is owned by the archdiocese, run by the Dominican sisters. The small complex consists of three areas: the chapel, museum/reliquary/bookstore, and St. Catherine's cell. As you enter through a gated courtyard, the Chapel is on your far right, the museum is to the left, and the cell of St. Catherine is down the stairs to the left of the museum.

The chapel (Chiesa del Crocifisso) contains the cross that St. Catherine was praying to when she received the stigmata in Pisa at the Church of Santa Cristina, April 1, 1375. St. Catherine asked that

La Casa di Santa Caterina

the stigmata be invisible, and they only appeared after her death. There are brochures on the right of the chapel as you come in, and sometimes there are some in English.

Directly across from the church is the museum named

"L'Oratorio della Cucina." The room is adorned with frescoes of Catherine's life and under the altar is a view of the original kitchen of her home. A small room next door contains items that the saint used. The adjacent bookstore is open at various times. (There is also a good bookstore at San Domenico.)

Down the stairs to the left of the museum is Catherine's cell, called "Oratorio della Camera." This is the room where Catherine secluded for three years before she started her mission in the world. Here she spent her time in prayer and meditation, and experienced many visions and miracles. The walls of the room are covered with beautiful frescoes portraying scenes from her life. This is a wonderful place to meditate; even though many pilgrims come and go, people attempt to be quiet. Over her cell is a sign that says "silentium"—silence. This is our favorite place in Siena to spend time with St. Catherine, for the power of her presence is very tangible.

The stairs that continue down past the cell labeled "Nobile contrada dell'oca oratorio cantina prodigiosa" are not currently accessible. St. Catherine's father and brothers had their wool dying business here, and beneath these rooms is the cellar, which was the site of many miracles.

SHRINE INFORMATION

Shrine: The House and Sanctuary of St. Catherine (Casa di Santa Caterina)

Address: Via Santa Caterina, 53100 Siena, Italia

Phone: 057 7288175 **Fax:** None

E-mail: associazione_caterinati@virgilio.it

Website: www.caterinati.org — Official website.

Quiet areas for meditation: St. Catherine's cell downstairs (Oratorio della Camera). The chapel (Chiesa del Crocifisso) is less intimate, but a good alternative if St. Catherine's cell is crowded.

English spoken: Rarely

Hours: Summer 9AM–12:30PM; 2:30PM–6:00; Winter 9AM–12:30PM; 3:30PM–6:00

Feasts and festivities: April 29 — Feast day

Accessibility: There is a ramp that provides access to "L'Oratorio della Cucina" through a side door to the chapel. Call 057 7288175 or ask the tourist office to call for you.

Tours: None

Bookstore: On the main floor to the left as you enter. Irregular hours.

Lodging: Hotel Alma Domus/Via Camporegio 37/53100 Siena/Italia. Email: incoming@terresiena.it Phone: 057 744177 or 057 744487 Fax: 057 747601. With San Domenico at your back, take the street downhill to the right. Take the first right down some stairs, and on the left will be the gate to the hotel. You need to ring the bell and they buzz you in. The same Dominican nuns that run St. Catherine's house operate this lodging. The two buildings are next to each other, but you still have to walk around the block to get from one to the other. The nuns do not speak English, but sometimes there will be a layperson working there that does. Plan to speak in Italian. Ask for a room on the upper floors to have a beautiful view of the Duomo. Curfew is 11:30PM. You can drive your car there to unload only.

Directions: The Casa di Santa Caterina is on Costa di Sant'Antonio, an easy walk down from San Domenico taking Via della Sapienza. As you leave the Basilica, take the street downhill to the right.

OTHER PLACES OF INTEREST IN SIENA

EUCHARISTIC MIRACLE OF SIENA
THE BASILICA OF ST. FRANCIS
Basilica di San Francesco

The Basilica of St. Francis is across town from San Domenico on Piazza San Francesco at the end of Via dei Rossi. The Eucharistic Miracle of Siena is in the Chapel of the Holy Hosts located in the left transept. There is usually a sign indicating the location of the Eucharist. The hosts are only displayed on special occasions or if pre-arranged for groups. The container holding them had been stolen in 1951, so they are kept secure in the tabernacle.

The history of the Eucharistic miracle begins in 1730, when 223 hosts were stolen from their silver container. The hosts were found three days later in a nearby church in a donation box. Collected from the dirty box, they were cleaned, counted and examined, then brought back to San Francesco. Over time, it was discovered that the hosts never deteriorated. They have been scientifically examined many times throughout the years and have always been found to be fresh, physically incorrupt and chemically pure.

Shrine: Basilica of St. Francis — Eucharistic Miracle of Siena (Basilica di San Francesco)

Address: Father Rector/Piazza San Francesco/53100 Siena/Italia

Phone: 057 7289081

Hours: 7:30AM–12; 3:30PM–7:00

Mass: 8:30AM, 11, 6:00PM; Eucharistic Miracle displayed after evening mass.

COMING AND GOING

SIENA

Car: Follow signs to Stadio (stadium). The symbol is a soccer ball. San Domenico and St. Catherine's house are near the stadium in the southwest area of Siena. Cars are restricted from driving through the town unless you are dropping off your luggage at lodging. You will get a ticket if you leave your car for more than five minutes. There is free parking near the Forte di Santa Barbara close to San Domenico.

Train: Stazione Siena is 1.5 miles northeast from the city center. Buses from the station shuttle to Piazza Matteotti, which is within walking distance of San Domenico.

Bus: Buses from out of town arrive and leave from a station near San Domenico. There is an information center across from San Domenico where you can buy tickets in advance, and they usually speak English.

TOURIST INFORMATION

❉ APT — Agenzia Turismo/Piazza del Campo 56/53100 Siena/Italia Phone: 057 7280551 Fax: 057 281041 E-mail: infoaptsiena@terresiena.it www.terresiena.it.

❉ APT — Tourist Information/Via di Città 43/53100 Siena/Italia Phone: 057 742209 Fax: 057 7281041.

WEBSITES

Basilica Cateriniana di San Domenico www.basilicacateriniana.com — Official website.

Christian Classics Ethereal Library www.ccel.org/ccel/catherine/dialog.html — The complete *Dialogue* online.

Comune di Siena www.comune.siena.it — Disabled traveler info: Click on "Il Turista," "English Version" "Siena for all."

ANOTHER ST. CATHERINE OF SIENA SHRINE IN ITALY

ROME

BASILICA OF HOLY MARY ABOVE MINERVA
Basilica di Santa Maria Sopra Minerva

Santa Maria Sopra Minerva contains the remains of St. Catherine of Siena on the main altar in a glass urn. The "Room of St. Catherine" consists of the reconstructed walls of the room in which she died. See the chapter on Rome for more detailed information. www.basilicacaminerva.it Italian.

Stadio

Piazza G. Matteotti

P. d. Salimbene

Via Vallerozzi

San Francesco

V. dei Mille

Buses.

Via Curtatone

Via della Sapienza

La Casa di S. Caterina

San Domenico

Via di Fontebranda

P. del Campo

Duomo

SIENA

0   100   200 M

Umbria

The Region of Umbria is known as the "green heart of Italy," for its central location and its rolling, woodland areas. The Apennine mountains in the north and east give way to the Umbra and Tiber (Tervene) valleys of the south and west, creating scenic drives over rambling hills, past quaint walled cities perched on the hillsides. Perugia is the capital of the region, with Terni, Assisi, and Foligno being other major cities. On a short visit to Italy, an itinerary including Umbria and Tuscany would give the pilgrim a complete experience of the country, for the two regions display a natural splendor and exquisite towns, as well as profound spiritual sites. Umbria is also called the "land of saints," for it is the home of St. Francis and St. Clare of Assisi and scores of other saints who have sanctified this mystical land with their spirit and love.

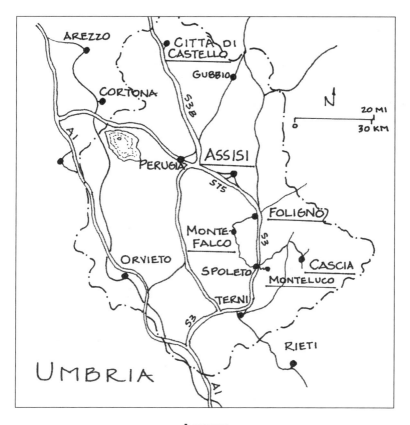

ASSISI
St. Francis of Assisi
St. Clare of Assisi

CASCIA
St. Rita of Cascia

CITTÀ DI CASTELLO
St. Veronica Giuliani
Blessed Margaret of Metola

FOLIGNO
Blessed Angela of Foligno

MONTEFALCO
St. Clare of the Cross

Assisi

Population 26,196

Nestled against Mt. Subasio and overlooking the Spoleto Valley, Assisi is one of Umbria's most beautiful and mystical hill towns. The superbly maintained medieval city is the home of St. Francis and is known worldwide as "The City of Peace" for it often accommodates ecumenical and interreligious conferences. The Basilicas of St. Francis and St. Clare, along with San Damiano, grace the city with their architecture, art and relics. Assisi has abundant housing for pilgrims and is an excellent hub from which to visit many of the shrines of central Italy described in this book.

ST. FRANCIS OF ASSISI
San Francesco 1182-1226

"Where there is peace and meditation, there is neither anxiety nor doubt."

St. Francis is known throughout the world as the saint of ultimate humility, simplicity and joy, yet his life hardly started out that way. Born in Assisi to a wealthy merchant family, Francesco lived a life of prosperity and worldly pleasures. Known for his enjoyment of song, music and libations, he was quite popular among his peers. Around his 20th year, this easy life changed abruptly when war broke out with the neighboring city of Perugia. He enlisted in the struggle and went to battle in hopes of returning a hero. Instead, he was captured and held prisoner for an entire year. Upon returning home, Francis became very ill and withdrawn, depressed by the world he now saw around him. After many months he regained his health and ultimately gained a new perspective on life. One day, while passing a leper on the road, he initially felt repulsion at the hideous sight. Then, feeling deep compassion for the leper, he returned and kissed him, offering his love and understanding. This was a turning point in Francis's life, for by showing compassion, he felt a love greater than his own.

Shortly after this incident, while Francis prayed in a dilapidated church just outside the walls of Assisi, Christ spoke to him from the crucifix there, and asked him to rebuild His church. Christ was referring to the greater body of the Church, but Francis took the command literally, and began rebuilding San Damiano, the church housing the miraculous crucifix. To raise money for the project, Francis stole fabric from his father's warehouse and sold it in the neighboring town of Foligno. His father was furious over the betrayal, and disowned his son in public before the local Bishop of Assisi. In response, Francis removed his clothing and offered it to his father saying that, henceforth, his Heavenly Father would provide for all his needs. From this point forward, Francis possessed nothing except the ragged clothes on his back and his great love for God and Christ. Thus, at the age of 25, he began the life of a beggar, administering to the poor and the lepers, and working to rebuild the churches around Assisi.

After three years, Francis received an inward calling to serve the people directly, and started to preach on the streets of Assisi and nearby towns, where he was often ridiculed for his appearance and behavior. At this time, a wealthy man of Assisi was so deeply impressed by the sincerity and joyous nature of Francis, that he, too, gave away all his possessions to the poor and joined Francis, becoming Brother Bernard. Together they preached on the streets, and slowly, one by one, more people began to hear their message and join the little band of souls. Thus, a force for spreading the gospel of simplicity and humility began to grow and infect the countryside with the good news.

Within a year, they were twelve brothers strong, so they went to Rome to receive the blessings of the Pope upon their order. The Pope accepted the Simple Rule of 1210, and he blessed their fledgling order, the Friars Minor, and prayed that it would be an inspiration to the masses

Bust of St. Francis

and to the Church itself. Returning to Assisi, the men lived at Rivotorto just east of the city, dedicated to poverty and service. Ultimately they moved to the property surrounding the Porziuncola, a tiny church in Santa Maria degli Angeli just south of Assisi, which became their permanent home. The Benedictine monks of Mt. Subasio gave the property to Francis, but Francis refused to own any property outright, so he agreed to lease the land for the yearly fee of a basket of fish and some bread. This arrangement is annually celebrated to this day!

The Franciscan order continued to gain new members and also attracted women to the work. A nineteen-year-old girl of Assisi, Clare Favarone, asked to join the group and was accepted as the founding member of the Second Franciscan Order of cloistered nuns.

Francis was forever traveling, preaching the gospel of simplicity and love throughout Italy, in Spain and North Africa. He joined the crusades in 1219 and traveled to Egypt, even speaking before an Islamic Sultan. The constant travel took its toll, and he returned to Italy seriously ill with glaucoma and malaria.

In Italy there was then much upheaval and infighting among his fellow brothers over the direction of the Order. Francis was deeply worried for the future, because he felt Christ had called him to create a mission with specific guidelines. He gave up the leadership of the Order and continued to worry about its future. Finally, during his deep despair, Christ appeared to Francis and assured him that He would always be the inspirational head of the true followers of Francis.

This released Francis of his burden, and he emerged ever more empowered by his personal relationship with Christ. He lived in almost constant communion with Christ, having countless experiences of His presence. On Christmas Eve, 1223, Francis prepared a replica of the manger scene in the small church at Greccio, creating the first crèche scene in history, at which time he had a vision of holding the infant Jesus in his arms. The following year, while in seclusion at La Verna, Francis received the stigmata, the wounds of the crucified Christ, and bore these blessed wounds for the final two years of his life.

In his last years, Francis performed many miracles, predicted the future, healed the sick, and lived in ecstatic communion with Christ. He preached to the birds of Avalon, tamed the wolf of Gubbio and wrote his beloved "Canticle of the Creatures." Finally, after only 20 years of service to God, his body ravaged by illness, he returned to the Porziuncola to die, but not before singing to his brothers in joyous ecstasy from his deathbed. He died on October 3, 1226, at the age of 44, and was canonized two years later.

THE BASILICA OF ST. FRANCIS
Basilica di San Francesco

The Basilica of St. Francis is composed of three levels, the upper and Lower Basilica and the Crypt. The lower Romanesque basilica was started in 1228, two years after St. Francis's death, and the upper Gothic basilica was started in 1230. This multi-faceted structure was completed in 1239 and the interiors in 1253. St. Francis' body was moved to the Basilica in 1230 from San Giorgio's (which is now the Basilica of St. Clare). St. Francis was buried in the lower church several meters under the high altar to prevent theft of the body.

In 1818, the Pope gave permission to build a chapel under the high altar so people could view the stone sarcophagus, since the trend of robbing saints' graves had passed. The crypt is entered in the middle of the lower church from stairs on the right hand side. St. Francis's tomb is behind the altar and his disciples Blessed Rufino, Leone, Masseo, and Angelo are entombed in the surrounding outer walls. Lady Jacoba, whom Francis called "Friar Jacoba," is laid to rest on the entrance stairway facing the altar. There are pews for praying, and even though it is very busy with many tourists and can be very stuffy, try to spend some time here, for there are many blessings to be received. You may also wish to go upstairs to pray before the high altar over St. Francis' crypt, which is more open and less crowded.

The Chapel of Relics is in the lower church on the main

Basilica di San Francesco

floor, to the right of the main altar and down some stairs. If it is dark, the motion sensors will turn on the lights when you enter. This room contains St. Francis's tunic and sandals, and a handwritten blessing for Brother Leo, among other relics. Usually this room is not very crowded, and there are chairs to sit and meditate.

The Upper Basilica contains restored frescoes by Giotto, Cavallini, Cimabue and others. Some of these beautiful frescoes were damaged in the earthquake of 1997. The frescoes along the walls depict the life of Saint Francis taken from the Legenda Major written in 1263 by Saint Bonaventure. *The Basilica of Saint Francis: A Spiritual Pilgrimage* is a great little booklet you can buy at the bookstore describing the artwork and layout of the Basilica.

St. Joseph of Copertino had a special spot in the Lower Basilica where we like to spend time in meditation. St. Joseph lived at the Basilica for 14 years and, when no one was around at night, he would go to pray in the "Cappella dell'Immacolata" (next to Cappella San Martino Di Tours). This side chapel is up the first stairs on the left as you face the main altar. Here St. Joseph would pray to the statue of the Virgin Mary (La Statua della Vergine), which is the same one currently on display. Because it is slightly out of the way, this spot is one of the only somewhat quiet areas we found in the Basilica to meditate, and it has a bench to sit on. Another special place to visit, if you can arrange a tour, is the five rooms St. Joseph of Copertino lived in from 1639 to 1653 in the Sacred Convent (Sacro Convento). Getting to see his rooms might be difficult since they are not officially

Cappella dell'Immacolata

open to the public. Ask at the information booth to see if a priest is available to escort you there. Consider yourself lucky if they can, but don't expect it. A prayer may help!

I would like to visit the rooms that St. Joseph of Copertino lived in.
Vorrei visitare le stanze dove ha vissuto San Giuseppe.

SHRINE INFORMATION

Shrine: The Basilica of St. Francis (Basilica di San Francesco)

Address: 06081 Assisi (PG) Italia

Phone: 075 819001 **Fax:** 075 8155208

E-mail: assisisanfrancesco@krenet.it/sacroconvento@sanfrancescoassisi.org

Website: www.sanfrancescoassisi.org — Official website: Basilica and Sacred Convent of St. Francis in Assisi.

Quiet areas for meditation: You can avoid the crowds by arriving when the Basilica opens at 6:30AM and before 8:30AM, but crowds are hard to avoid at any time. St. Joseph of Copertino had a favorite spot for meditation in the Lower Basilica in the "Cappella dell'Immacolata." The Chapel of the Relics is in the Lower Basilica, right off the main altar and down some stairs. There are chairs there, and it is not too busy.

English spoken: Occasionally

Hours: Daily 7AM–7PM

Mass: Sun: 7:30AM, 9, 10:30, 12, 5PM, 6, 6:30; Daily 7:15AM, 11, 6PM; Celebrate the Eucharist 7:30AM, 9, 10:30, 12, 5PM, 6:30; Canto dei vespri 6PM.

Feasts and festivities: October 3 & 4 — Festival of St. Francis (Festa di San Francesco); September 17 — Impression of the Stigmata.

Accessibility: Both the Upper and Lower Basilica, but not the tomb of St. Francis.

Information office: To the left of the main entrance to the Lower Basilica. Open 9AM–12, 2PM–5:30. Closed Sunday.

Tours: Tours are available in English given on the outside of the Basilica or inside with headphones. To prearrange, Phone: 075 819001 Fax: 075 8155208.

Bookstore: A large bookstore is behind the church, between the upper and lower church levels, facing the cloister. The information office, located near the entrance to the Lower Basilica, has a few books also. Ask at the information office for directions to the bookstore, as it is a little tricky to get there.

Recommended books: The booklet, *The Basilica of Saint Francis: A Spiritual Pilgrimage*, describing the Basilica and its artwork is available at the bookstore. Other books available in Assisi: *Assisi in the Footsteps of Saint Francis*, by P. Theophile Desbonnets and *The Land of Saint Francis: Umbria and Surroundings*, by Luciano Canonici.

Lodging: None

Directions: The Basilica di San Francesco is at the west end of the city on Via San Francesco.

ST. CLARE OF ASSISI
Santa Chiara 1193–1253

*"They say that we are too poor, but can a heart
which possesses the infinite God be truly called poor?"*

In the early thirteenth century, the nobility of Assisi consisted of only five families, so each son and daughter played an important part in their family's social role, especially if that daughter was of marrying age. One of the most sought-after young women of her day was the eighteen-year-old Clare Favarone. So it was alarming to her family when she fled their privileged home during the night of Palm Sunday, 1212, to join the poor friar Francis and his band of followers at the Porziuncola outside Assisi. Here the young Clare was greeted with great respect and joy, being the first woman to join with Francis's legion. After taking vows of poverty, obedience and chastity, her hair was shorn and she was clothed in a habit of sackcloth. Thus she became the first member of what was later called the Second Order of St. Francis, consisting of cloistered nuns.

Clare began her life of service at St. Paul's in nearby Bastia, but her quietude was disturbed when her family discovered her whereabouts, and tried to persuade her to return home. She adamantly refused, and soon after was relocated to St. Angelo of Panzo. Causing further grief within the Favarone family, Clare's fifteen-year-old sister Agnes joined her at St. Angelo, and together they practiced the life of poverty and devotion. In 1215, they were reassigned to San Damiano in Assisi, with Clare installed as superior. Eventually, their mother, younger sister Beatrice, and Aunt Bianca also entered the order. Thus the noble family of Assisi became a most noble family of God!

Clare remained cloistered at San Damiano for the remaining forty years of her life. A living example of humility, she refused to be served by her sisters, and instead insisted on serving them, even though she was their leader. She developed the Order of the Poor Clares under the strict rules of Francis, and expressed this rule by not wearing shoes, sleeping on the floor, abstaining from meat, and practicing "holy silence." Clare's personal austerities were often severe and were finally modified by Francis and the Bishop of Assisi to include sleeping on a straw mattress and eating at least one thing a day.

Clare's leadership was inspiring to many women of her day, and as a result, other monasteries were founded in Italy, France and Germany. The Poor Clares followed the rule of Francis (although technically it was the rule of St. Benedict as decided by the Pope), particularly the rule of not owning property or accepting money. This was a difficult way of life, but Clare thrived spiritually on it, and refused to compromise her stance, even under pressure from the Holy Father. Pope Innocent IV wanted to provide the sisters with some form of income, but Clare would not allow it. After many years of fighting for approval for her austere Rule, the Pope finally granted Clare's request just two days before her death. (She was the first woman to create a rule for women in the Roman Catholic Church that was approved by the Pope.) This act completed her life of service.

Crypt of St. Clare

St. Clare was cloistered most of her adult life, still she performed many quiet miracles. When the Pope visited her at San Damiano, he asked her to bless the bread they were about to eat. Clare humbly accepted his command and after she blessed the bread, all the loaves were adorned with slices in the crust in the shape of the cross. This convinced the Pope of Clare's sanctity, although he had already felt her divine essence. On another occasion, Assisi was in danger of being attacked by the mercenary army of Saracens. The army was marching through the Spoleto Valley, leaving towns afire in its wake. As they approached Assisi from the south, they came first upon the convent at San Damiano. There they were greeted by the sight of Clare standing at the door of the monastery, holding the blessed host before her and praying for salvation of her cloister and the city behind her. Miraculously, the army retreated, by-passing the convent and the city, moving on to plunder less fortunate neighboring towns.

Although Clare was cloistered, she allowed herself to see Francis, for he was the Father of her Order. She greatly enjoyed his spiritual company and counsel. At one meeting between the two great souls, they had a picnic near the Porziuncola. Their feast was shared with another brother and sister of the Order, and, prior to eating, they all sang praises to God for the beauty that surrounded them. Their joy was so great and their songs so inspired that they began to emanate a divine light. This light became so bright and tangible that the people of Assisi thought the forest was on fire. When they rushed to extinguish the flames they simply found the small band of devotees ablaze with the light and love of God.

As Clare approached the end of her life, she often experienced illness and pain. However her experience was not one of suffering but of joy. She said, regarding her health, "… Ever since by means of His servant Francis I have known the grace of our Lord Jesus Christ, I have never in my whole life found any pain or sickness that could afflict me." Thus she lived a life of joy in God until her passing at the age of 60, on August 11, 1253. At her deathbed was her sister Agnes, along with Brothers Leo and Juniper, who read to her the Passion of Christ according to St. John, as they had done for their brother Francis at his death, twenty-seven years earlier. St. Clare was canonized two years after her death, as was St. Francis, demonstrating their powerful spiritual influence during their lifetimes.

BASILICA OF ST. CLARE
Basilica di Santa Chiara

The Basilica of St. Clare was built over San Giorgio Church in 1257–1260. The body of St. Francis was kept in San Giorgio's until his Basilica was completed in 1230. St. Clare's body was also kept in San Giorgio until her Basilica replaced it and her body moved there in 1260. San Giorgio's is the church where St. Clare first heard St. Francis give a sermon, and made the decision to follow him. St. Clare's incorrupt body was discovered buried underneath the high altar in 1850 and placed in a newly constructed Chapel downstairs in 1872. In 1986, her body was encased in a ceramic mold due to deterioration and returned for public viewing in 1987. The current Basilica contains the crypt of St. Clare downstairs. Near her crypt are stairs leading up to the stone coffin her body resided in for 600 years. The crypt also contains the relic shrine of St. Francis and St. Clare, including: the breviary which Francis and his brothers used; the 1253 Bull from Pope Innocent IV approving Clare's Rule; Clare's hair and remnants of clothing; and a slipper Clare made for Francis.

The Crucifix of San Damiano that spoke to St. Francis is in a small chapel on the right side of the main floor. This crucifix was moved here from San Damiano, along with the Poor Clare nuns, around 1260–63 when the Basilica was completed. It has been on display to the public since 1957.

The chapel of St. Agnes on the left of the church contains the bodies of St. Agnes and Blessed Ortolana, the sister and mother of St. Clare, who were members of St. Clare's order, the Order of the Poor Clares (Ordine delle Clarisse). Also buried here is Bl. Benedetta, Clare's successor as abbess. Today, the Clarissians live cloistered in the convent next to the Basilica.

The Basilica is very busy and active, because

Basilica di Santa Chiara

it is fairly small and a primary pilgrimage stop, especially for tour buses. As a result, it is difficult to find a quiet place to meditate, as people are constantly coming and going. Sitting in the Chapel of the Crucifix is a true blessing, but one must really go inward to avoid the clamor. Earplugs are a good idea!

SHRINE INFORMATION

Shrine: Saint Clare Basilica (Basilica di Santa Chiara)

Address: Piazza Santa Chiara/06082 Assisi (PG) Italia

Phone: 075 812282 **Fax:** 075 816827 Speak in Italian

Contact for Information: Friars Minor Community - St. Clare

Address: 06081 Assisi (PG) Italia

Phone: 075 812216 **Fax:** 075 8198623

E-mail: None

Website: www.assisiofm.org Friars Minor of Umbria website

Quiet areas for meditation: None really. Silence is to be maintained in the Chapel of the Crucifix, but it is usually noisy with pilgrims coming and going. There are moments when it is peaceful, so enjoy it when the opportunity arises.

English spoken: Rarely

Hours: 6:30AM–12; Summer 2PM–7, Winter 6.

Mass: Sun/Hol 11:30AM; Weekdays 5:30PM.

Feasts and festivities: August 12 — Feast day; October 3 — Feast of Translation of Body; September 23 — Feast of Finding Her Body in 1850.

Accessibility: The side entrance leads to the main floor of the Basilica, with access to the Crucifix of San Damiano. There is no access downstairs to the tomb.

Tours: Contact the Friars Minor Community to see if you can arrange a tour: Phone: 075 812216 Fax: 075 8198623

Bookstore: A book in English on the life of St. Clare is sold along with booklets in several languages.

Lodging: None

Recommended book: *In the Footsteps of Saint Clare: A Pilgrim's Guide Book*

by Ramona Miller, O.S.F. The Franciscan Institute, St. Bonaventure University. Buy at home and read before you go on the trip. You can find it at www.stfrancisonline.com.

Directions: Basilica di Santa Chiara is on Piazza Santa Chiara, off of Via Santa Chiara. It is in the southeast area of Assisi, close to the entrance of the walled city called Porta Nuova.

SAN DAMIANO

The Convent of San Damiano is less than 1 mile (1.5 km) from Porta Nuova in Assisi and was built between the eighth and ninth centuries. This is the first church St. Francis restored after Christ spoke to him in 1205 from the cross in the chapel. The chapel now contains a replica of the crucifix, the original having been taken to the Basilica of St. Clare when the Poor Clares left San Damiano after St. Clare's death. This is a powerful place to feel the presence of both St. Francis and St. Clare.

St. Francis wrote the Canticle of the Creatures in a hut near here in 1225. On the day of his death, October 3, 1226, St. Francis's body was brought here for Clare and her sisters to see.

St. Clare and the Poor Clares lived at San Damiano from 1212–1253. The nuns slept on straw mats in the dormitory, and St. Clare died in that room on August 11, 1253. The dormitory is a good place to linger awhile even with pilgrims flowing through. A corner has been roped off indicating St. Clare's bed. The refectory is where St. Clare blessed the bread in obedience to the Pope and the miracle of crosses appeared on all the loaves of bread.

There is also a special shrine room for St. Clare's sister Agnes. The room is upstairs near the refectory, and requires special permission to get there, but it is a very quiet place to meditate.

San Damiano

SHRINE INFORMATION

Shrine: Convent of San Damiano (Convento San Damiano)

Address: 06081 Assisi (PG) Italia

Phone: 075 812273 **Fax:** 075 8198007

E-mail: guardianosandamiano@libero.it

Website: www.assisiofm.org Friars Minor of Umbria website

Quiet areas for meditation: San Damiano is smaller and quieter than most shrines. You can find time for contemplation here even with people passing through. The chapel with the replica of St. Francis's crucifix is especially nice, as is St. Clare's dormitory, and St. Agnes' room.

English spoken: Rarely

Hours: Summer 10AM–12:30PM, 2PM–6; Winter 10AM–12:30PM, 2PM–4:30.

Mass: Sun/Hol 7:15AM, 9:30PM; Weekdays 7:15AM.

Feasts and festivities: August 11 — Feast of Saint Clare; June 22 — Festa Del Voto (of the Vow) when St. Clare chased away the Saracens; Third Sunday of September (Canticle of the Creatures); October 4 — Feast of St. Francis.

Accessibility: The ground floor has one step here and there, and there is no access upstairs.

Tours: Ask at the information booth to the left of the main entrance for any tours in English, between 10AM–12 and 2PM–4. Be sure to get the free tour guide in English. For additional inspiration, ask about joining the monks for Vespers around 5PM in the winter and later in the summer.

Bookstore: None

Lodging: None

Directions: San Damiano can be reached walking 15 minutes downhill from Assisi south of Porta Nuova. By car, after exiting the city from the Porta Nuova gate, take the street "viale Vittorio Emanuele" leaving Assisi. Take the first road to the left and follow signs to "Convento di San Damiano."

Other places of interest in Assisi

Cathedral of Assisi
Duomo di San Rufino

San Rufino is on Piazza San Rufino and was built in 1140. It contains the baptismal font (to the far right as you enter) where St. Francis, St. Clare, and other local saints were baptized. Legend has it that the same angel that told St. Francis' mother, Donna Pica, to give birth in a stable, appeared to her at his baptism and asked to hold the baby. There is a stone behind a grate near the font that has the angel's impression made from kneeling. St. Clare's family home was connected to the church, on the left before you enter. Although nothing remains of her original home, there is a small altar commemorating the location of the house. St. Clare lived here until she was nineteen years old. It is a private home now and not open to pilgrims. Duomo di San Rufino/Piazza San Rufino/Assisi/Italia Phone: 075 812283 Fax: 075 815312 www.assisimuseocattedrale.com

Sanctuary of Chiesa Nuova
Chiesa Nuova, located on piazzetta Chiesa Nuova, off Piazza del Commune, was built in 1615 over the foundation of what is believed to be the home of Pietro di Bernardone and Donna Pica, St. Francis's parents. You can visit rooms in the house and visit the museum. St. Francis is thought to have been born in the nearby Oratorio di San Francesco Piccolino. Piazza Chiesa Nuova, 7 – 06081 Assisi (PG) Italia. Phone: 075 812339   Fax: 075 8155050 e-mail: info@assisichiesanuova.it www.assisichiesanuova.it Italian.

#2c via Portica
According to historical research, this address may be the original home of St. Francis of Assisi, but is not yet recognized officially. It is located west of Piazza del Commune, at #2c Via Portica, which is thought to have been the home and cloth shop of St. Francis' father, Pietro Bernadone. At the time of our visit, an American nun conducted tours in the summer. Since our last visit there, a candle shop has been installed and there is no access inside.

ST. MARY MAJOR
Santa Maria Maggiore

This is where the bishop asked St. Francis to return the money he had made selling his father's cloth. St. Francis returned the money and renounced his relationship to his father. As a symbol of his renunciation, Francis then took off his clothes and offered them to his father. The Bishop wrapped his cape around Francis, taking responsibility for him. Santa Maria Maggiore is on Piazza del Vescovado. Phone/Fax: 075 813085 smmariamaggioreassisi@libero.it.

LITTLE CHURCH OF ST. STEVEN
Chiesetta di San Stefano

According to certain legends, at the death of St. Francis the bells of San Stefano rang of their own accord. Built in the twelfth century, it is a sweet church to meditate in, with few tourists. San Stefano is in the middle of Assisi, off of Via Aluigi coming from either piazzetta Aluigi or Via A. Fortini. You will have to climb some stairs to get there. There is also a nice picnic area behind the church with a beautiful view of the valley below. Phone/Fax: 075 813085.

COMING AND GOING

ASSISI

Car: Assisi is located between Perugia and Foligno on highway S45. There are multiple exits from each direction, but the exit for Santa Maria degli Angeli is the most central and scenic. Follow the signs 3 miles (5 km) to Assisi. Note the Basilica of Santa Maria degli Angeli on your right as you pass through the small town. Assisi is 115 miles (185 km) from Florence and 105 miles (170 km) from Rome.

Train: The station, Stazione Ferroviaria, is located 2.5 miles (4 km) southwest of Assisi at Santa Maria degli Angeli. A shuttle bus from Assisi leaves every half hour from Piazza Matteotti. All major cities are accessible by train, but you will have to transfer to reach most major locations. Phone: 075 892021 www.trenitalia.it Italian.

Bus: ASP buses connect on a regular basis to Foligno, Perugia and other local cities, leaving from Piazza Matteotti. Daily buses connect to Rome, Florence and other major cities from Piazzale dell' Unità d'Italia.

TOURIST INFORMATION

✻ Assisi Promotion Agency/Piazza Del Comune 12/06081 Assisi
(PG) Italia Phone: 075 812534 Fax: 075 813727/E-mail:
info@iat.assisi.pg.it/ www.umbria2000.it

WEBSITES

Assisi Patriarchal Basilica of St. Francis www.sanfrancescoassisi.org
— Official website of the Basilica and Sacred Convent of St. Francis
in Assisi.

Franciscan Institute Outreach www.christusrex.org/www1/ofm/
fra/FRAmain.html — Comprehensive Franciscan cybercourse.

Friars Minor of Umbria www.assisiofm.org — Click on "Sanctuaries"
for a list of these sanctuaries cared for by the Friars Minor Order.

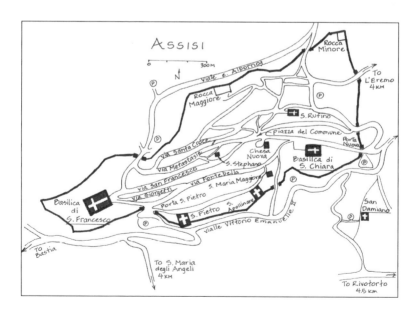

PLACES OF INTEREST NEAR ASSISI

BASILICA OF ST. MARY OF THE ANGELS
Basilica di Santa Maria degli Angeli

Shrine of the Porziuncola

The Porziuncola was built in the fourth century and is a small free-standing chapel in the center of the Basilica di Santa Maria degli Angeli. It was the first church given to St. Francis and his followers. They restored it in 1209, and it became the center of St. Francis's work in his lifetime. The first Franciscans lived in huts in the woods surrounding this chapel. A convent and the Basilica were eventually built around the Chapel of St. Mary of the Porziuncola in the sixteenth century. In 1832, a large portion of the Basilica was destroyed in an earthquake, and rebuilt.

Basilica di Santa Maria degli Angeli

The Porziuncola was said to be St. Francis's favorite place. The entire building, including the frescoes, has recently been restored to its original beauty. There are benches outside the Porziuncola for sitting. Many pilgrims flow through this blessed place, but you can stay inside as long as you want.

Behind the Porziuncola, on the right, in the place now marked by the Chapel of the Transitus, is where St. Francis died on October 3, 1226. In this area there are signs leading you to the rose bush without thorns (Roseto) that grew from the bramble bush St. Francis rolled in naked to fight temptation. There are signs here also directing the way to other small chapels of the Basilica.

The Pardon of Assisi: Jesus Christ and the Madonna surrounded by angels appeared to St. Francis in 1216 above the altar in the small church of the Porziuncola. The Lord asked St. Francis, "Ask whatever you desire, because it will be granted through the mediation of my Mother," and Francis responded, "Grant that all who come into this church having confessed and repented, may receive a bountiful and generous pardon, with the full remission of all faults." The Lord granted his request with the condition that Francis would consult his vicar on earth for this indulgence. He received permission from the Pope, and a few days later, announced to the population who had gathered around the Porziuncola, "My brothers, I want to send everyone to Heaven!" The Indulgence of the Porziuncola is celebrated on August 2nd.

The Porziuncola

There is an excellent bookstore before you enter the Basilica on the right. There is also a souvenir shop inside the Basilica after you take the tour to the Roseta bush and through the other chapels. The Porziuncola is in the town of Santa Maria degli Angeli about 3 miles (5 km) south of Assisi. It is close to the train station, which is accessible by frequent buses. Buses from Assisi also stop frequently at the Basilica.

Convento Porziuncola/P.za Porziuncola 1/06088 S. Maria degli Angeli/(PG) Italia Phone 075 8051430 - Fax 075 8051418 Email: info@porziuncola.org / basilica.porziuncola@libero.it Hours: 6:15AM–1PM; 2:30PM–8 www.porziuncola.org.

CASA GUALDI

On the road between Assisi and Santa Maria degli Angeli, at the crossroad Via Francesca, Casa Gualdi was built on the site of a thirteenth-century leprosarium. This area is thought to be the most likely place for St. Francis's conversion after meeting the leper, because lepers were not allowed to wander far from the leprosarium. St. Francis continued to serve the lepers, and his Order of the Friars

Minor was required to serve in the leper hospitals. When St. Francis was near death and carried from Assisi to the Porziuncola on a stretcher, he asked to stop at the Leper Hospital and face the city of Assisi to give it his final blessing. There is a plaque on the wall of Casa Gualdi to commemorate this event.

THE CARCERI HERMITAGE
L'Eremo delle Carceri

L'Eremo delle Carceri

L'Eremo is approximately 2.8 miles (4.5 km) east of Assisi on the road to Mount Subasio (Strada Subasio). There are many caves here that St. Francis and his followers retreated to for seclusion and prayer. It is the most peaceful St. Francis shrine in Assisi, with trails leading through the forest to the caves of St. Francis and his brothers. St. Bernardino of Siena built the current buildings you walk through in the fifteenth century around the ancient chapel that dates back to St. Francis's time. They have tours in Italian only. Ask in the information office. People do walk from town, but it is a major uphill hike. Even if you drive there, you must be prepared to hike up and down the paths to the caves. Wear comfortable shoes and warm clothing. There is no bus service so you must drive or take a taxi. Open the beginning of summer until Oct. 4th.

Eremo delle Carceri/06081 Assisi (PG) Italia Phone/Fax: 075 812301 E-mail: eremo.carceri@tiscali.it www.eremocarceri.it

CHURCH OF ST. MARY OF RIVOTORTO
Chiesa di Santa Maria di Rivotorto

Chiesa di Santa Maria di Rivotorto

Rivotorto is about 2 miles (3 km) east from the Porziuncola and 2.8 miles (4.5 km) southeast from Assisi. The church, built in the nineteenth century, has replicas of two stone huts that are believed to be built on the same spot where St. Francis started his mission with eleven brothers. St. Francis led his friars here after the Pope gave his approval for the Rule, and before they were given the Porziuncola. There is a bench on which to sit and meditate in front of the huts. There are very few visitors to this church since it is out of the way, and it is, therefore, very quiet. www.sanfrancescoassisi.org Italian Email: rivotorto@sanfrancescoassisi.org

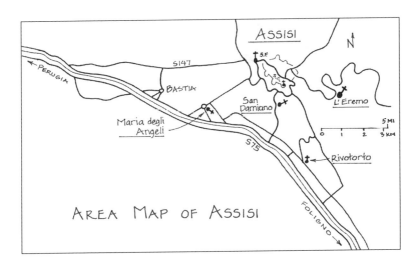

MORE ST. FRANCIS SHRINES IN UMBRIA

MONTELUCO (OUTSIDE OF SPOLETO)

Cave of St. Anthony, Monteluco

Monteluco is 34 miles (55 km) south from Assisi, and 5 miles (8 km) from Spoleto, just east of highway S3. St. Francis first arrived here with his brothers in 1218, seeking solitude in the caves (grottos). Other saints lived here, including St. Anthony of Padua. You have to explore this place on your own, as there is no one to show you where to go and very little signage. Inside the hermitage are cells to visit, which are replicas of the original cells. If you are adventuresome, you can follow the path to the caves. You might find a cave that St. Anthony stayed in, along with several other meditation caves. There are two hotels, camping areas and restaurants in this remote spot. A car is recommended, but Monteluco can also be reached by bus from Spoleto. Spoleto is on the Rome-Foligno-Ancona rail line.

Convento S. Francesco di Monteluco/06049 Spoleto Italia Phone/Fax: 074 340711 Email: fratimonteluco@assisiofm.org www.assisofm.org.

LAKE TRASIMENO
Lago Trasimeno

The island of Isola Maggiore is 11 miles (18 km) from Cortona and 12 miles (20 km) from Perugia. Legend has it that St. Francis spent the Lenten season here in 1211 with only two loaves of bread, fasting for 40 days. A chapel has been erected where he is said to have landed on the island and another chapel houses the stone he slept on. The boatman who picked Francis up reported that Francis calmed the stormy lake with the wave of his hand, and soon thereafter people made the island a pilgrimage destination. You can reach it by ferry, and it is a very pleasant day trip to walk around the island and enjoy a picnic lunch. By car, exit S75 and follow signs to Passignano sul Trasimeno, where the ferry is located with hourly service. By train, take the Ancona-Foligno-Terontola line and get off at Passignano sul Trasimeno. Servizio Turistico Territoriale del Trasimeno Phone: 075 9652484 Fax: 075 9652763 E-mail: info@iat.castiglione-del-lago.pg.it www.lagotrasimeno.net.

MORE ST. FRANCIS SHRINES IN ITALY

CORTONA

HERMITAGE OF THE CELLS
L'Eremo delle Celle

St. Francis heard about "Le Celle" as a secluded place for solitude, and he was eventually given the land. He first arrived in 1211 and his last visit was in 1226 when he was near death. You can visit his cell and the dormitory of his brothers. This is a fascinating place to visit, for it is still occupied by Franciscan Brothers and has the feel of an authentic cloister. Le Celle is located 2 miles (3 km) east of Cortona in the region of Tuscany, which is west of Assisi about 51 miles (82 km). Refer to the chapter on Tuscany/Cortona for more information. Email: eremo@lecelle.it www.lecelle.it Italian.

LA VERNA
Santuario della Verna

This is where St. Francis received the stigmata and is one of the most inspirational places in all of Italy. It is very quiet and peaceful, a perfect place for meditation and contemplation. The monastery is still run by monks and nuns of the Franciscan order, and the vibration of St. Francis is particularly tangible. La Verna is a small monastery in the mountains in the region of Tuscany about 72 miles (116 km) northwest of Assisi, and 37 miles (60 km) north of Arezzo. Refer to the chapter on Tuscany/La Verna for more information. www.santuariolaverna.org Italian.

RIETI VALLEY

St. Francis of Assisi traveled by foot and donkey throughout Italy spreading his doctrine of love. He visited the Rieti Valley on many occasions and founded several hermitages. It is called the Sacred Valley due to the presence of the Saint and for the deep vibrations of devotion he infused into the area. There are four hermitages in the valley that are associated with St. Francis: Fonte Colombo, Greccio, Poggio Bustone, and Convento Foresta Giaccomo. Refer to the chapter on Latium/Rieti Valley for more information.

ROME

ST. FRANCIS OF ASSISI BY THE RIVER
San Francesco d'Assisi a Ripa

When St. Francis of Assisi came to Rome, he stayed at 88 Piazza San Francesco d'Assisi. You can visit his cell and relics. Refer to the chapter on Latium/Rome for more information.

Cascia
Population 3,300

This small town that lies east of Spoleto in rural southeast Umbria began as a medieval village, growing up around an ancient castle in the Corno Valley. Little of the original settlement survived, having been destroyed by frequent earthquakes or remodeled into modern facilities. What remains are two quality medieval churches: San Francesco and San Antonio.

The modern Sanctuary of St. Rita, built between 1937 and 1947, is the primary attraction of the town, drawing thousands of pilgrims each year to this remote area to celebrate the life of the saint. The older parts of the town are charming in a typically rural Italian way. Roccaporena, the birthplace of St. Rita, is located 4 miles (6 km) west of Cascia, at the end of a narrow meandering road that winds its way through the ragged hills and sharp peaks of the area, culminating in the tiny picturesque village.

St. Rita of Cascia
Santa Rita da Cascia 1381–1447

"Sisters, I am not afraid to die. I know already what it is to die.
It is to close the eyes to the world and open them to God."

While some saints enter into a cloistered life at an early age and live in relative innocence of the world, others experience all the trials and tribulations of secular life before they are called to a life in God. Such is the story of St. Rita: daughter, mother, wife, widow, nun, saint. She experienced it all, transcended it all, and is therefore a wonderful channel of grace to those with similar challenges. St. Rita is known as the "Saint of the Impossible" for her many intercessions in seemingly impossible situations.

Rita did not become a nun until her late years, but throughout her life she sought God. As a child she spent many hours praying in her room in the tiny village of Roccaporena, and had a great desire to lead the devout life of a nun. But her parents were very old and feeble, and demanded that she stay home to care for them and to marry in order to fully support them. This she did out of duty, but she still craved God.

Rita's marriage was tumultuous as her husband was violent and frequently unemployed, which caused Rita and their two sons to live in constant fear and uncertainty. For years, Rita prayed daily for her husband's soul and a softening of his heart. After eighteen

St. Rita of Cascia

years, he finally opened himself to grace, and asked her forgiveness. But shortly thereafter, he was murdered by bandits, leaving Rita alone to care for her sons.

Her sons then angrily vowed revenge and plotted to kill the murderers. Rita was afraid that they would only reap damnation for their revengeful acts, and prayed for divine intervention. Her prayers were again answered and, within a year, both sons died, leaving Rita completely on her own. With her earthly responsibilities behind her, she could now live for God alone.

Rita traveled to nearby Cascia to seek admittance into the monastery of Saint Mary Magdalene. Each time she asked permission to enter, she was denied because she was a widow and a woman of the world. After a third request was denied, Rita prayed deeply for help, and experienced a vision of St. Augustine, St. Nicholas of Tolentino and John the Baptist. In vision, Rita saw them escort her into the monastery. In the morning, the nuns were amazed to find Rita inside the walls, and realizing her zeal for God was greater than they imagined, admitted her to the order. Rita was an example of righteous living, becoming an inspiration to her sisters. She fasted, practiced severe austerities, slept little and battled the devil, all of which strengthened her spiritually.

Rita experienced the Divine in many different ways. During Holy Communion, she often went into ecstasy, becoming completely immobile, engrossed in an internal state of rapture. Once, she was in this state for such a long time her sisters thought her dead, and were prepared to give her last rites before she finally returned to her body. Rita spent the long nights in meditation and prayer, often staying up till dawn, only to be inconvenienced by the morning sun. "Why do you come so quickly?" she would say. "Do you wish to deprive me with your small light of the delights my soul is enjoying? Let me pray, O sun! Let me meditate. My soul sees more when it contemplates under the shadows of the night, than my eyes do when aided by your splendor."

Another time, after hearing a sermon about the passion of Christ, she prayed to share in Christ's suffering. Her prayer was answered in the form of a thorn in her forehead. This was both a blessing and a curse, for she keenly felt the suffering of Christ, but the wound festered and putrefied, isolating her from the other nuns. Once a group of nuns were to travel to Rome on pilgrimage and Rita wished to go along, but she was told she could go only if her wound healed. The wound miraculously healed for the duration of the journey, but when she arrived back at the convent, it returned just as before.

Four years following her return from Rome, Rita suffered from increasing pain in her wound, and felt the approach of death. At this time, Rita asked a cousin who was visiting to bring her a rose from her old garden in Roccaporena. The cousin said she would try but that it would be impossible since it was winter. Rita replied; "My dear cousin, there is nothing impossible to God." The cousin went where she was directed and found a red rose in bloom, which she brought to Rita. On another occasion, Rita asked her cousin to pick two figs from a frozen fig tree in the same garden, and this time the cousin dutifully went and retrieved the figs. Rita saw these miracles as a sign that she would soon die. A few days before her passing, she had a vision of Jesus and Mary confirming that they would soon be united in eternity.

In 1446, Rita died at the age of seventy-six, accompanied by a sweet perfume filling her cell, a light emanating from her wound, and the bells of the town ringing of their own accord. Shortly after death, her body was transformed, becoming more youthful and her face more beautiful. Many miracles surrounded her death, and her body was seen to elevate, and move from side to side. At the time of her beat-ification, her eyes opened and they remained open for some time. Because Rita was a wife and a mother, many women relate to and find comfort in her life story. When a miracle happens by her interces-sion, her devotees say a sweet perfume fills Rita's shrine.

THE BASILICA OF SAINT RITA
Basilica di Santa Rita

The building of the Basilica began in 1937 and it was consecrated on May 19, 1947. On August 1, 1955, it was declared a Basilica. The design is of a modern eclectic style in the shape of a Greek cross, composed of a central dome and four main apses. The interior orna-mentation is very contemporary, including two-dimensional frescoes. The Monastery of St. Rita and information center is outside the Basilica, on the left, as you face it. They do not speak English, but the information center provides a "Guide to the Sanctuary of Saint Rita" in English. We recommend that you purchase this comprehensive guide before visiting the Basilica. It will provide you with all the details of the Basilica and Monastery of St. Rita.

Basilica di Santa Rita

When you walk into the Basilica, on your right is the main altar and on the left is the Chapel of St. Rita. Behind the grill in the Chapel of St. Rita is the incorrupt body of St. Rita, placed there in 1947. There are a couple of benches, but for the most part people come up to the grill and pray or stand around. This chapel is always busy, but we found at the end of the day there were fewer people. Sometimes you will see a nun on the left side of the grill place a gray walking stick with a metal tip through the grate for pilgrims to touch. This cane is filled with St. Rita's relics. Every fifty years, they change St. Rita's habit and cut it up for relics.

Enter the Lower Basilica (La Basilica Inferiore) by following the road to the right of the Basilica to the side door. The Lower Basilica is a good place for quiet meditation since there are many rooms and it is not as crowded as the Upper Basilica. As you enter, on the right are the Chapel of the Eucharistic Miracle and the remains of Blessed Simon Fidati resting inside a stone sarcophagus. The crypt of Blessed Mary Theresa Fasce is in the left transept along with a painting by Vincent Cesarini depicting St. Mary Magdalene in tears.

The Eucharistic Miracle contained in the stone crystal tabernacle originated in Siena. In 1330, a priest was called to take Holy Communion to a sick person. In an act of disrespect, he put the Host into his breviary. Upon his arrival he noticed the Host had liquefied and bled. The remorseful priest confessed to Simon Fidati, who eventually took one page of the breviary to Cascia. Pope Boniface IX confirmed the authenticity of the miracle in 1389. Looking at it against the light, the stains of blood are said to make a human outline.

Blessed Simon Fidati (1285-1348) was highly regarded as a preacher and spiritual counselor. He wrote many theological books and founded two monasteries. Born in Cascia, he entered the Order of St. Augustine in his early twenties. His writing focused on devotion to Christ's humanity: "It is absolutely necessary to make oneself similar, in soul and body, to Christ, just as He made himself similar to us, if we want to be crowned with Him." He died in Rome in 1348, was beatified in 1833, and his feast day is celebrated February 16th.

Blessed Mary Theresa Fasce (1881-1947) was born in Torriglia, near Genoa, in 1881, and died in Cascia on January 18, 1947. She was beatified on October 12, 1997. She dedicated her life to spread the devotion of St. Rita and was the moving force behind the construction of the Basilica, overcoming great obstacles in the process. The monthly bulletin, *From the Bees to the Rose,* was started by Blessed Mary Fasce in 1923 and is published today in five languages to spread the devotion of St. Rita around the world. In 1938, she founded the girls' orphanage, Saint Rita's Hive, which still receives the "Little Bees of Saint Rita," girls from the ages of 6-18 years.

Crypt of St. Rita

Blessed Mary Fasce was known for her tremendous courage and tranquility, especially facing her own ill health and pain. She demanded much from herself and others, but was also well respected and loved for her sweetness. She was elected abbess of the convent nine times. In her characteristic devotional style, she was noted for saying to her sisters while in between tasks, "While we wait, let's talk about God."

The original Church of Blessed Rita (1577) is located to the left of the

The well, Monastery of St. Rita

basilica, as you are facing it. Behind the bronze gate is the portal of the church where the remains of St. Rita were venerated from 1577 to 1947. The building was so severely damaged by the earthquake of 1703 that the body of St. Rita was kept in a wooden hut in the garden of the monastery for four years. In order to build the new sanctuary, the original building was demolished. The portal that you see and some altars are all that remain of the early church.

Just to the left of the Church of St. Rita is the ancient Monastery of St. Rita (1200) originally dedicated to Saint Mary Magdalene. The monastery was enlarged during the first half of 1700 due to the generous donation of King John V of Portugal, who recovered from cancer of the eye through the intercession of St. Rita. It has been further expanded in the last ten years. This monastery is where St. Rita lived for 40 years and currently houses about 40 cloistered Augustinian nuns. It can be visited only in groups and at scheduled times. You can find out about the schedule inside the information center to the left of the entrance, but you will have to speak in Italian.

When is the next tour in English?
Quando ci sarà la prossima visita guidata in inglese?

If you can't wait for the next tour in English, ask,

When is the next tour in Italian?
Quando ci sarà la prossima visita guidata in italiano?

Do you have a guidebook in English?
Avete una guida scritta in inglese?

Be sure not to miss the tour of the Monastery, even if it's in Italian. What you will see downstairs is the well that Rita used, the "Bees of the Wall," the 200-year-old grape vine, and the "Ancient Choir" where St. Rita took the habit and prayed. Upstairs you will find the Oratory of the Crucifix where it is thought that Rita received the stigmata consisting of one thorn in her forehead from Christ's crown of thorns.

There is also St. Rita's cell and a reliquary with the saint's wedding ring, made of two hands together, and her rosary. The baroque gilded urn held St. Rita's remains from 1745 to 1930, and the monastic habit and crown were at one time on the body of St. Rita. She spent all her time in the cell and died there on May 22, 1457 at age 76. Above the altar are some other relics: her habit, a veil, bandages used to clean the wound on her forehead, and a cushion.

The wooden sarcophagus in this cell dates from 1447, and Rita's body was kept in it until 1745. This coffin was made by Master Cecco Barbaro of Cascia, who recovered from a deformation of his hands after visiting the saint. The painting on the coffin is the oldest known of Rita. This is the end of the tour, and we suggest staying here until your guide tells you it is time to go. Since St. Rita lived here for forty years, it is a good place to feel her presence, if there is the opportunity.

SHRINE INFORMATION

Shrine: Sanctuary of St. Rita of Cascia (Santuario di Santa Rita da Cascia)

Address: The Right Reverend Mother Abbess/Suore Agostiniane Monastero di Santa Rita/06043 Cascia (PG)/Italia

Phone: 074 376221 (no English spoken) **Fax:** 074 376630

E-mail: mon.santarita@tiscali.it You can e-mail in English, and they will get it translated.

Website: www.santaritadacascia.com — Official website for the Sanctuary of St. Rita.

Quiet areas for meditation: The Lower Basilica is generally quieter as it is not as crowded. In the Upper Basilica the area in front of St. Rita's crypt (Chapel of St. Rita) although not quiet, is particularly devotional.

English spoken: The nuns in the monastery do not speak English, but in the Basilica they usually have a priest who speaks English for confession.

Hours: See the website or ask at your lodging.

Mass: There are many masses throughout the day. Check their website under "Schedules."

Feasts and festivities: May 21–22 — Festival of St. Rita; May 21st — The Fire of Faith (Incendio di Fede) is a torchlight procession on the feast of St. Rita and starts at 8:00 pm.

Accessibility: There is a ramp for the Upper and Lower Basilica, or an elevator through the sacristy. The Monastery is not accessible to wheelchairs, but there is a room available to view a video of the Monastery.

Tours: There are tours of the Monastery of St. Rita in English. Inquire at the information center to the left of the entrance of the monastery. They do not speak English, so refer to the Italian questions above.

Bookstore: There is a bookstore in front of the Basilica as you face it, on the right.

Recommended Book: *St. Rita of Cascia: Saint of the Impossible* by Fr. Joseph Sicardo, O.S.A. Tan Books. (Not available at shrine; buy before you go.)

Lodging: Hotel Delle Rose — House of the Pilgrim (Casa del Pellegrino), owned by the monastery, is directly across from the Basilica. It is the most convenient lodging for visiting the shrine of St. Rita. It is a large hotel with parking provided underneath the building. It is open from Palm Sunday until November 1st. (It is not recommended to stay during Holy Week because of an annual youth congress that is held in the hotel.) We recommend staying at least one night to visit all the sights related to St. Rita, including Roccaporena. Ask for a room with a view. The small town of Cascia is quiet and pleasant to wander around in.

Hotel Delle Rose/ViaFasce 2/06043 Cascia (PG)/Italia; Phone: 074 376241 Fax: 074 376240/ E-mail: info@hoteldellerose.com www.hoteldellerose.com

Parking (Parcheggio): If you are not staying at Hotel Delle Rose, there is a large parking lot on the left hand side at the switchback of the road several blocks before the Basilica.

Directions: Once you arrive in town follow the signs on the major road that leads up to the Basilica of St. Rita (Santuario di Santa Rita da Cascia.) It is a small town and easy to get around.

COMING AND GOING

CASCIA

Car: Cascia is a remote 31 miles (50 km) east of Spoleto. It can be reached from Terni and Spoleto on winding roads. Cascia is on S471 from the south and S320 from the north. It is 124 miles (200 km) from the Rome airport.

Train: Spoleto is the closest train station (31 miles (50 km) away) and is on the Rome-Foligno-Ancona line. Buses make connections to Cascia 6 times a day from this station.

Bus: Cascia is served by buses from Rome, Perugia, Terni and Spoleto. The local bus (Spoletina) makes trips to Roccaporena.

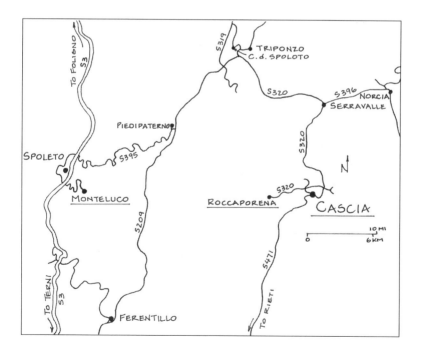

TOURIST INFORMATION

❋ Ufficio Informazioni Turistiche dell'A.P.T./Piazza Garibaldi 1/Cascia/Italia Phone: 074 371147 Email: info@iat.cascia.pg.it.

❋ Servizio Turistico Territoriale — IAT della Valnerina-Cascia/ViaG. Da Chiavano 2/06043 Cascia (PG)/Italia Phone: 074 371401 Fax: 074 376630.

OTHER PLACES OF INTEREST

ST. AUGUSTINE CHURCH
Sant'Agostino

Sant'Agostino is up the hill from the Basilica. You can walk, drive, or take a bus called the Spoletina. It is thought that St. Rita was christened in the St. John the Baptist's chapel and that she frequented this church.

ROCCAPORENA

Roccaporena, about four miles (6 km) west of Cascia, is where St. Rita was born and lived until entering the monastery in Cascia. It is a small town and, although there are many pilgrims, you can catch some quiet time in any of the churches or chapels. Below are the major points of interest pertaining to the life of St. Rita.

❋ Parish church of St. Montano (Chiesa Parrocchiale di San Montano) — This is where St. Rita got married and where her relatives are buried.

❋ Sanctuary of St. Rita (Santuario Santa Rita) — On the right there is a side chapel that contains the leather mantle of St. Rita ("Manto di Santa Rita" – Religuia veste al Pelle usate da Santa Rita) This chapel is relatively quiet for meditation.

❋ On the left of Casa dei Ricordi there is a sign saying "Nativa," which is the house where St. Rita was born (Casa Nativa di Santa Rita).

❋ There is a path labeled "Lazzareto" that leads to a statue of St. Rita.

❋ House of St. Rita (Casa di Santa Rita) — This is now a chapel, but was the house St. Rita lived in with her husband and children.

❋ As you walk through town there will be a sign, "Scoglio de Santa Rita della Preghiera," directing you to the Rock of St. Rita. It is a steep walk up the mountain with Stations of the Cross along the way. At the top is the Rock of St. Rita enclosed in a small building.

Città di Castello
Population 38,500

Sixteenth-century walls circumscribe and embrace this city of the Upper Tiber Valley, and give it a charming urban character. Located east of Arezzo and north of Perugia, the city is well known for its quaint commercial areas. Though originally a thriving pre-Roman town, its glory now is found in its well-preserved medieval and Renaissance buildings. The city is easy to walk around, sprinkled with small piazzas and enlivened with street markets alongside modern shops. The Monastery of St. Veronica Giuliani (Monastero Santa Veronica Giuliani) and the Church of San Domenico (Chiesa di San Domenico) are not major tourist sights in the city, but they house two of Italy's great mystical saints.

ST. VERONICA GIULIANI
Santa Veronica Giuliani 1660–1727

"Let everyone know that I have found Love.
This is the secret of my joy and my suffering, I have found Love!"

The story of our own lives, and how we are striving to know God, is often a story of the heart. For the heart must be open and receptive to grace, and learn how to triumph over the critical mind. The story of Veronica Giuliani is one of these, for she transformed her heart of steel into one of compassion and ecstatic love.

Orsola Giuliani was one of five girls born to the Mancini family of Mercatello, Italy. Even as a young child she was given a spiritual test, for she felt both compassion and spiritual pride; giving away her clothes and food to the poor, while still criticizing those who were not as devout and pious as she. Soon after, a vision revealed to her a heart of steel within her own chest, making clear that her primary task was to forge that heart of steel into one of sweetness. This process required many years of devotion and prayer, but she transformed herself, becoming a saint of grace and empathy.

At age seven, her mother died, leaving the family to fend for itself. Three of Veronica's sisters became nuns, and she would soon follow. Prior to entering the cloister, she experienced two visions of Christ, visions which opened her understanding to His suffering and passion, and more importantly, to His great love. Though her father

Crypt of St. Veronica Giuliani

wanted her to marry, and even brought her suitors, Veronica entered the convent of the Poor Clares in 1677 at the age of seventeen. In the following year, she took vows as a Capuchin Poor Clare in Città di Castello, and took the name Veronica. The Bishop of the city was taken by the depth of Veronica's spirituality and predicted that she would become a saint. This was another test for the young novice, for the Bishop's prediction resulted in resentment from Veronica's fellow sisters and superiors, and they made her first years in the convent very difficult.

Veronica also received tests in more tangible forms, being tested by Satan with temptations, visions and even physical abuse. She had many visions throughout her life, but the satanic visions of her early years were the most arduous, for she was still learning to discern true spiritual visions from ones fostered by evil. Veronica overcame these trials by developing a deeper yearning for Christ and by experiencing His divine love. In one vision, she was offered a chalice of Christ's suffering, and she chose to receive the taste of suffering in order to become closer to him. Finally, her longing became so intense that she directly experienced the suffering of Christ on the cross. In the following year, the imprint of the crown of thorns appeared on her head, causing her great physical pain but also deep inner joy. Ultimately, her identification with Christ became so complete that, on Good Friday in 1697, the five stigmatic wounds of Christ appeared on her body.

Veronica received the wounds with reverence and humility, but the new Bishop viewed them with skepticism and doubt. He ordered examination of the wounds, and many medical procedures were conducted to verify the authenticity of her afflictions. Veronica was under constant surveillance, always in the company of a fellow nun, assuring that no actions were taken to deceive the examiners. She accepted her role with great patience, for she was told in vision, "you are to become an ardent flame of love which will speak to your fellow man."

Veronica was ordered by her superiors to write a spiritual diary to record her many insights and visions, which she commenced on December 13, 1693. She made entries faithfully until completing it on March 25, 1727. The diary portrays a deep inner life of visions and communion with Christ. It is one of the most insightful treatises ever written, but unfortunately, it has never been translated into English in its entirety. Veronica often wrote while in ecstasy, stating: "For the most part I write estranged from myself, and I don't know what I'm saying." In her later years, Veronica attributed many of her entries as direct dictation from the Virgin Mary. As her visions became ever deeper and her experiences of divine love more profound, she wrote: "My love of God is so intense that already on earth I live a heavenly experience, becoming kind and gentle through Divine love."

Veronica was eventually allowed to return to a normal conventional life, but her stigmata and visions continued throughout her final 30 years. Although a deep mystic, she was also very practical. Veronica was the novice mistress for 34 years and the abbess for her last eleven years. She was also responsible for bringing a clear source of water to the convent and enlarging the facilities of the monastery.

Suffering of the physical body accompanied Veronica's stigmatic wounds, yet she felt that compassion and love were the essence of her life. She had succeeded in transforming her hardened heart into one of infinite love and joy. At the age of 66, she suffered a stroke and died 33 days later, on July 9, 1727. She was canonized on May 26, 1839.

MONASTERY OF ST. VERONICA GIULIANI
Monastero Santa Veronica Giuliani

The church and monastery are nondescript and are easy to miss while walking along "ViaXI Settembre." The tiny church contains the urn with St. Veronica's bones, encased in wax, on the main altar. A death mask was made of the saint, so the wax figure is an accurate representation of Veronica. There is a small urn with the remains of Beata Florida Cevoli on the left side of the church.

Beata Florida Cevoli (1685–1767) was born Lucretia Helen in Pisa to a family of nobility on November 11, 1685. On June 3, 1703, at the age of 18, she entered the Capuchin Poor Clare monastery in Città di Castello and took the name Florida. Sister Florida held many jobs and offices, including that of vicar after St. Veronica was elected abbess. She assisted St. Veronica for eleven years, becoming her closest confidant. When St. Veronica died, Sister Florida became abbess at age 42. She had "one hundred eyes and as many hands" when dealing with her sisters and the poor who asked for help. She was very generous in helping those in need, especially with prayers and intercessions. Beata Florida was greatly admired for her wisdom and generosity of spirit within the convent and in the community at large.

This is a quiet church with some local people coming and going, so you can take all the time you need to meditate and pray. On the right side of the church is the monastery entrance. You can enter the monastery's vestibule from the street or from inside the church. From inside the vestibule, ring the bell, and after some time a sister will come and talk to you from behind the wooden wheel. They do not speak English, so you will say in Italian,

Can I see the relics of St. Veronica?
Posso vedere le reliquie di Santa Veronica?

The sister will open the door to the left of the wheel. When you enter, there is a display of postcards, pictures and pamphlets about the saint. You can review their selections before or after visiting the museum. Ask if they have any books in English. They have a small booklet in English (the only English translation of her life that we have found) on the life of St. Veronica, *Saint Veronica Giuliani, the Nun of Fire.*

Do you have any books in English?
Avete libri in inglese?

You will be led through the courtyard to a small museum where the saint's relics are displayed in glass cases. Everything is in Italian, but make sure you see the reliquary with the saint's incorrupt heart with an imprint of the cross. You will probably be left alone with the relics, so you can stay as long as you like. On one visit a sweet nun talked to us in Italian the whole time we were there, but another time we were left alone.

Remember that you are in a cloistered monastery, so be respectful of the nuns' privacy. After you have seen the museum, you may leave on your own. As you walk back to the entrance, look through the courtyard on your left, to the second floor, and you will see a sign that says, "Cella di Santa Veronica Guiliani." No one is allowed to visit her cell,

Monastero Santa Veronica Giuliani

but this is where she received the crown of thorns from Christ and later His other wounds. There is a postcard with a picture of her cell in their bookstore. You pay by donation for the postcards and pamphlets. If no one is around when you leave, just leave the money on the table.

SHRINE INFORMATION

Shrine: Monastery of St. Veronica Giuliani (Monastero Santa Veronica Giuliani)

Address: Via XI Settembre 21-A/06012 Città di Castello (PG)/Italia

Phone: 075 8550956 Italian only **Fax:** None

E-mail: None

Website: None

Quiet areas for meditation: The church is very small with locals coming in and out, and very suitable for meditation. When you are in the museum there is no place to sit, so the church is the best place.

English spoken: Rarely

Hours: 8:30AM–12:00; 3:00PM–6:30.

Mass: 7AM

Feasts and festivities: July 9 and June 30

Accessibility: There is one step outside and two inside.

Information office: None

Tours: None

Bookstore: Once you are let into the cloister, there are postcards and a booklet called *Saint Veronica Giuliani, the Nun of Fire* that you can pay for by donation.

Recommended booklet: *Saint Veronica Giuliani, the Nun of Fire* published by the Monastery of the Capuchinesses, Città di Castello. Available in their bookstore.

Lodging: None

Directions: To find the Monastero Santa Veronica Giuliani, start in Piazza Matteotti, at the center of town. Take ViaM. Angeloni, which becomes ViaXI Settembre. The Monastery is on the right, #21. It is easy to miss. Look for a simple cross on the side of a terra-cotta-colored building.

BLESSED MARGARET OF METOLA
Beata Margherita de la Metola 1287–1320

There is a spiritual axiom that states "All circumstances are neutral; it's our reaction that makes them good or bad." Margaret of Metola became saintly because she perfected this tenet, by accepting her difficult circumstances as God's will and by reacting to all situations in a positive manner. If we ever find ourselves indulging in self-pity, meditating on the life of Margaret can inspire us to see God's hand in all things, and teach us to accept our trials and tests as gifts from God.

Crypt of Blessed Margaret of Metola

Margaret was born into wealth and nobility in rural Metola in 1287, being the first child born to the local nobleman Parisio and his wife Emilia. Their great anticipation turned to great disappointment when the newborn was a girl instead of the longed-for first son, and then even greater agony when her body was discovered to be deformed and her eyes void of sight. Margaret's very existence was an embarrassment to her aristocratic parents, so she lived hidden away in the back rooms of the castle, never allowed to be seen in public.

Despite her parents' neglect, Margaret's early childhood was happy, for she was joyful at heart, playing and living in a delightful world of her own making. One day, at the age of six, when wandering too far from her allotted rooms, she encountered a local noblewoman and, in playful conversation, Margaret almost revealed her heritage. Her father was furious about the incident and decided it was too "dangerous" to have Margaret in a situation where her true identity could be easily discovered. As a solution to his problem, he had a small cell built a short distance from the castle and placed Margaret inside, permanently walling her into the tiny prison.

Two small windows were her saving grace. One window faced the adjacent church, and here she would receive the sacrament from Padre Capellano. The other small aperture was used to pass Margaret her daily meals. Her truest window was her inner window to God, for although she couldn't understand the actions of her parents, she opened her inner sight to the omnipresence of God and found solace in that joyful experience.

Margaret lived in abandonment for a total of twelve years until the age of eighteen, with her only personal contact being with Padre Capellano. The only break in the monotony of her existence came when she was sixteen, when war broke out in the surrounding region and she was moved to another cell in the local town of Mercatello. Her situation was different, but worse, for she could no longer converse with her Padre or receive the Blessed Sacrament. After two years of war, peace returned to the area, but Margaret was forced to remain in her isolated cell.

When Margaret was eighteen, rumors of miraculous healings were reported from the nearby city of Città di Castello, and reached the ears of her family. The shrine of the deceased Fra Fiacomo of Castello was the site of these healings, and Margaret's parents decided to take her there secretly for one last chance at transforming Margaret into a "normal and acceptable" daughter. They took her to the shrine early in the morning, leaving her there, and instructing her to pray for healing of her small, feeble, hunchbacked body and for vision in her sightless eyes. Margaret prayed deeply, as she did every day, but she only prayed that God's will be done. If God wanted her healed, she would accept it, but if he wanted her to remain in her present physical condition, she would accept that, too.

She passed the entire day at the shrine and enjoyed being in a new environment, especially one as holy as this. When her parents returned later in the day they saw their daughter was not miraculously changed and decided to abandon her completely, leaving her to care for herself. Margaret was not aware of her parents' decision and waited all day for their return. Finally, at day's end, the shrine was closed and Margaret was ushered outside, forced to spend the night on the city streets.

As morning broke, two beggars, Roberto and Elena, discovered Margaret on the steps of the church. Margaret explained her situation to her new companions, and they were moved to help her. Elena taught Margaret to beg and introduced her to the streets and people of Città di Castello. Margaret's bright countenance and cheerful attitude impressed all those she met, and she was watched over by various poor families of the community. They would take her into their meager homes for a short period, then pass her on to another family when it became financially difficult. After some time, people began to notice that families that cared for Margaret received special blessings from her presence. Margaret's reputation as a deeply devout soul began to spread throughout the city.

Margaret eventually entered a local convent and took vows as a nun. After her acceptance as a novice, she was once again rejected, for Margaret believed in a strict interpretation of the order's rule while her fellow sisters preferred to practice a looser version. The devout nature of Margaret was an embarrassment to the less committed sisters, so she was expelled from the convent. Once again, various families took her in, but this time they were wealthy families who had by now heard of her virtue and were eager to help the cheerful Margaret.

She soon became a member of the lay order of the Penance of St. Dominic, serving the people of Città di Castello with love and devotion. As the first unmarried Dominican mantellate, Margaret followed the strict rule of St. Dominic, rigorously praying and fasting. After midnight prayers, she would not sleep but would remain in prayer and meditation long into the night. She also practiced severe austerities, and when friends approached her to stop, she said "If by undergoing suffering I can help save just (one) soul, I would gladly endure the utmost agony from now to the day I die!"

Miracles began to happen around Margaret, for she predicted future events, cured a fellow tertiary of blindness, and put out a raging fire with her cloak. She was also well known for her compassion, especially for those in prison, as she could relate directly to their suffering and isolation. When hearing of the deplorable conditions in the jails, she visited the cells to comfort the prisoners. Upon witnessing their suffering, Margaret would think of Christ's suffering and levitate, rising high in the air above the dank prison floor. Her frequent visits and levitations became quite a phenomenon among the townspeople, so much so that they began to come to the cells just to see her levitate, despite their revulsion at the prison conditions. In this way, Margaret was able to help the prisoners and raise the consciousness of others about the conditions in the prison.

When Margaret was thirty-three, she had a premonition of her approaching death and requested the last rites. She died on April 13, 1320. In keeping with the rule of the Dominicans, a rule of simplicity and poverty, Margaret was to be buried without a coffin in the cloister cemetery. The citizens of Città di Castello objected and had other ideas. When the friars attempted to take the body outside of the church to be buried, the huge crowd demanded she be buried in the church because she was a saint. A standoff ensued between clergy and congregation, until a couple with their crippled, mute child made their way through the crowd. They devotedly knelt in front of the corpse of Margaret and began to pray for a miracle. The crowd and the friars all began to pray with them, pleading for Margaret's intercession, when suddenly Margaret's arm reached out and touched the child, instantly curing her. This miracle changed the Prior's mind, and Margaret was laid to rest in a coffin inside the church. Pilgrims came from all over Italy to venerate Margaret. Over two hundred miracles were documented following her death and many blessings are still felt today when visiting her shrine. In 1558, her body was exhumed and found to be incorrupt after more than two hundred years, and is still incorrupt today. Because of the plague and wars, the procedures for Margaret's formal recognition as a saint were not begun for nearly 300 years. Finally, in 1609, she was beatified.

MONUMENTAL CHURCH OF SAN DOMENICO
Chiesa Monumentale di San Domenico

Chiesa Monumentale di San Domenico

The Church of San Domenico is large and uninhabited except for the urn of Blessed Margaret of Metola on the altar. It was built in the fourteenth century and "has a single aisle and a cross-shaped choir, revealing a structure that is both severe and solemn." Since our last visit, we have heard that because of numerous thefts the church is open only limited hours (see hours below). When we were there you could kneel in front of the urn and view Blessed Margaret's incorrupt body, which is in perfect condition, considering she died in 1320. There is a brochure in Italian and English to the side of the altar. We could take all the time we needed here to pray and meditate with few interruptions. So take a chance, and hopefully the church will be open, and you will have an opportunity to spend quiet time with Blessed Margaret.

SHRINE INFORMATION

Shrine: Church of San Domenico (Chiesa di San Domenico)

Address: Via Luca Signorelli 8/06012 Città di Castello (PG)/Italia

Phone: 075 8554389 **Fax:** None

E-mail: None

Website: None

Quiet areas for meditation: The church is large with very few visitors, so as long as they are open, you can stay as long as you want.

At first, the church appears dark and somber, but after you sit and close your eyes, you can focus on the inner light of Blessed Margaret's unique life.

English spoken: Rarely

Hours: There have been numerous thefts since we were there, so they don't keep it open much anymore. The church is closed in winter. At other times it is open from 10am–12 and sometimes from 3:30–5:30pm. It is possible to phone a parish priest and arrange a visit, but they only speak Italian.

Mass: Sundays 8:30AM, 11; Winter 8:30AM

Feasts and festivities: April 13

Accessibility: There is a side entrance from Via Luca Signorelli in front of Piazza San Giovanni in Campo.

Information office: None

Tours: None

Bookstore: None

Recommended book: *The Life of Blessed Margaret of Castello* by Father William R. Bonniwell, O.P.

Lodging: None

Directions: To find Chiesa di San Domenico, start in Piazza Matteotti in the center of town. Take corso Vittorio Emanuele to Via Signorelli and turn right. The church is several blocks down on your left.

Coming and Going

Città di Castello

Car: Città di Castello is north of Perugia on E45 about 46 miles (74 km). There are multiple exits from the north and south. Park outside the city walls and walk into town.

Train: Sansepolcro-Terni Line to Arezzo, then by bus to Città di Castello.

Bus: Accessible by bus with connections to major cities.

TOURIST INFORMATION

❋ Servizio Turistico Territoriale — IAT dell'Alta Valle del Tevere/Piazza Matteotti/06012 Città di Castello (PG)/Italia; Phone: 075 8554922 Fax: 075 8552100 E-mail: info@iat.citta-di-castello.pg.it – Italian www.english.umbria2000.it

❋ Servizio Turistico Territoriale (IAT) Perugia/Piazza Matteotti, 18/06100 Perugia/Italia; Phone: 075 5736458 Fax: 075 5720988 E-mail: info@iat.perugia.it www.english.umbria2000.it

WEBSITES

Città di Castello www.cittadicastello.com — Italian.

Comune di Città di Castello www.cdcnet.net/en — Tourist info.

Umbria Regional Tourism Board www.english.umbria2000.it — Tourist info.

Foligno
Population 53,000

One of the region's larger urban areas, Foligno rests in the plane of the Umbrian Valley nestled between Mt. Subasio, Mt. Aguzzo, and the Topino River. The city is easily accessible, located just east of Assisi on major highways and rail lines. Known for its handicraft industries, Foligno is primarily an industrial hub with modern buildings and business areas. The heart of the city resides within the walled town center, containing the central Piazza della Repubblica with its Romanesque duomo, and other medieval structures. A few blocks away is the Church of St. Francis, which houses the sanctuary of Blessed Angela, the city's saintly mystic.

BLESSED ANGELA OF FOLIGNO
Beata Angela da Foligno 1248-1309

"Lord tell me what thou dost want of me; I am all Thine."

Saints are not usually born into this world as such, but evolve by overcoming all obstacles along their path to God. Even after reaching higher levels of spiritual consciousness, they are often given more severe tests to purify their souls of any remaining shortcomings. We, too, may know this roller coaster ride of the spiritual life. But we can gain solace by studying the life of Blessed Angela of Foligno, for she transcended both the heights and depths of spiritual trials.

Angela's journey began on a seemingly high note, for she was born to a prosperous family of Foligno and grew up enjoying the pleasures and passions of a worldly woman. By her own account, she was sinful and vain, completely indulging in the pleasures afforded by her station in life. Her mother encouraged this worldly life, and Angela eventually married a wealthy nobleman. Together they produced a family with several sons and lived contentedly in a castle nearby.

Unexpectedly, at the age of thirty-seven, Angela's world was shattered by a vision of light which showed her the futility of her earthly ways and the joy of love she could experience in the presence of the divine. This was her first taste of ecstatic vision, and her first look into her future life. Though her inner world went through a metamorphosis, for a time Angela's outer world of family and position remained the focus of her life. But not long after this first vision, Angela's circumstances changed dramatically, for her mother died, then her husband, and finally her sons. Angela felt great sorrow at the loss of her family, but she was gradually able to transform this feeling of loss into the joy of giving all to God. She then realized the blessing of being free to follow her soul call.

Six years after her dramatic vision, Angela went on pilgrimage to Assisi to visit the Basilica of St. Francis, home of her spiritual mentor. She had joined the Third Order of St. Francis as a tertiary, and wished to pray to the saint at his crypt. Upon entering the shrine, Angela had an ecstatic mystical experience, falling to the floor and shouting incomprehensibly. The attending priest was embarrassed by the display and expelled her from the Basilica, forbidding her to return.

The following year, this same priest, Brother Arnold, went to Foligno to interview Angela, for he had heard of her continuing ecstatic episodes and suspected that evil spirits were at work. Instead of finding a case of possession, he was so taken with her sincerity and spiritual depth, that he became her scribe and confessor. For many years he recorded the divine experiences and visions of Angela in

Crypt of Blessed Angela

what is called her *Book*. Due to his dedication, we are fortunate to have a thorough record of her inner conversations with God, and a detailed insight into the development of a devout soul.

In these writings, Angela described her evolution as a series of steps, which took her from a life of sinful preoccupation with the world to one of unification with God. These eighteen steps included the painful understanding of the emptiness of a life without God, the comfort of living in God's mercy, the joy of complete self-knowledge, and finally, the deep love experienced in comprehending the passion of Christ.

As her inner life evolved, so did her outer life change. After joining the order of St. Francis, she embraced Lady Poverty and eventually shed all her earthly possessions. Her toughest test was to relinquish her beloved castle. Brother Arnold tells us that Angela gave up her possessions against the advice of the friars and her family, following a vision of St. Francis in which he instructed her to follow him in absolute poverty.

Angela's example of righteous living attracted a pious family of lay men and women, so she created a fellowship called the "Cenacolo" (Last Supper) to foster a more spiritual life. The Cenacolo continued throughout her life but faded after her death. In 1989, the Cenacolo became active again, encouraging a life in God for the citizens of Foligno.

After reaching a high state of awareness, Angela was once again tested. From the heights of ecstatic communion with God, she fell into a chasm of doubt, surrounded by darkness and despair. She felt nothing of the presence of her beloved God, feeling only loss and emptiness. Her visions turned to wild temptations, and she was keenly aware of her worldly past corrupting her inner peace. For two full years she lived in this tormented state, praying for redemption, but receiving only silence. At long last, she beheld another vision of God, and the power of His love broke through the veils of darkness, lifting her out of the abyss of despair. She at last fully understood the teachings of St. Francis and saw love as the binding force that "makes all things one."

In 1308, at age sixty, Angela knew she was near death. In vision, God presented her with a robe of light that clothed her soul, and said to her, "Come to me, my beloved, my beautiful one, my dearest, whom I love so much. Come, for all the saints are waiting for you with great joy." Shortly thereafter, she gathered her spiritual children together and blessed them, exhorting them to be charitable toward everyone. For many days before her death she was consumed with pain, but on the day she died, January 4, 1309, she was in a "joy-filled state" of great peace and happiness, and passed on to a life enveloped in God. One of her disciples commented simply that Angela was a "great teacher in the discipline that leads to God."

Blessed Angela demonstrates that no matter what our past, we can always change direction and seek God. No matter what our tests, we can pass them by clinging to the knowledge that we are always supported by the love of God. We can choose at any time to turn toward living our life for God and, in that divine pursuit, find lasting contentment.

THE CHURCH OF ST. FRANCIS
Chiesa di San Francesco

Chiesa di San Francesco

Inside the walls of Foligno, the Church of St. Francis is on Piazza San Francesco and houses the remains of Blessed Angela of Foligno and Blessed Angelina da Marsciano. The church was built in honor of St. Francis in 1309 over the previous Church of San Matteo. It was modified in the nineteenth century in the neo-classical style. The apse of the interior of the church remained Gothic and displays the urn of Blessed Angela of Foligno located on the left, halfway into the church. Angela's body was interred here on the day of her death. In 1961, her skeleton was covered in wax.

Blessed Angelina da Marsciano (1357-1435) is interred in an urn on an altar opposite Blessed Angela's. Born into wealth, married at fifteen, widowed at seventeen, Angelina embraced the life of a Franciscan tertiary. She and her small group were so successful at preaching celibacy to young girls that she was charged with sorcery.

Summoned before the King of Naples, she explained herself, declaring that she was ready to be punished if she was in error. The charges were dismissed, but she was eventually exiled. After reaching Assisi, she established the first enclosed monastery for tertiaries.

SHRINE INFORMATION

Shrine: The Church of St. Francis (Chiesa di San Francesco)

Address: Convento San Francesco, Piazza San Francesco 9/06034 Foligno (PG)/Italia

Phone: 074 2351402 **Fax:** 074 2344080

E-mail: direttore@beataangeladafoligno.it

Website: www.beataangeladafoligno.it — Official website: La Beata Angela da Foligno.

Quiet areas for meditation: When we visited, the church was under repair following an earthquake, so we did not see the inside of the building. However, a friendly priest took us to a side room where Blessed Angela was temporarily placed. We assume that the church is suitable for quiet contemplation.

English spoken: Rarely

Hours: 7AM–12:30PM; 4PM-7.

Mass: Weekdays: 8AM, 9, 6PM; Sun/Hol: 8AM, 10, 11:30, 6PM.

Feasts and festivities: February 28 — Feast day; January 3 & 4 — Transit and liturgical feast; Every Friday, 4:30PM-6:30 — Contemplative adoration of the Holy Sacrament; Last Sunday of September — Pilgrimage on foot from Foligno to Assisi.

Accessibility: There is access in front of the church on Piazza San Francesco.

Information Office: None

Tours: None

Bookstore: In the convent, Cenacolo Beata Angela Da Foligno, there is a small booklet in English.

Where is the bookstore? Dov'è il negozio con i libri?

Do you have any books in English? Avete libri in inglese?

Recommended book: The only book we could find in English is *Angela of Foligno: Complete Works*, Transl. Paul Lachance, O.F.M. Paulist Press. It is a big hardbound book (not available in the church bookstore), so we suggest reading it before you go.

Lodging: For groups only, in the convent. Phone: 074 2354459 / 074 2349854 Fax: 074 2340545.

Directions: Walk into the center of the city and find Piazza della Repubblica. Follow corso Cavour in the direction of Porta Romana. Turn right on Via Rutili ending up at Piazza San Francesco.

COMING AND GOING

FOLIGNO

Car: Foligno is at the intersection of S75 and S3. Leave the highway at any exit with signs to Foligno "Centro." Follow signs to "Centro" and park outside the walls of the city.

Train: Foligno is accessible from all major cities. From Stazione F.S. it is a short walk to Piazza della Repubblica in the center of the walled city.

Bus: Accessible by bus with connections from all major cities.

TOURIST INFORMATION

❋ I.A.T. Ufficio Informazioni Turistica /Corso Cavour 126/06034 Foligno (PG)/Italia Phone: 074 2354459 Fax: 074 2340545 Email: info@iat.foligno.pg.it.

❋ Comune di Foligno Ufficio Stampa Palazzo Comunale/Piazza della Repubblica 10/06034 Foligno (PG)/Italia Phone: 074 2330269 info@commune.foligno.pg.it www.comune.foligno.pg.it – Italian

Montefalco

Population 5,700

This prototypical medieval hill town is called "the balcony of Umbria," for it rests atop one of the highest hills in the Umbrian valley, providing wonderful panoramic views. The distant cities of Perugia to the northwest, Assisi to the north, and Spoleto to the south can all be viewed from various vantage points around the diminutive municipality. The rolling hills surrounding Montefalco are adorned with ancient olive groves and abundant vineyards, making the short drive from Assisi or Foligno a pleasant ride. In the middle of the walled settlement is a circular piazza, the Piazza di Commune, which is fronted by historical buildings, both civic and religious. The medieval Church of St. Francis now contains the city's art collection, including splendid fifteenth-century frescoes.

ST. CLARE OF THE CROSS
Santa Chiara della Croce 1268–1308

"The life of the soul is the love of God."

While some saints grow into their lives of piety over time, others seem to be born into the role. Clare was one of the latter, for the devout young girl was only six when she entered the cloistered hermitage outside the small town of Montefalco. The hermitage was built by her father Damiano Vengente and established by her twenty-year-old sister Giovanna. Clare was the first candidate accepted into the cloister, and she filled her new home with her youthful energy, intelligence and devotion to spiritual practices. The hermitage of Damiano still stands today, now known as the Church of Santa Illuminata.

The small band of devotees soon attracted others to the sacred life and began to outgrow their humble abode. Damiano Vengente once again took on the task of building a new home for his daughters, but this time closer to the city. The new project was ill fated from the beginning, for Damiano died halfway through construction, and there was much local resistance to the new cloister. The townspeople of Montefalco and other existing monasteries were opposed to the convent, for they felt another religious group reliant upon the charity of the town was too great a financial burden for the small population. As a result, the women were persecuted for several years, exiled from the community, and forced to forage in the countryside for their meager sustenance. The half-built hermitage also lacked many comforts, being open to the various torments of the seasons. Clare offered to do her part for the survival of the group and willingly ventured into the countryside to beg for food. She was often met with denigration and disrespect, but she bore the tirades with humility and love. Her fellow sisters felt it was too dangerous for a young girl of fifteen to venture alone into the hostile countryside, so they ordered her to remain in the cloister. She thus remained cloistered from the age of fifteen until her death at the age of forty.

After several years, the hostilities receded, and the sisters were able to complete the hermitage of Santa Caterina. Up to this point, the women were not a formal part of the church, for they were self-evolved and not under the direct auspices of any order. In 1290, they chose to accept the rule of St. Augustine and became an official monastery, with Giovanna elected as their abbess. Eighteen months later Giovanna died, leaving Clare alone to grieve for her beloved sister. "I weep neither for her soul nor her body, but only for myself. Giovanna was to me an example and a mirror of life and every day she spoke to me of God and of always new and profound spiritual matters." Though only twenty-three, Clare was elected as the new abbess. She humbly attempted to refuse the responsibility, but her sisters insisted upon her appointment.

St. Clare of the Cross

Clare had no formal education, but she was blessed with infused spiritual knowledge of theology and the scriptures. She was well known for her insights and intuition, and attracted many theologians, religious and lay people from all over Umbria. She would graciously serve as counselor and guide to anyone who asked. Clare spoke freely to both men and women, but only through the cloth-covered grill of the interview room, because she was very aware of the sensual magnetism of the secular life. She was very serious about her spiritual practices and spent eight to ten hours a day in prayer, and would sometimes fall on her knees a thousand times in the night reciting the Lord's Prayer. Clare always gave willingly to the poor and sick, even though she had very little herself. Even to those who were against her, she would offer help when they were ill or in need in any way.

In 1294, Clare fell into a deep interior crisis, feeling the loss of God's presence in her inner life. She prayed fervently for resolution. Finally, on the Epiphany, she went to confession and became absorbed in a profound ecstasy. She remained absorbed in God's presence for over two weeks, living only by His grace, and the small amounts of sugar water administered to her by the other nuns. While entranced, Clare beheld a vision of herself in judgment before God, and witnessed heaven and hell, seeing how she must live in order to be fully in God. When she recovered, she resolved never to think, say or do anything contrary to that understanding. In another vision, she beheld Christ searching for a place to set his cross, but finding no place strong enough. Later on, she envisioned Christ placing the cross in her own heart, saying "I have found a place for my cross." From this time on, Clare continually experienced the interior presence of Christ and felt the cross impressed upon her heart. After her death, her heart was removed, and an actual imprint of the cross was seen upon it. This is how she became known as St. Clare of the Cross.

At age forty, Clare became increasingly weak and was confined to a bed consisting of boards and a blanket. There was great concern for her well being, but she refused all care, sending the doctors away. Though ill and weak, Clare still experienced frequent ecstasies. At times her great inner joy caused her to break into song: "We are all happy and sing Te Deum Laudamus that my Jesus reveals himself to me." One evening, in August of 1308, Clare called all her sisters to her and gave them her final spiritual testament. She received the last rites, and appeared ready to die. But the next morning, she unexpectedly sat upright in the Chapel of the Holy Cross looking healthy and well. Clare called for her brother, Francis, and held a lengthy discussion with him. Finally she said to her sisters, "Now I have nothing more to say to you. You are with God because I am going to Him." She then turned her eyes upward toward heaven and quietly left her body. It was Saturday morning, August 17th.

St. Clare of Montefalco demonstrates to us that a person can be holy from a very young age, and if nurtured on the spiritual path, can become a beacon of light for all those who are seeking God.

CHURCH OF ST. CLARE
Chiesa di Santa Chiara

The Church of St. Clare was initially built by the saint in 1303, but the nun's choir and cloister are all that remain of the original structure. A larger church was started in 1615 and completed around 1643. The present church is from the eighteenth century. The incorrupt remains of St. Clare of the Cross rest inside a side altar, to the right of the main altar. If the small doors on the altar are not open to the saint's urn, ring the bell to the convent on the right of the main altar and ask to see the remains of St. Clare. They will open the doors to the crypt and the lights will go on, enabling you to see the saint. The nuns will also open the windows on either side of the crypt to view other relics: the saint's heart imprinted with the passion of Christ and her three gallstones representing the trinity. Also ask to see the Chapel of the Holy Cross, decorated with frescoes from 1333, which is to the left of the main altar. They will buzz you into the chapel. This is where

Chiesa di Santa Chiara

St. Clare experienced visions of Jesus and the Virgin Mary, and where the saint died in 1308.

Can I see the saint's relics?
Posso vedere le reliquie della santa?

Can I see the Chapel of the Holy Cross?
Posso visitare la cappella della Sacra Croce?

SHRINE INFORMATION

Shrine: Monastery of St. Clare of the Cross (Monastero Santa Chiara della Croce)

Address: Via Giuseppe Verdi, 23/06036 Montefalco (PG)/Italia

Phone: 074 2379123 **Fax:** 074 2379848

E-mail: scdcroce@tin.it — Italian

Website: www.chiesainrete.it/chiaradamontefalco — Official website: Monastery of St. Clare of the Cross, Italian.

Quiet areas for meditation: The church is very quiet, with few visitors. The Chapel of the Holy Cross, to the left of the main altar, is accessible by ringing the bell to the convent and asking in Italian to see the chapel. They will buzz you in. You can stay and meditate only for a short while, because they keep a close watch on you from their cloister. Picture taking is not allowed in the Chapel of the Holy Cross.

English spoken: Rarely

Hours: 9AM–11:30; 3:30PM–6

Mass: Weekdays 7:45AM; Sun 6:30PM

Feasts and festivities: August 17

Accessibility: There are a few steps into the church.

Tours: None

Bookstore: As you enter the church, to the right is a bookstore down some stairs. The lights might be off, but just ring the bell for assistance. There is a small booklet, *St. Clare of the Cross of Montefalco Augustinian*, and a brochure in English on the life of St. Clare of the Cross.

Lodging: None. See Tourist information.

Directions: The Church and Monastery of St. Clare of the Cross are just outside the city walls of Montefalco at the corner of Via Cavour and Via Giuseppe Verdi. It is a short walk from the town center. Beginning in the center of town at Piazza del Comune, to the right of the Town Hall, take Corso Goffredo Mameli to Porta San Agostino. Go through the wall, take a short right, then a left on Borgo Garibaldi. The city wall will be to your left. After several blocks you will see Santa Chiara Church on your right.

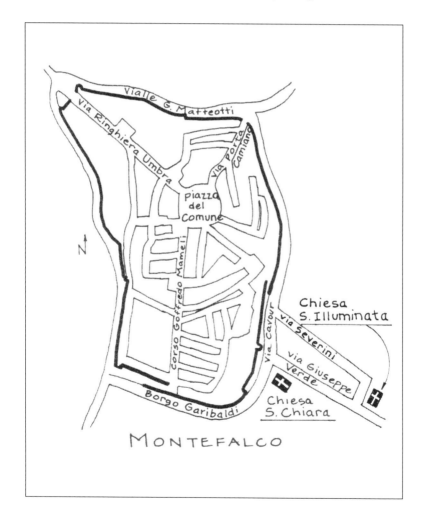

COMING AND GOING

MONTEFALCO

Car: Take SS316 from Foligno 5 miles (8 km) to Bevagna. Follow signs to Montefalco about 4.5 miles (7 km).

Train: Closest train station is Foligno with frequent buses connecting to Montefalco.

Bus: Accessible by bus with frequent connections to and from Foligno with transfers to major cities.

TOURIST INFORMATION

❋ Comune di Montefalco/Piazza del Comune/ 06036 Montefalco (PG)/Italia Phone: 074 2378673 Fax: 074 2379506 www.comune.montefalco.pg.it/www.english.montefalcodoc.it Email: info@comunemontefalco.it

❋ Museo Civico di San Francesco/Via Ringhiera, 6/06036 Montefalco (PG)/Italia. Phone: 074 2379598 www.sistemamuseo.it

❋ Ufficio Informazioni Turistiche dell'A.P.T./Palazzo Comunale /Montefalco/Italia. Phone: 074 2354459 / 074 2349854

WEBSITES

Monastery of St. Clare of the Cross
www.www.chiesainrete.it/chiaradamontefalco — Official website, Italian.

B&B antico Frantoio Brizi www.frantoiobrizi.it — Lodging across from the Monastery of St. Clarre of the Cross. Ask for a special price for visiting the shrine. They speak English. Phone: 074 2379165 Email: frantoiobrizi@libero.it

Umbria www.english.umbria2000.it — Tourist information.

Veneto

The northeast region of Veneto is diverse in its area and population. The region ranges from the Adriatic Sea and the unique city of Venice, through the wide Venetian plains to end in the Dolomite Mountains and the Carnic Alps of the Austrian border. A scenic drive from the sea to the stunning alpine mountains shows off the rich beauty of the region and the variety of landscapes. There is no one center of population as the three major cities are Venice, Padua and Vicenza, each with populations of several hundred thousand. While visiting this area it is easy to be enamored by the beauty of Venice and the grandeur of the Alps, but don't forget to experience the quiet power of St. Mark and the saints of Padua.

PADUA
St. Anthony of Padua
St. Leopold Mandić

VENICE
St. Mark the Evangelist

Padua
Padova
Population 225,000

Padua is an ancient Roman city dating back to 89 B.C. Always subject to the power of Venice, the city has grown up as a distant suburb of the city of canals. In renaissance Italy, Padua was known for its university, and Galileo taught there. The town is now industrial based, and is off the beaten path of most tourists, so it actually gives one a good feel for the metropolitan Italian lifestyle. The city is not too large, and is very easy to navigate using public transportation. St. Anthony is simply known here as "il Santo" (the Saint) and a visit to his Basilica is highly recommended. It is an easy thirty-minute train ride from Venice.

ST. ANTHONY OF PADUA
San Antonio di Padova 1195-1231

*"May He steer our boat away from worldly things
toward the heights of contemplation."*

St. Anthony of Padua is venerated worldwide as the "Wonder Worker," a saint whose presence is invoked for healing and resolving difficult situations. But the real St. Anthony was a very quiet yet purposeful man, whose love for prayer and contemplation helped to elevate him to the level of sainthood.

St. Anthony of Padua

St. Anthony was born in Lisbon in 1195, the first son of a noble Portuguese family. He was baptized Ferdinand and spent his youth studying with the clergy at the cathedral of Lisbon. By age fifteen, he was ready to enter the religious life. Against his parents' wishes, he joined the Augustinian order at the nearby abbey of St. Vincent.

The close proximity of his parents and family proved to be a problem for Ferdinand, as they visited him often, distracting him from his studies and prayer. He tolerated the situation for two years, then after asking to be transferred, was relocated to the quiet monastery at Coimbra, the capital of Portugal at that time. Here Ferdinand dove deep into his studies and received one of the best educations offered a cleric. His teachers noted his gift of intelligence and excellent memory as he became completely absorbed in his study of the Bible. After eight years of intense study, he was ordained at the age of twenty-five.

The scholarly life became boring for Ferdinand, and he longed to give his life to God in a more active manner. Shortly after his ordination, a group of Franciscan friars were martyred in Morocco and their relics brought to a nearby Franciscan monastery for veneration. Ferdinand was inspired by the devoted life of the monks and soon joined their order with visions of following in the martyrs' footsteps.

Now known as Brother Anthony, he departed his native land for the African continent, ready to preach the Gospel to the Moors. Arriving in Morocco, Anthony immediately became very ill, suffering from the high fever of malaria. He remained ill for several months and finally accepted the fact that he must return home to recover his health. God seemed to have other things in store for this ambitious monk!

Bound for home in 1221, Anthony's ship was blown off course in a storm, and he landed in distant Sicily. Coincidentally, he learned from the local friars that the general chapter meeting of the Franciscans was soon to occur in Assisi. Anthony made his way to the central Italian city and joined the throng of monks gathering to renew their spiritual lives. Among them was St. Francis himself. Anthony was subsequently assigned to a remote hermitage near Foli, north of Assisi, where he performed mundane duties but experienced ever-deepening prayer.

The quiet life of the hermitage aided Anthony's healing from malaria, and he was again full of energy. One day he attended an ordination for Franciscans and Dominicans and was asked to speak when no one came prepared to give the sermon. The quiet Anthony reluctantly obeyed delivering a powerful speech that greatly impressed his peers with his eloquence and knowledge.

Anthony was soon assigned to preach in northern Italy and France. He traveled from town to town teaching the Gospel and quickly built a large following of converts. He filled the churches to overflowing and often had to preach in the town squares in order to accommodate the multitudes. The friar became known for his stirring oratories and opened the hearts of believers and non-believers alike. Anthony was especially known for his ability to verbally spar with non-believers and convince them rationally of the merits of a God-filled life. He succeeded in converting many souls in this rational way, but he also attracted many with his caring heart and love for the poor.

Anthony came to St. Francis's attention and was asked by him in a letter to "teach sacred theology to the brothers, as long as, in the words of the Rule, you do not extinguish the Spirit of prayer and devotion with study of this kind." He was the first to fill this post in the Franciscan order. Anthony produced many theological documents and was one of the primary writers in early Franciscan history. Some of his writings discussing the various forms of prayer ring with the truth of his personal experience. He wrote about contemplative prayer (what we would refer to as meditation): "Contemplative prayer does not use words or thoughts, but involves an awareness of the presence of God, apprehended not by thought but by love." During this period, Anthony also developed a close inward connection with Francis and found him to be a great source of inspiration. This connection became evident when, during one of Anthony's sermons, a brother monk saw St. Francis appear and bless Anthony.

He continued to teach in the French cities of Montpellier and Toulouse, and in the Italian cities of Bologna and Padua. At the death of St. Francis, Anthony was recalled to Italy and asked to take on a supervisory commission, but he chose to concentrate on preaching and working directly with the people. Thus Anthony was assigned to the city of Padua, where the faithful welcomed him with open hearts and celebration.

Anthony was a tireless worker for God and gave his all to the people of Padua. One of the brothers said of him, "Preaching, teaching, hearing confessions, it happened often that the sun had already set, and he had not yet eaten." A constant flow of people sought out Anthony for confession, even though he was known for his rather strict advice. Having never completely recovered from his bout with malaria, Anthony's exhaustive lifestyle eventually wore him down. After five intense years in Padua, his health began to diminish.

To regain his strength and take more time for contemplation, Anthony secluded at a hermitage in Camposampiero, outside of Padua, that was donated by his disciple, Count Tiso. While walking through the wooded retreat, Anthony noticed a large walnut tree and decided to have a cell built high up in the branches. Here he would spend his days in contemplation, and return to the hermitage in the evening. One night the Count approached Anthony's room, attracted by a bright light, and witnessed Anthony in ecstasy embracing the infant Jesus.

Shortly thereafter, Anthony realized his time of death was drawing near, and wanted to return to Padua. He was only able to reach the outskirts of town, an area in Padua now called Arcella, before he became too weak to continue. After being given the last rites, he gazed longingly upward and invoked Mother Mary. When his brothers asked what he saw, he replied; "I see my Lord." Anthony died peacefully on June 13, 1231. After much debate, his body was taken to Padua where the town mourned the passing of their saint. He was canonized within a year of his death, on May 30, 1232, and declared a Doctor of the Church in 1946.

St. Anthony was indeed a highly intelligent man, but his heart quality is what makes him revered throughout the world, even by devotees of other religions. The essence of St. Anthony is very tangible when visiting his relics in Padua, for his love permeates the shrine. Regardless of location, to meditate on St. Anthony is to feel the sweetness of divine love.

THE BASILICA OF ST. ANTHONY
Basilica del Santo

The Basilica of St. Anthony, commonly called Basilica del Santo, was built in many stages starting in 1232 and continuing in the fourteenth, sixteenth and eighteenth centuries. The façade is an eclectic mixture of Lombard, Tuscan and Byzantine styles, and the Basilica is crowned by eight domes and two bell towers that are uniquely eastern. In 1263, St. Anthony's body was transferred to this new church, accompanied by St. Bonaventure. When they opened the sarcophagus, St. Anthony's tongue was found to be incorrupt. Today, St. Anthony's skeletal remains rest in the Chapel of St. Anthony to the left of the main altar. The power of St. Anthony's love is very present around his

Basilica del Santo

altar, and there are always many pilgrims praying here. Although very active, the atmosphere is one of devotion and love. The Chapel of the "Madonna Mora" is all that remains of the small Church of Santa Maria where Anthony's body was buried from 1231-1236. The Chapel of the Reliquaries behind the main altar contains his tongue, vocal cords and lower jaw, along with other relics. The Chapel of Blessed Luke contains the tomb of Blessed Luke Belludi of Padua, a disciple and companion of St. Anthony. The Chapel of St. James contains the relics of the martyr St. Felix under the altar. You can pick up a short guide in English to the Basilica at the information office.

SHRINE INFORMATION

Shrine: Basilica of St. Anthony (Basilica del Santo) – Office for Anthonian Pilgrimages (Opera Pellegrinaggi Antoniani)

Address: Piazza del Santo 11/35123 Padova/Italia

Phone: 049 8789722 information office **Fax:** 049 8789735

E-mail: contattaci@santantonio.org / infobasilica@santantonio.org

Website: www.saintanthonyofpadua.net Go to "Visit the Basilica."

Quiet areas for meditation: The large size of the Basilica seems to absorb much of the sound of the multitude of visitors, so you can find many places to sit throughout the Basilica. There are two cloisters that can also be used for meditation and prayer.

English spoken: At the information office of the Basilica, on the westside of Magnolia Courtyard. Open in Winter: 8AM - 6:30PM Summer: 8AM - 7PM.

Hours: Summer 6:20AM–7:45PM; winter 6:20AM–7PM. Sat/Sun close at 7:45PM after the last mass.

Mass: Sun/Hol: 6:30AM, 7:15, 8, 9, 10, 11, 12:15, 4PM, 5, 6, 7; Weekdays: 6:30AM, 7, 7:30, 8:15, 9, 10, 11, Winter 4PM, Summer 5PM,6; Prayer at the tomb 5:45PM; English-speaking priests are available for confession; Groups accompanied by a priest can celebrate Mass in their own language call to arrange.

Accessibility: Wheelchair accessible at main entrance.

Feasts and festivities: June 13 — Feast day.

Tours: Book an English tour a couple of weeks in advance at the information office.

Bookstore: Souvenir shop is on the south side of Magnolia Courtyard.

Recommended book: *Life of St. Anthony – Assidua* written by an unknown Franciscan friar a year after St. Anthony's death.

Lodging: Hotel Casa del Pellegrino on Via Cesarotti, next to the Basilica. Privately owned, but recommended on the Basilica's website; Phone: 049 8239711 Fax: 049 8239780 www.casadelpellegrino.it.

Directions: The Basilica of St. Anthony is located on Piazza d. Santo with detailed directions on the website.

OTHER PLACES OF INTEREST

CAMPOSAMPIERO

ANTHONIAN SHRINES
Santuari Antoniani

St. Anthony spent his final days in Camposampiero just twelve miles (20 km) north of Padua. For peace and quiet, he had built a small cell in a walnut tree which is now called the Shrine of the Walnut Tree (Il Santuario del Noce). Another church is the Shrine of the Vision (Santuario della Visione), where St. Anthony was observed holding the baby Jesus. The Anthonian Shrines are open every day from 6:45am-12pm and 3:30pm-7. Casa de Spiritualita, Santuari Antoniani/Via S. Antonio, 2/35012 Camposampiero PD Italia. Phone: 049 9315711/049 9303003 Fax: 049 9316631 Email: spirituale@tin.it Italian. www.saintanthonyofpadua.net/portale/camposampiero.asp

ARCELLA

SANCTUARY DELL'ARCELLA
Santuario dell'Arcella

Arcella is located within the city of Padua and contains the Cell of Transit (La Cella del Transito) where St. Anthony died inside the Church of Arcella. Blessed Elena Enselmini, a nun living at the time of St. Anthony, is also buried here. Open daily 7:30am-12pm, 3:30pm-7. Santuario dell'Arcella/Via Bressan 1/35137 Padova PD 35137 Italia. Phone 049 605517. www.saintanthonyofpadua.net/portale/camposampiero.asp

ST. LEOPOLDO MANDIĆ
San Leopoldo Mandić 1866-1942

St. Leopoldo Mandić was a small frail figure, but big in spirit. Standing only four and a half feet tall, he spiritually towered over less devoted souls. Born in Herzegovina, Montenegro on May 12, 1866, he was the youngest of twelve children. His mother was a "woman of

St. Leopoldo Mandić

outstanding piety," and later he stated that he owed what he was to her. Named Bogdan at birth, which means "given to God," he was a fragile child and given to contracting maladies. While one would think the children would call him names, they sensed his sincerity and would say, "Bogdan is a saint!"

By age eight, Bogdan realized that he wanted to become a friar and confessor, so by age sixteen he was ready to enter the Capuchin seminary at Udine, Two years later he took vows in Bassano del Grappa, Vicenza and assumed the name

Brother Leopoldo. Shortly thereafter, on June 18, 1887, Leopoldo heard a voice from God telling him to bring the "separated brothers of the East" back to the church. He was attracted to the ecumenical movement of the time, and desired to be a missionary to his native land and promote unity between the churches. Because of his delicate health, Leopoldo knew he was destined for the confessional. He spent the next nineteen years at various friaries and was sent to Padua in 1909, where he remained until his death in 1942. Leopoldo's notoriety came from his work in the confessional, where he served for 34 years, often counseling people for more than 12 hours a day.

The people of Padua were drawn to Leopoldo by his pure saintliness. His advice from the confessional was often very simple—"Faith. Have faith,"—but people were transformed and received great blessings merely by being in his presence. He was always advising his penitents to pray, saying "God's promises are bound up with our prayers," and he was found praying at all hours when others were asleep.

The greatest joy for Leopoldo was to feel the presence of God, and he vowed to live in that presence at all times. He said, "We work with our bodies here on earth, but our soul should always be in the presence of God." When his mind would stray from God, he would excuse himself and ask the Lord's forgiveness. Leopoldo was extremely humble and rarely spoke of his experiences or premonitions. Still, many heard his true predictions, witnessed his miraculous healings, listened to him intuitively read their souls or saw his blissful face after the consecration of the Mass.

Leopoldo's living shrine was his confessional, for this was where he channeled his passionate love for God. His cubicle was adorned with an image of Mary, and he would place fresh flowers in a vase before her statue every day. He predicted that his cell and confessional would be spared during the bombing of World War II saying, "The church and friary will be hit by the bombs, but not this little cell. Here God exercised so much mercy for people, it must remain as a monument to God's goodness."

After serving as a priest for fifty-two years, Leopoldo was overcome by cancer of the esophagus and collapsed in the sacristy while preparing for the liturgy. Taken to his tiny cell, he was given the last rites and passed quickly on July 30, 1942. Leopoldo was beatified in 1976 and canonized in October 1983.

SANCTUARY OF LEOPOLDO MANDIĆ
Santuario di San Leopoldo Mandić

This Capuchin church is on the site of the sanctuary where Leopoldo served for the last thirty-one years of his life. Most of the church and monastery were bombed out during the Second World War and reconstructed shortly thereafter.

Santuario di San Leopoldo Mandić

Leopoldo's cell and confessional remained intact, just as he predicted. The simple church remains a shrine to Leopoldo and is adjacent to confessional. To visit the cell of the saint, look for the sign on the left of the sanctuary, and proceed down the corridor. You will find a gift shop and the reconstructed cell and confessional of St. Leopoldo. The saint is buried in a chapel near the church that is always open.

SHRINE INFORMATION

Shrine: The Sanctuary of St. Leopoldo Mandić (Santuario di San Leopoldo Mandić)

Address: Piazzale S. Croce 44/35123 Padova/Italia

Phone: 049 8802727 **Fax:** 049 8802465

E-mail: info@leopoldomandic.it Italian.

Website: www.leopoldomandic.it - Italian, working on English version.

Quiet areas for meditation: None

English spoken: Rarely

Sanctuary hours: 6:30AM–12; 1:30PM–7

Church hours: 6:30AM–12; 3PM–7

Mass: Weekdays: 7AM, 8:30, 10, 6PM; Sun/Hol 6:30AM, 7:45, 9, 10:15, 11:30, 4PM, 6.

Feasts and festivities: May 12.

Accessibility: There is a ramp on the side of the church at the left of the entrance. The saint's cell and confessional are not accessible to wheelchairs because the doors are too narrow.

Tours: None

Bookstore: To the left of the sanctuary towards the saint's cell.

Recommended books: *Leopoldo Mandić Saint of the Reconciliation*, by P.E. Bernardi, a large book with complete biography, and *Father Leopoldo: Saint of the Reconciliation*, by Leo Lazzarotto, a picture book. *A Poor Man and his Hope: the Ecumenicalism of St. Leopold Mandić* by Lorenzo da Fara, a small book. The books are available at the shrine.

Lodging: None

Directions: The Sanctuary is less than three quarters of a mile (1 km) from St. Anthony's Basilica. By bus: From the railway station take the number 8 bus that passes St. Anthony's Basilica. Four or five stops after St. Anthony's, the bus stops near the Sanctuary, which is on Piazza S. Croce. Ask your fellow bus riders for assistance, they will be very helpful.

COMING AND GOING

PADUA

Car: Padua is on Autostrade A4 between Vicenza and Venice, at the intersection with A13 from Bologna and Florence. From the south, take SS516/SS309 Coast Road Via Chioggia from Ravenna. Padua is 25 miles (40 km) west of Venice. The Basilica is in the walled city, on the southern side. Follow the yellow signs for Basilica del Santo.

Train: Trains to Venice arrive and depart every thirty minutes and the ride is about thirty minutes long. The train station, Piazza Stazione, is outside the city's walls and has local bus and tram stops outside. Buy your local tickets in the station. For the Basilica of St. Anthony, ask your fellow riders to tell you when to get off at the "Basilica del Santo" or "Santo." It's about a ten-minute ride. After you exit, the Basilica is a block further down, then a block to your left.

Phone: 1478 88088 toll free in Italy. To Santuario di San Leopoldo Mandić take the electric tram to Capolinea sud (S.ta Croce Station) www.tramdipadova.it click on "Visitare la città in tram" Italian.

Bus: The main bus station is five minutes from the train station, near Piazza Boschetti at ViaTrieste 42. Phone: 049 8206844. From the train station, bus #8 takes you to the Basilica of St. Anthony. Four or five stops after St. Anthony's, the same bus stops near the Santuario di San Leopoldo Mandić that is on Piazza S. Croce.

TOURIST OFFICE

✿ Azienda Promozione Turistica di Padova N.8/Padua Tourist Board/Riviera dei Mugnai 8/35137 Padova/Italia Phone: 049 8750655 Fax: 049 650794 E-mail: apt@padovanet.it www.apt.padova.it

❊ IAT/Uffici di Informazione ed Assistenza Turistica/Information Offices 1/Stazione FS/Railway Station Phone: 049 8752077 Fax: 049 8755008.

WEBSITES

Accessible Italy www.tour-web.com/accessibleitaly/venetia.htm — Accessible info for the traveler with disabilities in Padua.

APT Padua Tourist Board www.apt.padova.it — Padua tourist info.

Venice

Venezia

Population 68,200

Venice is a premier tourist town, holding the unique distinction of being the only town strictly for pedestrians. Of course, boats and gondolas take the place of the usual buses, taxis and cars. The city is always alive with throngs of tourists and is very active. But behind the glamour is a subtle spiritual side of which not many people take advantage. Venice is home to the relics of St. Mark the Evangelist, housed in the famous San Marco Basilica. The Basilica and San Marco square are the center and main focal point of the city and very easy to find from anywhere in the city. The sights of the city are fantastic, but don't forget to slow down and experience the presence of the city's patron saint, St. Mark.

ST. MARK THE EVANGELIST

San Marco 74 A.D.

To uncover the life of St. Mark the Evangelist is to take on the role of a detective, for there is very little solid evidence about his birth, life or death. There are several versions of his life story, and even some discrepancy about his name – was he Mark and also known as John Mark? For all the controversy, the only real thing of importance is that he was the author of one of the four Gospels of the New Testament, and that he is enshrined at St. Mark's Basilica in Venice. As for his biography, what follows is only one version!

Mark was of Jewish decent, probably a Levite, and did not become a disciple until after Christ's resurrection. He is mostly

Mosaic of St. Mark

known for his association with the apostle Peter, and traveled some with him, spreading the new teachings of Christianity. Around 49 A.D., the two apostles were together in Rome, and this is where Mark wrote the Gospel, at the request of the Roman faithful and as approved by Peter. It is most likely that the Gospel according to St. Mark is a written version of the story of Christ as told by Peter. For Mark was Peter's interpreter, and his Gospel contains details of some stories of Christ that were known only to Peter. For example, it is only in Mark's Gospel that the details of Peter's denial of Christ are told.

After writing the Gospel, Mark was sent by Peter to support the Christian communities in Egypt and he was appointed Bishop of Alexandria. Alexandria was a large ancient city, populated by many pagans and governed by superstition. Mark was very active in his missionary work, denouncing the beliefs of the local people and teaching the gospel of Jesus. He was successful in converting many to Christianity but he also made many enemies among the pagans. Eventually, they rose against Mark and sought him out in order to kill him. He escaped their wrath for a time, but was finally caught, bound by ropes and dragged behind horses through the streets of Alexandria. After dying a martyr's death, Mark's remains were gathered by the Christians and buried in nearby Bucoles. This became a place of sanctity and prayer for the community, and a marble monument was built at the site.

Mark's body remained in Alexandria until 828, when Venetians sacked his shrine and stole the body. Mark's body was delivered to the Doge of Venice and placed in his private chapel, where it was secretly kept until a proper church was constructed. Mark has been the celebrated patron of Venice for the past fourteen centuries, and his symbol, the winged lion, is visible throughout the city. Though not much is known about the man, his legacy as saint and evangelist lives on.

ST. MARK'S BASILICA
Basilica di San Marco

Legend has it that St. Mark was in Venice, when he was visited by an angel who indicated that Venice was to be his final resting place. Two Venetian merchants took the legend seriously and stole St. Mark's body from his tomb in Alexandria, Egypt around 828 A.D. On their return to Venice, the thieves encountered a storm that threatened to sink the ship. St. Mark appeared to the captain and told him to strike the sails in order to avoid the rocks hidden below. After their safe arrival in Venice, the relics were given to the Doge, and St. Mark was declared their new patron saint.

Initially St. Mark's remains were buried in the chapel of the Doge's Palace. The original church was begun upon the arrival of the remains of St. Mark. This church was destroyed in 976 by fire and St. Mark's body was lost for a time. The three people who knew the hidden location of the body died with their secret unrevealed. When the church was being rebuilt and consecrated in 1094, a portion of a pilaster crumbled to reveal St. Mark's arm. His relics were then placed in another secret crypt until discovered again in 1811, when they were placed under the high altar. The Basilica was the Doge's private chapel until 1807 when it became the cathedral of Venice. The Basilica was originally built in the traditional Greek cross form modeled after the Church of the Holy Apostles in Constantinople (536-46). Through the centuries it has been through many alterations, combining the Byzantine, Romanesque and Renaissance styles, and has been decorated with treasures plundered primarily from Constantinople.

The high altar of St. Mark's contains the skeletal remains of St. Mark. There is a fee to enter on the right of the altar to see the famous gold and jeweled altar screen, Pala d'Oro (1000-1300 A.D.), behind the tomb. St. Mark's remains are under the altar. Quite

High Altar with the Crypt of St. Mark

astonishingly, no one pays attention to his crypt. We felt somewhat awkward praying in front of the tomb, while people were filing by to see the golden screen and wondering what we were doing. There is not even a sign indicating that the altar is the resting place for St. Mark. But, we both felt a special blessing and recommend braving the questioning stares. There is a side chapel, Chapel of the Blessed Virgin Nikopeia, to the left of the altar where you can spend time with St. Mark from a distance.

Before you reach the entrance to the high altar on the right, you'll see the Treasury (Tesoro), which contains treasures from a raid on Constantinople in 1204, including a thorn from Christ's crown of thorns. Don't miss the Loggia dei Cavalli upstairs (enter inside front entrance) which displays gilded bronze horses originally made in the time of Alexander the Great, fourth century B.C., and a closer view of the incredible 4000 square meters of mosaics on the ceiling and walls dating back to the thirteenth century. Step outside on the balcony with replicas of the bronze horses for a nice view of San Marco Square. See below for times when the ceiling mosaics are lit up, and English-speaking tours that are given two times a week.

There is no opportunity for quiet contemplation with the ever-present stream of tourists. St. Mark's is really more like a museum than a sanctuary, but we feel it is well worth the visit for the beauty of the art and the presence of St. Mark. Appropriate dress is required: no shorts, bare shoulders or bare midriff.

Where is the schedule for English-speaking tours?
Dov'è l'orario per le visite guidate in inglese?

SHRINE INFORMATION

Shrine: Basilica of St. Mark (Basilica di San Marco)

Address: San Marco 328/30124 Venezia/Italia

Phone: 041 5225205 **Fax:** 041 5208289

E-mail: biblioteca.proc@patriarcatovenezia.it

Website: www.basilicasanmarco.it

Quiet areas for meditation: None, but you can pray on the left of the high altar in the Chapel of the Blessed Virgin Nikopeia.

English spoken: Occasionally

Hours: The areas requiring entrance fees are open Sun/Hol 2PM–4:45; Mon–Sat 9:45AM–4:45PM; mosaics lit up Mon–Fri 11:30AM–12:30PM and during Mass on the weekend.

Mass: Weekdays: 7AM, 8, 9, 10, 11, 12, 6:45pm; Sun/Hol: 7AM, 8, 9, 10:30, 12:00, 6:45PM.

Feasts and festivities: April 25 — Feast day; January 31 — translation of St. Mark's relics to Venice.

Accessibility: There is a guide published by "Venezia Accessible," available for people with special needs at the tourist offices. You can also ask to borrow a key for the wheelchair lifts around San Marco square. We were told there is an entrance on the left of San Marco Basilica. There always seem to be stairs some place, and the floor in San Marco Basilica is very warped from the yearly flooding. Venice is particularly difficult for people in wheelchairs because of the pedestrian bridges that have steep stairs, but some now have lifts. The website for the City of Venice has "Itineraries without Barriers" (see "Websites" below). The Venice train station has assistance for people with disabilities: Phone: 041 785570.

Tours: Free tours daily at 11AM except Sundays & holidays from April to October. Meet in the atrium (front hall) on the right side. You can book a tour two days ahead online www.basilicasanmarco.it, click on "Plan your visit" and "Reservations." Groups need to make reservations for 10AM -12PM/Mon-Fri Phone: 041 2413817.

Bookstore: On the left as you enter the Basilica.

Lodging: None

Directions: Transportation is by boat in the form of taxis (higher prices) or public boats called vaporetto, motoscafo and motonave run by the ACTV (least expensive). Then, of course, the famous gondola rides (highest prices) are available everywhere. Vaporettos run to San Marco Square every 10-12 minutes. See the website for more detailed directions under "Plan your visit" and "How to reach the Basilica."

COMING AND GOING

VENICE

Car: Of course you cannot drive in Venice, but you can certainly drive to it on Autostrada A4, approaching from west or east. Follow the sign towards the city, and when you arrive at Piazzale Roma, leave your car in one of the parking lots or go to Tronchetto Island. From Tronchetto you can reach Venice by Vaporetto # 3 (only in the morning) and # 4 (only in the afternoon). Otherwise you can take a ferry boat (line # 17) from Tronchetto to the Lido. An alternative is to leave your car in Mestre. There are both open and covered parking areas directly in front of the train station, and they cost a fraction of what it costs to leave your car in Venice. You can then reach Venice by train (departure every 5-10 minutes) or by numerous buses.

Parking Garages:

Venezia Tronchetto Parking Phone: 041 5207555 Fax: 041 5285750 Email: info@veniceparking.it www.veniceparking.it.

Terminal Fusina Venezia Phone: 041 5470160 Fax: 041 5479133 Email: fusina@terminalfusina.it www.TerminalFusina.it.

Garage San Marco Phone: 041 5232213 Fax: 041 5289969 Email: info@garagesanmarco.it Italian www.garagesanmarco.it.

Terminal Punta Sabbioni Phone: 041 5301096 Fax: 041 5300455 Email: acipuntasabbioni@libero.it www.acivenezia.it click on "Parcheggi e navigazione."

Train: S. Lucia (Stazione Ferroviaria S. Lucia) is the name of Venice's train station. If you get off in Mestre, Venice station, you haven't reached Venice yet! From the train station, take the various forms of water transportation to your destination in the city, or walk. Information about train timetables: Phone: 041 2381560 (24 hours a day).

Bus: Buses arrive at Venice from all major cities, but the only way to get around Venice is by gondola, water taxi or public boats run by ACTV. ACTV Information Service: 041 5287886.

Plane: Marco Polo Airport, located about 13 km from Venice, is connected to the city by bus # 5 (departures at intervals of every half hour), by airport shuttle (faster but more expensive, leaving every hour), and by water taxi www.veniceairport.it.

TOURIST INFORMATION

✳ APT — Azienda di Promozione Turistica/Castello, 5050/Venezia/ 30122 Italia Phone: 041 15298711 Fax: 041 5230399 E-mail: info@turismovenezia.it www.turismovenezia.it

✳ IAT — Ufficio Informazioni e di Accoglienza Turistica. There are many of these tourist offices around town: Piazza San Marco, Marco Polo Airport, Santa Lucia train station and Piazzale Roma bus station. Use the contact information above.

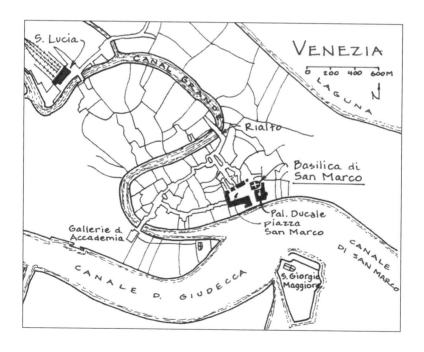

WEBSITES

Accessible Italy www.tour-web.com/accessibleitaly/infovene.htm — Accessible info for the traveler with disabilities in Venice.

ACTV www.actv.it — Public transportation timetables.

Alata www.alata.it — Alata is a consortium of Communes and Provinces of the Northern Adriatic area. Helpful information for parking, booking and purchasing the Venice Card. Phone: 041 5459611 Fax: 041 5459601 E-mail: alata@alata.it.

Association of Venetian Guide Lecturers www.guidevenezia.it — Licensed Venice guides: Phone: 041 5209038 Fax: 041 5210762 Email: guide@guidevenezia.it.

City of Venice www.comune.venezia.it — Accessible Venice maps and itineraries: Click on "I am a disabled person," then "Informahandicap", then "Accessible Venice." Phone: Mestre 041 2746144 Venezia 041 2748144 Fax: 041 2746145 Email informahandicap@comune.venezia.it.

Venetia www.venetia.it — Transportation info; everything you need to get around in Venice.

Veneto Between Earth & Sky www.veneto.to — Tourist info.

Venice World www.veniceworld.com — Tourist info on Venice, lodging, descriptions of sites, visitor info, etc.

Italy's Ancient Pilgrimage Routes

VIA FRANCIGENA

The act of pilgrimage was a deep test of faith in the middle ages, and countless seekers made personal sojourns to one of three major holy destinations. Rome was one of the primary destinations in Europe, and pilgrims from the western reaches of the continent found their way to the city of St. Peter by walking the Via Francigena. The ancient pilgrim's route originated in Canterbury, England, then wound its way through the plains and hills of France before climbing the mountains of Switzerland and descending the Italian peninsula, to complete the journey in Rome. The name "Via Francigena" has many translations but it literally means the French road or the route of the Franks. The first historical mention of the route was recorded in 876 AD in the Actum Clusio, a parchment discovered in the Tuscan Abbey of San Salvatore al Monte Amiata. The Archbishop of Canterbury, Sigeric the Serious, wrote an initial description of the route in 990 AD. The Archbishop traveled to Rome to receive his ecclesiastical vestments from Pope John XV and on his journey home to Canterbury he recorded the intricacies of the route and the first map was created.

The Via Francigena reached its peak of popularity in the thirteenth century, but through the years its use declined, until the knowledge of its existence became just a dim historical footnote. It wasn't until 1994 that the embers were rekindled into flames of renewal, and a revival was planned by the Italian Ministry of Tourism and the Committee for Cultural Itineraries of the Council of Europe. This initiative sprang to life after the Italian Prime Minister Romano Prodi made his own pilgrimage to the Spanish city of Santiago di Compostela, and realized the power and vitality of the modern day pilgrimage movement. He vowed to put the Via Francigena back on the map.

HISTORICAL PILGRIM ROUTES AND SYMBOLS

The historical medieval pilgrimage routes of Europe led to one of three sacred sites: Santiago di Compostela in Spain, Jerusalem in the Holy Land, and Rome. The resurgence and tremendous popularity of the Spanish route began in the late twentieth century, and it continues to thrive as people from all over the world come to take part in the ancient ritual. This unprecedented renaissance has ignited interest in all the ancient pilgrim routes that once criss-crossed Western Europe. In 2006 alone, over 100,000 pilgrims registered to walk the Compostela, along with thousands of other hikers and non-registered pilgrims. In that same year, only 8,000 people walked the Via Francigena as very few pilgrims were aware of its existence. This is slowly changing as the Italian and European cultural and religious agencies get out the word about this beautiful, often neglected trail.

Each of these pilgrimage routes has an artifact or symbol associated with it, and this is often carried by each of its travelers. In Spain, the Cathedral of Santiago de Compostela is the goal, and the pilgrims carry a shell. This symbol is also seen in many towns and villages along the route, and metal castings are often embedded in the road. A Christian pilgrim in the Holy Land is bound for Jerusalem, and he carries a crucifix. On the Italian Via Francigena, the Basilica of St. Peter in Rome is the final destination, and the symbol carried by the pilgrim is a key. For the Catholics who make the spiritual journey, they seek forgiveness of their sins. For non-Catholics, the routes offer their own individual meanings, both spiritual and personal.

THE ITALIAN ROUTE

The Via Francigena enters Italy in the Alpine passes of the northwest, descending through the region of Val d'Aosta and the town of Aosta. It then makes its way through the western provinces, passing Pavia, Lucca, Siena, Viterbo and ultimately ending at the Vatican City in Rome and St. Peter's Basilica.

There are many small towns and villages along the way that you would seldom visit as a casual tourist, but they contain beautiful churches, holy relics and sites of miracles. For example in Lucca, St. Martin's Cathedral houses a crucifix called the Holy Face (Volto Santo) that legend tells us was made by Nicodemus at the time of Jesus. Another account tells of St. Catherine of Siena praying to the Holy Face and Jesus speaking to her. Exploring this pilgrimage route is not only an opportunity to test your spiritual strength and receive its many blessings; it is also a means of encountering the hidden side of Italy and experiencing the Italian people and their culture.

Once arriving in Rome there are seven churches dedicated to pilgrimage: St. Peter's Basilica, St. Paul Outside the Walls, St. John Lateran, St. Mary Major, St. Lawrence Outside the Walls, St. Sebastian Outside the Walls, Basilica of the Holy Cross and Our Lady of Divine Love.

PLANNING YOUR VIA FRANCIGENA PILGRIMAGE

The routes are mainly footpaths and in some areas they are not well maintained. About 8% of the paths are actually considered dangerous! Although the Italian government has allotted over 1500 signs to be installed along the paths, you will still need detailed maps, since the Via Francigena is not yet well marked. Also, there are alternative routes to consider, so careful planning of your itinerary is recommended. Excellent advice is available on the many websites listed below, and you should take advantage of their local expertise.

While the Via Francigena is becoming more organized, lodging is not consistently available. You will need to make plans and reservations in advance and not expect to find accommodations as you arrive in each town or village. You may consider including stops at some of the natural hot springs along the way. The springs at Bagnaccio near Viterbo and the thermal baths at Bagno Vignoni, near Siena, offer weary pilgrims much appreciated respite and rejuvenation.

Finally, make a concerted effort to get in shape before your trip. A typical day includes up to 20 miles (30 kilometers) of walking for the experienced hiker, so develop a training schedule to get prepared. You may hike less so plan accordingly. Begin developing the specifics of your journey at least a year in advance, and utilize the websites listed below for their maps, itineraries, and expert advice. The websites also describe how to obtain a pilgrim identity card. The monasteries and churches along the route recognize this card, and they will provide accommodations for one night of your sojourn, as space is available.

WEBSITES

Associazione Europea delle Vie Francigene
www.associazioneviafrancigena.com — Excellent site once you learn
how to navigate the tabs in English. Interactive maps, detailed history,
contact info, pilgrim ID card, and how to walk the route. Association of
Municipalities on the Via Francigena, Piazza Duomo, 16, 43036, Fidenza,
Parma, Italy. Email: segreteriagenerale@associazioneviafrancigena.it

Cammini d'Europa www.camminideuropageie.com — Drop down
menu top of page for English. Only one page of English but an excellent guide "European Pilgrimage routes" in English with detailed info
about all the routes in Europe. E-mail: pattoneri@soprip.it.

Canterbury City Council
www.canterbury.gov.uk/buildpage.php?id=1218 — Accommodation
along the Via Francigena between Canterbury and Dover and details
of the route of the Via Francigena in the Pas-de-Calais area of France

The European Institute of Cultural Routes www.culture-routes.lu
— Based in Luxembourg the EICR is in charge of ensuring the
continuity and development of the cultural routes program of the
Council of Europe. Go to "media library" and do a search for "The Via
Francigena" for publications in English.

Eurovia www.eurovia.tv — Austrian website created by pilgrims to
promote pilgrimage with postings from pilgrims, history, maps,
pilgrim ID card, books and DVDs.

International Association Via Francigena www.francigena.ch
www.francigena-international.org — Excellent website with history,
manuscripts of ancient pilgrim routes, road maps of Italy, and advice
on routes. Order maps, the Guide Vademecum A in English and the
Dormifrancigena (lodging) in Italian. Association Via Francigena,
Lgo Ecuador 6, I-00198 Roma, Italia
Email: info@francigena-international.org.

La Via Francigena www.viafrancigena.com — Itineraries of the
towns in Italy and describes the stages and ancient maps.
Email: francigena@linkey.it.

La Via Francigena www.giovannicaselli.com/francigena/ — Great maps covering England, France, Switzerland and Italy with detailed segments of the Italy route. English on main pages.

Opera Romana Pellegrinaggi www.orpnet.org — Vatican Pilgrimage travel agency. Italian with a little English. Cammini d'Europa - Opera Romana Pellegrinaggi, Uff. S.Pietro, Piazza Pio XII, n.9, Roma, Italia. Phone: 39 06 698961 Email: info@orpnet.org. Their office in St. Peter's square provides assistance for pilgrims with their catalogue "I Cammini d'Europa."

Sapori Via Francigena www.saporiviafrancigena.com — Lodging and restaurants on the Via Francigena route.

The Magazine of the Great European Culture Route www.rivistaviafrancigena.it — A bi-annual magazine in Italian and English about the Via Francigena Email: info@rivistaviafrancigena.it.

CAMMINO DI FRANCESCO

The Rieti Valley is home to several ancient hermitages visited by St. Francis of Assisi. Each of these sanctuaries in this Sacred Valley has a story to tell of St. Francis and his time spent there. Santuario di Greccio was witness to the first Nativity scene created in 1223, and Santuario di Fonte Colombo is where St. Francis wrote the Rule of the Franciscan Order. In the Grotto of Revelations at the Santuario di Poggio Bustone, St. Francis received pardon for his sins. He performed the miracle of the wine in Santuario Santa Maria de La Foresta. Refer to page sixty-eight for more details on each of these shrines dedicated to St. Francis.

The fifty-mile (80 km) footpath inaugurated in 2003, retraces the footsteps of St. Francis between the sanctuaries, and is divided into eight stops. The path is well marked with arrows and wooden sign-posts. Your first stop is at the Rieti Tourist Board on Via Cintia, 87, in Rieti. They will give you a free Pilgrim's Kit or you can have it mailed to you before you come by emailing: colaianni@apt.rieti.it.

There is an excellent website, Cammino di Francesco (see below), with "Practical Tips" for walking, riding your mountain bike, horseback riding or driving by car for people with special needs. If you complete the walk in no less than two days you also receive a Pilgrim's Certificate from the Rieti Tourist Board.

WEBSITES

Cammino di Francesco www.camminodifrancesco.it — Comprehensive website for walking the trail to all the sanctuaries in the Rieti Valley Email: info@camminodifrancesco.it.

APT Rieti Tourist Board www.apt.rieti.it — Main office for St. Francis walk. Via Cintia, 87 Rieti 02100 Italia Phone: 074 6201146/7 Fax: 074 6270446 Email: colaianni@apt.rieti.it.

A Guide to Meditating with the Saints

PRACTICE BEFORE YOU GO

A peaceful environment is usually necessary for meditation. Unfortunately, with their many distractions, the shrines are not always the most suitable environments for focusing inwardly. But, with practice, you will learn to shut out most external disturbances. You also do not need to visit saints' shrines to experience their grace. In fact, you should practice before going on pilgrimage by meditating on the saints you will be visiting. Because the large shrines are filled with many pilgrims and tourists, you will sometimes feel like you have connected to a saint better at home than halfway around the world in a noisy environment. Each way of experiencing the saints is valid. Even with a lot of noise, we have often felt the saints' special presence pierce through the commotion and move us to tears by their sweetness.

At first, it is a good idea to start meditating at home for short periods of time (five to ten minutes), and then lengthen the time as your body becomes accustomed to sitting quietly for longer periods (half hour to an hour). With any new behavior, it is a good idea to form the habit of meditating at the same time of day or night. Good times to meditate are upon awakening, before lunch, after work, or before retiring at night. Make the time convenient for yourself, and when you won't be disturbed.

When you are ready to meditate, find a quiet room, unplug the phone, and use headphones or earplugs if your surroundings are noisy. Dress comfortably or loosen your belt, and use a light blanket for warmth if needed. Sit on a straight-backed chair with your spine upright, and away from the back of the chair. Experiment with using a small pillow under your sit bones, to slightly raise and tilt the pelvis forward. Your feet should be flat on the floor. Put your hands, palms up, resting on the crease between the thighs and the hip. This will help keep your shoulders back and chest open.

If you are accustomed to sitting on a cushion on the floor, or you have special needs, experiment and choose the sitting position that works best for you. On pilgrimage, you will mostly be sitting on hard wooden benches or standing. So, even though you might not think that sitting with your spine straight is comfortable now, you will have less creature comforts at the shrines. That is why sitting for longer and longer periods will train your body to be accustomed to meditation, and after awhile it will not protest so much.

RELAX

When you are comfortable, close your eyes and mentally relax each body part, slowly, one by one. Focus on relaxing your head, neck, face, and jaw and so on, all the way down through your body to your toes. You will be surprised how much tension you hold in the different muscles.

If you find it difficult to relax, do some yogic stretching that involves deep breathing and slow, conscious movements. A simple stretch is bending forward from the waist while standing, until your upper body is hanging loosely with neck and shoulders relaxed. Continue to breathe and relax a bit more with each exhalation, allowing your head and shoulders to sink toward the floor. Then, on a final exhalation, slowly return to standing, bringing your arms up over your head and slightly back with your palms together, bending the

Meditating at L'Eremo

spine just a few inches in the opposite direction of the forward bend. Return to standing with your arms down at your side. Only go as far as is comfortable, never forcing the movement or bouncing.

Another easy technique for relaxation is to take a deep inhalation, hold the breath and tense the entire body. Then release the tension by forcing the breath out on the exhalation. Do this two or three times. When you feel relaxed, return to sitting upright with eyes closed.

In order to meditate, the body must be relaxed, or it will distract you with all its aches and pains. But you don't want to be so relaxed that you fall asleep. That is why it is important that you remain in an upright position with your spine straight, shoulders slightly back and chin parallel to the floor. In the beginning, you might spend more time relaxing than focusing inwardly, but eventually you will be able to develop the habit of relaxation immediately upon sitting.

FOCUS INWARD

Sitting in an upright position, begin to be aware of your breathing by focusing on your breath going in and out of the lungs. Follow the breath from the nostrils into your lungs, then follow the breath out again. Instead of just breathing from the top of your chest, your chest and stomach should move in and out together, stretching the diaphragm. If your stomach is not moving in and out, practice breathing into your stomach by gently pushing it out on the inhale.

Eventually, your breaths will become longer and deeper, similar to when you are sleeping, which in turn will help you to relax even more. Check in with your body from time to time to see if it is relaxed, with a straight spine. If you continue to be tense, imagine breathing into that area of tension, and letting go of the tension on the exhale. Then return your attention to the breath.

Another simple technique to help you focus is to inhale through the nose to a count that is comfortable for you (6-8 or 8-10), hold the breath for the same count, and then exhale through the nose on the same count. Continue immediately with your next inhalation. You can practice this three or more times.

As you continue to watch the breath, you are learning how to focus. It seems like a very simple exercise and that not much is happening. But as you try to meditate on your breath for any length of time, you will notice how much your mind can wander. This can be frustrating in the beginning because the mind, like a wild horse, does not want to be tamed. But, with patience, and most of all practice, you will begin to notice that you are more peaceful and calm. Each time you catch your mind going hither and yon, gently bring it back to your breathing.

OPEN YOUR HEART

We have all had the feeling of openheartedness when we see a smiling baby, a playful puppy, or a beautiful sunset. This feeling is in us all the time, and we can practice in meditation opening up to our inner sweetness and joy. Because of the hurts and traumas we have experienced in life, our hearts may have protective layers defending us against further pain. Through meditation and feeling the unconditional love of the Divine, the heart will begin to relax more. This might mean that tears of pain could flow, releasing old wounds. This is one of the great benefits of meditation. Our hearts learn to expand instead of contract, and we become more open and loving.

Humans want to be loved more than anything else, and when the heart contains so much pain, it is unable to receive the love we desire. The unconditional love of the Divine heals all wounds. The saints are good examples of how to let go of our attachments to the past and feel the presence of God in the present. Visualize offering your pain to the Divine on the exhalation, then allow unconditional love to replenish your heart on the inhalation. Continue imagining the Source of all Love filling you completely. Eventually, your tears will turn from those of grief to tears of gratitude. The heart will be touched with so much love your pain will eventually melt into joy.

After you are calm, relaxed and focused, visualize your heart open and loving. Imagine this love expanding out in concentric circles beyond your body to include at first your loved ones, then your community and eventually the world. Breathe naturally and be receptive to what feelings or intuitions come.

THE SPIRITUAL EYE OR CHRIST CENTER

As you become more focused in meditation, you may see some form of light when your eyes are closed. Within each of us is a spark of the Divine, and inherent in this spark is the ability to feel connected to the Divine light. In order to perceive this light, we need to practice bringing our focus inward toward the spine and upward toward this inner light. We can do this by focusing on what is called the spiritual eye, third eye, or Christ Center that is located at the point between the eyebrows. You see this portrayed in pictures of the saints with their eyes lifted upwards. The Eastern saints are sometimes painted with a ray of light radiating from their spiritual eye. Jesus explained this technique when he said, "If therefore thine eye be single, thy whole body shall be full of light." (Matthew 6:22)

With eyes closed, turn your eyes slightly upward, focused about an arm's length away, but looking through the point between the eyebrows. Do not strain or cross your eyes; your eyes should feel comfortable and relaxed. As your practice deepens, you may feel sensations or a slight tingling at the point between the eyebrows. At some point, you may begin to see light at the spiritual eye, and eventually a five-pointed silver star in a field of blue, surrounded by a golden halo. This representation is apparent to people of all faiths. Some people see this light early on in their meditation practices and others never see it. It is not necessary to see this light to feel a Divine connection, so don't be concerned if you are not able to. It is not an overt sign of your depth of spirituality. Focus on the spiritual eye as often as you can, especially while practicing all your meditation techniques.

Bring your attention now to the air passing through your nostrils, and focus on it flowing to the point between the eyebrows. It might help to put your finger at the point between the eyebrows at first to help you visualize the air reaching its destination. As you do this, repeat silently two or three words that have spiritual meaning to you. For example, on

Meditating at San Damiano

the inhale mentally repeat "Jesus" and on the out breath "Christ" or "A" - "men" or "I am" – "Spirit." Practice this for several minutes, or as long as you want, always bringing your attention back to the spiritual eye if it wanders.

FEEL THE SAINTS' PRESENCE

By using the above techniques of relaxation, focusing inward and opening, we are now more receptive to the saints' blessings. When you are open and calm it is a good time to pray to the saints, asking to feel their presence. Some qualities you might experience when feeling the saints' presence are joy, sweetness, unconditional love, or peace. These are actually manifestations of God's consciousness within us. Imagine that you are absorbing these qualities into every cell of your body. Open your mind, body and soul, absorbing the gift of grace that you have prayed for. Try not to let your mind wander and miss out on this opportunity. This special grace can disappear in a flash, and you will want to take advantage of each moment, bathing in the rays of the saints' blessings. Then hold on to the experience, carrying it with you as you go about your day. Any time, anywhere, by closing your eyes, and focusing on the spiritual eye, you can recall the partic-ular qualities you have felt.

ADDITIONAL TIPS

In the beginning of practicing meditation, the mind wants to stay active, so it helps to have some additional tools to train the mind to maintain focus.

1. Listening to, or singing, quiet devotional songs help to open the heart and invoke the presence of the Divine before meditation.

2. Creating an altar with pictures of your favorite saints or holy ones will assist you in focusing. Look into the eyes of the saints, and feel that they are sitting in front of you. Talk out loud or silently to them, recite prayers, mantras, or the rosary when your mind is distracted. If you are unfamiliar with praying, just converse with the saints, speaking to them from your heart: "I want to know you," or "Show me how to love God as you do." Then, close your eyes and bring your attention inward and upward, imagining the picture of one of the saints at the point between your eyebrows, the spiritual eye.

3. Another useful tool is to create a personal relationship with a saint. As you read about the saints' lives in this book, feel as if you know them and are familiar with what kind of people they were. What aspects of their experiences can you personally relate to? You might sense that a particular saint seems like a father, mother, grand-mother or grandfather to you. Then, as you meditate on them, you will begin to know their unique vibration. When you visit their shrines, you will find it easier to tune into their vibration because it will already be familiar.

4. It is generally not a good idea to meditate after a meal, when your body is preoccupied with digestion. Better to wait at least a half hour, or up to three hours, depending on how big the meal is. Caffeinated beverages speed up the body and mind, and are not conducive to a calm, meditative, mental state. We once made the mistake of having a strong cappuccino before we visited a shrine. Unfortunately, we were too wound up to focus inwardly and ended up leaving. Depending on how you react to caffeine, you might want to wait a half hour to an hour after consuming the stuff. In Italy, with the best cappuccinos available everywhere you look, that can be a challenge to your will power and your schedule!

5. When visiting the shrines, try to look for quiet places to sit and med-itate. In the description of the shrines at the end of each chapter, we make note of suitable places available for quiet contemplation. If one is not available, you won't regret bringing earplugs to help block out most sound.

For the purposes of experiencing pilgrimage, you will need just the basic meditation techniques described above. More in-depth methods are taught in many excellent books on meditation, some of which are in the resources section in the appendix. For further instruction, please refer to them when you are ready to move beyond these simple techniques. Joining a meditation group can be helpful not only because it is easier to learn to meditate with others, but also because a good group leader can guide you through the learning process. Meditation groups can be found through churches, spiritual book-stores and on the Internet.

TYPICAL MEDITATION ROUTINE

1. Find a quiet room where you will not be disturbed.

2. Do several stretches to release tension in your body, or inhale, tense all your muscles and then release the tension on the exhale.

3. Sit on a chair with your spine erect and not touching the back of the chair. Your chin should be parallel to the floor, feet flat on the floor, and hands with palms facing upwards, resting on the crease between your thighs and hip. Begin with a prayer from your own heart.

4. Close your eyes, breathe naturally, and check your body from head to toe for tension. Breathe into any areas of tension, relaxing the tension on the exhalation. Mentally relax by letting go of all worries, thoughts and distractions.

5. Inhale slowly through the nose to a count that is comfortable. Hold the breath for the same count and exhale for the same count. Repeat for several rounds.

6. Follow the breath entering the nostrils, traveling into the lungs and out again. The relaxation steps 1 – 6 should take about three to five minutes. With eyes closed, turn your eyes upward, looking through the point between your eyebrows (spiritual eye). Your focus should be fixed about an arm's length away and relaxed. Gaze at this point throughout your meditation.

7. Follow the air passing through the nose, to the point between the eyebrows, then back out again. Repeat "A – men," or other words that have spiritual meaning to you, on the inhalation and exhalation. Do this technique for half of your remaining meditation time.

8. When you feel calm and peaceful, invoke the presence of the saint by asking: "St. _____, help me to feel your presence and the grace of God that flows through you. Bless me and (others you are praying for), by guiding us on our spiritual path." Or pray in your tradition through the saint you have called upon. After invoking their presence, sit in the silence and absorb the peace and grace they are sharing with you. This should constitute the final half of your meditation time. End with a prayer of gratitude, bringing the peace and inner calmness of meditation into your daily activities.

Tips for Traveling in Italy

Traveling in Italy can be a pleasure if you are prepared and have the right attitude. It is all about understanding the rules, the norms, and going with the flow. Italians do things differently: breakfast is a croissant and coffee, the table of contents is in the back of the book, and lunch can take well over two hours. The tips below will help prepare you for some of these differences. Except on the highways, life is slower in Italy, and you can benefit more from your travels if you assume an Italian frame of mind. The Italians' friendliness, love of good food, and appreciation of art and saints makes visiting this beautiful country a complete and satisfying experience.

TRAVEL IN ITALY

If you will be driving in Italy, you need to be prepared to be assertive. Driving in Italy is not for the weak of heart! Italians drive very fast, and have the highest number of road deaths in Europe, more than 7,000 per year. Learn the rules of the Italian roadway before getting into your rental car. Outside the major cities, driving is not so different from what you are used to, just don't use the left lane of the Autostrada (freeway) unless you are passing. You will quickly notice small German sports cars flying down the left lanes at 100 mph, so beware! We suggest not driving in major cities, especially Rome. Park your car and use public transportation. After all, this is a vacation, not a lesson in survival! It is often difficult to know the speed limit because it varies, so drive at the speed of the other traffic. It may be helpful to check out the speed limits from the car rental agent when you rent your vehicle.

In many of the walled cities of central Italy you have to park outside the walls and walk into the city center. If you are staying in

Curious Italian cat, Deruta

the city, you can go to your hotel and get a pass to park, or unload your luggage and park outside the walls. Plan ahead for parking, so you don't have to figure it out while you're driving around in circles. We try to find lodging with its own parking, especially in the big cities.

It is essential to buy a good map of Italy. If you are traveling by car, you need a detailed map that shows all the highways. The maps provided by the rental agencies are fine for the major roads, but if you want to venture into the countryside to find some of the small shrines described in this book, you will need a better map. If you are traveling by train you need a map that shows train routes. We like Michelin maps, especially the ones that are spiral bound, for they are easy to use in the car and have great information for quick reference. The foldout maps are good too, but we found that they became torn, and are difficult to fold up in the car. One difference in getting around Italy is that signs do not typically include road numbers, but use names and arrows pointing towards the distant city. It takes some getting used to, but if you study your map, it will become clear. When looking for the center of town, follow the signs to "Centro" that have a black and white bull's eye.

Look for a map store in your yellow pages or do a search for maps on the Internet. Here are a few sites: www.viamichelin.com / www.hammondmap.com / www.maps.com.

Getting around the cities of Italy is another thing. There are many good maps of the cities, but the most difficult thing is to find an address. In Italy, street names often change every block, so finding a specific address can be a harrowing experience. Maps are essential but do not always show all the street name changes. You can save time wandering around looking for a shrine by getting a town or city map before you arrive in the city. We have included many maps in this book, but a greater level of detail will always be helpful. Contact the local tourist offices of the cities you will be visiting, and request a city map at least three months before you leave for Italy, or go directly to the local tourist office and get a local map upon your arrival. Then you will have a map of Italy, the city, and the map in this book for locating the shrine. For fun, view a satalite picture of where you are going by checking out Google Earth at www.earth.google.com.

When traveling, always give yourself enough time to get lost. Even with a map, you will find one-way streets going in the wrong direction, or there will be signs showing the way to a shrine that suddenly leave you guessing at the next crossroads. Take a deep breath and relax – you're on vacation! If you learn any Italian before you go, learn to ask directions and be able to understand the reply. You can always ask, "Dov'è il santuario...(insert the saint's name)?"

LANGUAGE

English is spoken quite often in the big cities, but in the smaller towns it will be the luck of the draw. Italians are very friendly and will go out of their way to help you, even if you don't understand, but they love it if you try to speak their language. We asked an Italian friend why Italians keep talking when we say we don't understand Italian, and she replied that they just can't believe we don't speak Italian!

Always be prepared with an English/Italian phrasebook. We provide some Italian phrases in the book, but you will need an English/Italian phrase book to learn how to pronounce the words.

LODGING

Staying in monasteries and convents is a wonderful way to make a trip to Italy affordable. You must understand though, these are not hotels, and they do not have the amenities of a hotel. The rooms are plain and simple, and there is no room service. However, we have found them to be clean, safe, and affordable. You can share a bathroom down the hall or ask for a private bathroom at an additional cost. The nuns and staff are usually very sweet and add to the quiet ambiance of the lodging. Most monasteries have a curfew, so find this out when you check in. If you are not back in time, you will be locked out for the night! Curfews are usually late enough to accommodate most pilgrims' lifestyles. See Resources in the Appendix for books and websites on lodging in monasteries and convents in Italy.

CHURCH ETIQUETTE

When Mass is being conducted, please be respectful. Do not walk around looking at the artwork, talking loudly or taking pictures. Though many churches are treated more like museums, they continue to be a house of God for the local people and all due respect is appreciated. Talking should be kept to a minimum, and whispering is preferred.

In the past, no one was allowed to approach the altar except for the priests and altar boys, but today, in the smaller churches, you are *usually* allowed to visit the altar and the reliquary of the saint. If you are unsure, you can look for clues from the other pilgrims.

When you visit a convent or a church, don't be afraid to ring the bell to the convent if you need assistance. The bell is usually next to a

Le Celle, Cortona

door on either side of the altar, or in a building adjacent to the church. A priest or nun will come and ask you what you want. If you do not speak Italian, be prepared with a script ahead of time, or show them written questions. The hardest part is in understanding their replies. You can just keep repeating that you do not speak Italian but that you want to visit the saint.

Because of thefts and lack of staff, many of the churches have video cameras in the churches to allow them to monitor activity from the convent. We meditated in one church for a long time thinking we were alone, when a nun came from the cloister and asked if we wanted to see a special chapel we didn't know about. So, even if the church looks empty, always conduct yourself properly.

In small churches where there is minimal staff, books and mementos for sale will be kept out on a table. You will be expected to pay the price of the book, leaving the money in a basket or in an indicated slot. When you light a votive candle, it is expected that you make a monetary offering.

Many of the large churches do not allow taking pictures inside the sanctuary. There are usually good postcards available for purchase that have better pictures than you could take yourself in a darkened church. Also, please turn off your cell phone before entering a church.

CLOTHING

You will be doing a lot of walking on uneven surfaces, so always wear comfortable walking shoes. Some of the larger basilicas (St. Peter's in Rome, St. Mark's in Venice) will not let anyone enter the church with shorts, miniskirts, sleeveless shirts, or a bare midriff. Dress appropriately when visiting the shrines: long pants or skirts to the knees. Sometimes bare arms are a problem, so bring something to put over your shoulders.

HOURS OF OPERATION

The one predictable thing in Italy is that the times for opening and closing will invariably change from what is printed here. Always check ahead for the hours of operation if you are on a tight schedule. Most churches and businesses are closed for two to three hours in the early afternoon, and stay open into the early evening. Know what holidays occur during your visit. Sometimes churches are closed on Sundays after Mass. If your itinerary is tight, you will need to check before you go, or at least upon arrival in town, so you won't be disappointed. The month of August is vacation for most Italians, and many places are closed or have limited hours.

NATIONAL HOLIDAYS

The national holidays in Italy are: January 1 & 6; Easter Monday; April 25; May 1; August 15; November 1; December 8, 25 & 26. On the feast day of a local saint many businesses will be closed.

ELECTRICITY & LIGHTS

Electric power in Italy is very expensive, and the lights are turned off in many churches in order to save electricity. At St. Mark's Basilica in Venice the lights are turned on at specific times to display the golden mosaics. In some of the larger churches, especially in Rome, there are coin-operated lights for small side chapels. We have found these well worth the price, because you see the beauty of these chapels in their entire splendor. A few places have motion sensors that turn the lights on when you enter the room. Sometimes you can ask the staff to turn the lights on for a short period of time. If they do, please make a donation.

TELEPHONES/FAXES

The country code of Italy is 39. The local area code is used before the phone number when calling outside and inside Italy. For calls within Italy, you will need to buy a phone card (carta telefonica) at a local tobacco shop (tabaccheria) or newsstand. With the advent of cell phones, numbers have been changing everywhere. Italian phone numbers contain a different quantity of numbers, so don't be confused by this.

While traveling in Europe, international telephone calls can be expensive, but the internet and cell phones offer a variety of options. Skype www.skype.com is the most popular internet phone service, but there are many others. Search online for "Compare internet telephone service." If you have a GSM network cell phone that operates in Europe, you can use a prepaid local SIM card to make calls. Check out your phone's capabilities for international calling or www.Telestial.com for more information.

When planning your trip, if you are not receiving a response from your emails, try sending a fax. Church staffs are small and sometimes they have to find someone to translate your message. So, wait a week and send again.

MONEY

For current exchange rates and a currency converter for the Euro, do a search for currency converter or check out the website www.xe.com. Be aware of your credit card bank fees for purchases and A.T.M. withdrawals made in Italy. Search www.Bankrate.com for "currency conversion costs."

Tourist Information

Research your trip before you go with the Italian Government Tourist Office's excellent website: (ENIT) Ente Nazionale Italiano per il Turismo www.italiantourism.com and the Rome website below.

Rome

(ENIT) Ente nazionale italiano per il turismo
ViaMarghera no. 2/6
00185 ROMA
Phone: 39 06 49711
Fax: 39 06 4463379
E-mail: sedecentrale@enit.it

Website: www.enit.it
Names of local tourist offices are:
APT — Azienda Promozione Turistica
IAT — Ufficio Informazioni e di Accoglienza Turistica
EPT — Ente Provinciale Turismo

New York City

Phone: 212 245-4822
Fax: 212 586-9249
E-mail: enitny@italiantourism.com

Chicago

Phone: 312 644-0996
Fax: 312 644-3019
E-mail: enitch@italiantourism.com

Los Angeles

Phone: 310 820-1898
Phone: 310 820-6357
E-mail: enitla@earthlink.net

London

Phone: 44 20 7408 1254
Fax: 44 20 7493 6695
E-mail: enitlond@globalnet.co.uk

VEGETARIANS

We include this topic because we are vegetarians. We see that more people are interested in learning how to eat well in general, but when traveling it can be more of a challenge. Fortunately, Italians always have good salads and one vegetarian pasta (pasta marinara) or vegetarian pizza on the menu. When we were in Italy for five weeks, we got tired of pasta and pizza, but relief came when we visited the larger cities and indulged in various ethnic foods, like Oriental and Indian. Vegans have to plan ahead, and people who are allergic to wheat will have to do their research on what is edible.

Refer to our Resources in the Appendix for Vegetarian Travel. There are websites that list the vegetarian restaurants in Italy.

If you don't drink caffeinated beverages, bring your own tea bags and ask for hot water. Herbal teas are not usually available. You can also ask for "decafinato" espresso drinks, but these are usually made from instant decaf, so don't expect quality coffee.

If you want to eat protein at breakfast, it will be difficult to find in Italy. Breakfast typically consists of a croissant and coffee. So, if you need protein, bring your own or purchase food the day before. We bring our own protein powder and mix it with water so we don't run out of energy in the morning.

At a café in Siena one morning, we eyed a big bowl of hardboiled eggs behind the counter and asked if we could buy some. They adamantly refused, for eggs are not to be eaten in the morning! Be prepared by understanding Italy's customs, and just go with the flow. You will have much more fun!

Time Line of the Saints

1st century St. Peter in Rome
1st century St. Paul in Rome
1st century St. Mark in Venice
1st century St. Andrew in Amalfi
1170-1221 St. Dominic of Bologna
1181-1226 St. Francis of Assisi
1193-1253 St. Clare of Assisi
1195-1231 St. Anthony of Padua
1227-1320 Blessed Margaret of Metola
1247-1297 St. Margaret of Cortona
1248-1309 Blessed Angela of Foligno
1268-1308 St. Clare of the Cross Montefalco
1268-1317 St. Agnes of Montepulciano
1347-1380 St. Catherine of Siena
1381-1457 St. Rita of Cascia
1387-1455 Blessed Fra Angelico
1389-1489 St. Antoninus
1413-1463 St. Catherine of Bologna
1491-1556 St. Ignatius of Loyola
1515-1595 St. Philip Neri
1522-1590 St. Catherine de' Ricci
1603-1663 St. Joseph of Copertino
1651-1711 Blessed Bonaventure of Potenza
1660-1727 St. Veronica of Giuliani
1866-1942 St. Leopold Mandić
1887-1968 St. Pio of Pietrelcina (Padre Pio)

Resources

INTERNET SITES

The Internet is an enormous resource for travel information. We have included sites for researching the cities and regions of Italy plus general travel information to get you started. For the English version of a website, look for the British Flag or the words "English Version." Sometimes a website in Italian will have English for parts of its website and not others. Italian websites are loaded with graphics, so be patient while they download. In the ever-changing world of the Internet, websites change, so if one we provide doesn't work, do a search, and let us know what the new site is. If you don't want to type in the website addresses below, go to our website **www.innertravelbooks.com** and click on **Links** for faster access.

REGIONS

Argoweb www.argoweb.it — Umbria Tourist info.

Bella Umbria www.bellaumbria.net — Umbria tourist info.

Emilia Romagna Turismo www.emiliaromagnaturismo.it — Emilia Romagna tourist info.

In Toscana www.intoscano.it — Toscana tourist info.

Marche Worldwide www.marcheworldwide.org — Marche tourist info.

Marche Voyager www.le-marche.com — Marche tourist info.

Puglia Turismo www.pugliaturismo.com — Puglia tourist info.

Umbria www.umbria2000.it — Umbria tourist info.

Umbria Tourism www.umbriatourism.com — Umbria tourist info.

Tourism in Tuscany www.turismo.toscana.it — Tuscany tourist info.

TravelCampania.com www.travel-campania.com — Campania tourist info.

Campania Region www.turismoregionecampania.it — Tourist info.

Tuscany.net www.tuscany.net — Tuscany tourist info.

Turismo Lazio www.turislazio.it — Lazio tourist info.

Veneto www.veneto.to — Veneto tourist info.

CITIES

About.com http://goeurope.about.com/od/italy — Tourist info.

The American Catholic Church in Rome www.santasusanna.org — Detailed tourist info, tickets for papal audiences, and lodging in convents (Go to "Coming to Rome").

World Guide Bologna www.bologna.world-guides.com — Tourist info.

Costa di Amalfi www.costadiamalfi.it — Tourist info for the Amalfi coast including Ravello.

Firenze by Net www.mega.it — Florence tourist info.

Firenze On Line www.fionline.it — Florence tourist info.

Florenceby.com www.florenceby.com — Florence tourist info.

In Roma www.inroma.it — Rome tourist info. Click "turismo" & "English version."

Italy Guide www.romeguide.it — Rome tourist info.

Move About Italy www.moveaboutitaly.com — Tuscany info.

Ravello www.ravellotime.it — Ravello tourist info.

Ravello www.ravello.it — Ravello tourist info.

Roma Turismo www.romaturismo.it — Rome Tourist info.

Romeby.com www.romeby.com — Rome tourist info.

Rome Buddy www.romebuddy.com — Rome tourist info.

Terre Siena www.terresiena.it — Official website APT Siena.

Tuscany Net www.tuscany.net/tourist/tour5.htm — Addresses and Mass times of Non-Catholic and Catholic Churches in Florence.

Veniceby.com www.veniceby.com — Venice tourist info.

Venice World www.veniceworld.com — Venice tourist info.

Your Way to Florence www.arca.net/florence.htm — Florence tourist info.

TOURIST INFORMATION

There are many websites on Italy. For lodging, search "Italy" and "lodging" for more than enough websites to explore.

Autostrade per l'italia www.autostrade.it — Highway maps to plan your trip. Click on "Plan your Journey" then search in Italian.

Avventure Bellissime www.tours-italy.com — Walking and road tours in Italy.

Camping Italia www.camping.it —Campsites throughout Italy.

Concierge.com www.concierge.com/italy — Search for destination.

Discover Italia www.discoveritalia.com — Tourist info.

Dorling Kindersley www.dk.com — Eyewitness Travel Guides.

ENIT Italian State Tourist Board www.enit.it — Click on "Tourist Offices" and search the town (in Italian) for tourist office.

Ferry Metrò del Mare www.metrodelmare.com phone — Campania region ferries. Phone: 19 9600700 Email: info@metrodelmare.com.

Fodor's www.fodors.com — Search for destination.

Frommer's www.frommers.com — Search for destination.

IgoUgo www.igougo.com — Tourist info & reviews from tourists.

In Italy Online www.initaly.com — Tourist info.

Insight Guides www.insightguides.com — Insight guides, maps and phrasebooks.

Internet Cafes in Italy http://cafe.ecs.net — Internet connections.

Italia Rail www.italiarail.com — Train information in Italy.

Italian Government Tourist Board North America
www.italiantourism.com — Same as ENIT tourist info.

Italian Tourist Web Guide www.itwg.com — On-line hotel reservations & tourist info.

Italy in a Flash www.italyflash.com — Tourist info.

Italy Tickets www.italytickets.it — Entertainment tickets in Italy.

Italy Travel www.justitaly.org — Tourist info.

Italy Travel Escape www.italytravelescape.com — Tourist info.

Italy's Monastery Hotels www.monasteryhotels.com Refurbished monasteries, now two to four star B&B's or hotels.

Let's Go www.letsgo.com — Written by young adults for budget travel.

Lonely Planet www.lonelyplanet.com — Guidebooks & tourist info.

Parks in Italy www.parks.it — Parks in Italy.

Planetware www.planetware.com — Tourist info.

Rail Europe www.raileurope.com U.S. company for online reservations for European railways.

Rick Steves www.ricksteves.com — Go to: Plan Your Trip.

Rome Guide www.romeguide.it — Ticket reservations and tourist info.

Rough Guides www.roughguides.com — Rough Guides, miniguides and phrasebooks.

Routes International www.routesinternational.com — Transportation links.

SITA Bus www.sitabus.it — Italian. Phone: 089 871016.

Sulga www.sulga.it Public transportation from Umbria to other parts of Italy.

Time Out www.timeout.com — Online travel guides and entertainment for major cities around the world.

Trenitalia www.trenitalia.com/en/index.html — Train tickets in Italy.

Via Michelin www.viamichelin.com — Online detailed maps.

Visit Europe www.visiteurope.com — European Travel Commission.

Welcome to Italy www.emmeti.it — All regions tourist info and religious itineraries.

SHRINE INFORMATION

Refer to individual chapters under Websites, or visit:
www.innertravelbooks.com and click on Links.

PILGRIMAGE

There are hundreds of pilgrimage tour operators. Do a search with
these words: Italy/pilgrimage/tours.

LODGING IN MONASTERIES AND CONVENTS

BOOKS

Bed and Blessings Italy: A Guide to Convents and Monasteries Anne and
June Walsh, Paulist Press $16.95.

Europe's Monastery and Convent Guest Houses Kevin J. Wright, Liguori
Publications $16.95.

The Guide to Lodging in Italian Monasteries Eileen Barish, Anacapa
Press $22.95. www.monasteriesofitaly.com.

WEBSITES

The American Catholic Church in Rome www.santasusanna.org —
Tourist info and lodging in convents under "Coming to Rome."

dell´Accoglienza Cattolica in Italia www.Hospites.it — Search for
lodging in convents, monasteries and other lodging. info@hospites.it

Italia Sixtina www.sixtina.com — A French booking service for lodging in convents and monasteries. You provide a price range and pay
them directly. If you don't have time to buy the books or do the
research, this is for you.

In Italy www.initaly.com/agri/convents.htm — A list of lodging in
convents and monasteries can be ordered for $6.00.

Monastery Stays www.monasterystays.com Booking service for
monastery lodging.

Reid Guides www.reidguides.com — Article on staying in convents.
Go to "Finding the Perfect Place to Stay' & "Alternative
Accomodations."

Santuario della Madonna del Rosario www.santuari.it — Search for
Sanctuaries in Italy: "Cerca un Santuario." Italian.

MEDITATION RESOURCES

BOOKS

Centering Prayer in Daily Life and Ministry by Thomas Keating. Christian contemplative meditation.

The Best Guide to Meditation by Victor N. Davich. Overview of different meditation techniques and their history. Good for beginners.

The Complete Idiot's Guide to Meditation by Joan Budlilovsky & Eve Adamson. Catalogue of meditation practices.

Discovering Jewish Meditation, Instruction & Guidance for Learning an Ancient Spiritual Practice by Nan Fink Gefen. Jewish Meditation for beginners.

How to Meditate: A Guide to Self-Discovery by Lawrence Leshan. A beginner's guide for the best meditation techniques available.

How to Meditate: A Practical Guide by Kathleen McDonald. Buddhist meditation.

How to Meditate: A Step-by-Step Guide to the Art and Science of Meditation by John (Jyotish) Novak. Yoga meditation techniques for beginners.

Insight Mediation: A Step by Step Course on How to Meditate by Sharon Salzberg. Buddhist Vipassana meditation.

Meditation for Beginners by Jack Kornfield. Buddhist Vipassana meditation, Audio CD.

Meditation for Starters by J. Donald Walters. Basic meditation techniques for beginners.

WEBSITES

There are many websites on meditation. Search for meditation, or for meditation and your particular religion, i.e., Catholic, Buddhist, etc.

Ananda Online www.ananda.org — Yogic meditation. Click on: Lessons in Meditation: Online meditation support & video.

Beliefnet www.beliefnet.com — Comprehensive info on all religions. Click on "Faith practices" then "Meditation."

Contemplative Outreach www.centeringprayer.com — Christian Centering Prayer as taught by Thomas Keating.

Dharma Net International www.dharmanet.org — Resources for Buddhist Meditation Centers worldwide.

The World Community for Christian Meditation www.wccm.org — Christian meditation as taught by Dom John Main OSB. Click on: How to meditate.

Vipassana.com www.vipassana.com/meditation — Buddhist meditation in the Theravada tradition. Online course in meditation.

MEDITATION RETREATS ITALY

Ananda Assisi www.ananda.it/en — A yoga and meditation retreat center just outside Assisi.

Casa della Pace www.casadellapace.org — Yoga and meditation retreat near Gubbio.

Migliara Retreats www.dallaluce.com — Retreats in southern Umbria.

Retreats Online www.retreatsonline.com/guide/meditation.htm

Sacred Travel www.sacredtravel.org — Assisi East - West Retreat Center, Meditation retreats in Assisi and other sacred sites.

RESOURCES FOR TRAVELERS WITH DISABILITIES

BOOKS

The Accessible Guide to Florence by Cornelia Danielson www.bftservices.it Email: info@bftservices.it.

Air Travel Guide for Seniors and Disabled Passengers: The Better Breathing Traveler The American Lung Association of San Diego 619 297-8402 / 619 297-3901

Barrier Free Travel: A Nuts & Bolts Guide for Wheelers & Slow Walkers by Candy Harrington 888 795-4274/215 923-4686 www.emerginghorizons.com

Disappearing Windmills - A Waist High View of the World's Hotspots by Kate Zee 800 882-3273.

How to Travel: A Guidebook for Persons with Disabilities Fred Rosen 636 394-4950

WEBSITES

Accessible Europe www.accessibleurope.com — Ttravel info.

Accessible Italy www.accessibleitaly.com — Non-profit tour operator for individuals with disabilities. Email: info@accessibleitaly.com.

Accessible Journeys www.disabilitytravel.com — Tours to Italy.

Accessible Rome www.coinsociale.it/tourism/accessiblerome/index.php — Tours and free equipment rental in Rome. Once in Rome, pick up their free "Roma Accessible" guide at COIN/Via Giglioli 54-a/00169. Phone: 06 7129011 Fax: 06 71290140 Email: info@coinsociale.it.

Access-able Travel Source www.access-able.com — Travel info.

CO.IN. www.coinsociale.it/tourism — *Cooperative Integrate ONLUS* is a nonprofit association based in Rome that provides services for people with disabilities. Phone: 06 7129011 Fax: 06 71290140 Email: info@coinsociale.it.

DisabledTravelers.com www.disabledtravelers.com — Travel info.

Disability Resources on the Net www.disabilityresources.org — Click on "Travel & transportation" "Travel guides foreign."

Emerging Horizons www.emerginghorizons.com — Comprehensive travel info for Italy: Go to "Travel Resources," "Destinations," "Europe," "Italy." Bookstore and newsletter. Phone 209 599-9409.

Global Access News www.globalaccessnews.co — Disabled travel network.

Paraplegia News www.pvamagazines.com — Click on "Resources" then "Travel."

Routes International www.routesinternational.com — Click on "Travel for the Disabled."

Society for Accessible Travel & Hospitality www.sath.org — Travelers with disabilities info. Phone: 212 447-7284.

VEGETARIAN TRAVEL

BOOKS

Vegetarian Europe by Alex Bourke Guidebook for vegetarian travelers to Europe.

The Vegetarian Traveler: Where to Stay if You're Vegetarian, Vegan, Environmentally Sensitive by Jed Civic International guidebook.

LODGING & RETREATS

Ananda Assisi www.ananda.it/en — A yoga and meditation retreat center near Assisi offering educational programs and vegetarian food.

B&B Corte Armonica Relais Fiesole www.cortearmonica.it — Tuscany B&B serving organic vegitarian food. Six miles (8km) from Florence Phone: 055 59334 Email: cortearmonica@tiscali.it.

Country House Montali www.montalionline.com — Umbrian country house near Lake Trasimeno serving gourmet vegetarian food Phone: 075 8350680 Email: montali@montalionline.com

Le Tortorelle www.sustenanceforthesoul.com — A vegetarian agriturismo on the Umbria Tuscany border. Phone: 07 59411564 Email: peter@sustenanceforthesoul.com.

Villa Orsini www.villaorsini.com — Tuscany vacation apartments serving gourmet vegetarian food.

WEBSITES

Happy Cow's Global Guide to Vegetarian Restaurants www.happycow.net — Click on "Travel" for vegetarian resources.

Veg Dining www.vegdining.com — Vegetarian restaurants around the world.

The Vegetarian Resource Group www.vrg.org/travel — Travel information, books, websites, tour operators, bulletin board, and articles.

Vegetarians Abroad www.vegetariansabroad.com — Establishments abroad that cater to vegetarians.

Glossary

Altar – A focus of spiritual devotion; in the Catholic Church altars are the center of focus for the building and where the Eucharist is kept for the celebration of Mass. In large Catholic churches, when there are other altars in side chapels, the main altar is called the "high altar." Personal altars can be made in a home with pictures of saints and symbols of one's faith as a source of focus for meditation and prayer.

Apse – An area of a church that is typically semi-circular and projects out from the building as part of the sanctuary or altar.

Basilica – A Roman Catholic church given certain ceremonial privileges.

Beatification – The step taken before recognition of sainthood, or canonization, of a deceased Christian. After a local church has organized a strong petition, then with papal approval, beatification takes place, allowing the person to be called "Blessed." With this designation the local church that organized the cause can venerate the Blessed.

Bilocation – Being in two places at the same time.

Blessed – The title given to a deceased Christian who has passed certain criteria in the beatification process, which is the step taken before recognition of sainthood, or canonization.

Breviary – A book of prayers, hymns, psalms, and readings for the canonical hours.

Canonization – In the Catholic Church, after extensive research, and proof of at least one miracle, the pope declares that a deceased Christian is a saint, allowing for universal veneration.

Cilice – Hair shirt used like other austerities to overcome bodily desires.

Cloister – An area within a monastery or convent to which the monks or nuns are normally restricted.

Convent – The building in which a religious community lives. Usually referred to as an establishment for nuns in the United States, but in Italy, convent and monastery are used for both nuns and monks.

Crypt – The burial place of a person in a church. Also called tomb, reliquary, mausoleum, sepulcher, and vault. These places usually are under the high altar, or under altars in side chapels, but they can also be in a room downstairs beneath the high altar.

Duomo – A cathedral, which is the principal church of a bishop's diocese, containing the Episcopal throne.

Eastern Orthodox – There was the "Great Schism" between the Eastern and Western Church in 1054 when the Orthodox Christians, primarily from Greece and Russia, and the Roman Catholics split off from each other. There were many disagreements, but the major difference was their concept of authority. The Eastern Church made decisions with an Ecumenical Council of sister churches, whereas the Western Church made decisions based on hierarchy, through bishops, cardinals and ultimately the pope.

Ecumenical – The general definition is the bringing together of all faiths in order to find common ground and purpose.

Eucharist – Also called the host, Holy Communion and the Blessed Sacrament. It is a wafer of bread blessed, consecrated, by a priest during the Mass. The consecrated bread is turned into the body of Christ and taken internally during mass. In the Roman Catholic Church the recipients must be Catholic, but other Christian religions have different criteria for receiving the host. The Eucharistic miracles are instances where the consecrated hosts have been scientifically proven to have turned into human flesh, to have shed blood or withstood the test of time by not decomposing.

Feast day – In the Catholic Church saints have a feast day where a special Mass is celebrated in their honor once a year. Usually the day is the date of their death, or near that date. There are more festivities around a feast day, birthday or the translation of their relics to the church for some saints.

Gothic – The style of architecture developed in northern France that spread to western Europe from the middle of the twelfth century to the early sixteenth century. It is characterized by pointed arches, the ribbed vault, and the flying buttress.

Inquisition – There are three eras of the Inquisition. Pope Gregory IX initiated the first in 1235 as a tribunal for the discovery and punishment of heresy that was carried out sporadically in different parts of Europe. The second was the infamous Spanish Inquisition authorized by Pope Sixtus IV in 1478 but controlled by King Ferdinand and Queen Isabella and terminated in 1843. The third was the Roman Inquisition established in 1542 by Pope Paul III to combat the Protestant heresy.

Levitation – To rise or float in the air in an ecstatic state.

Mass – The ritual that entails recitation of the liturgy of the Roman Catholic Church around the celebration of the consecration of the Eucharist. Mass is celebrated daily at most churches.

Nave – The perpendicular body of a cross-shaped church that connects to the horizontal wings, called the transept.

Novice – A person admitted into a religious community for a probationary period.

Novitiate – The time period that a person is a novice or a house where novices are trained.

Presbytery – The part of a church reserved for clergy.

Reformation – The creation of the Protestant church by Martin Luther and others who broke off from the Roman Catholic Church in the sixteenth century.

Renaissance – Beginning in Italy in the fourteenth century, and lasting into the seventeenth century, a period of transition from the Middle Ages into an era marked by a humanistic revival of classical influence expressed in a flowering of the arts and literature and by the beginnings of modern science. The neoclassical style of architecture was dominant during the Renaissance period.

Roman Catholic – The Western Catholic Church having a hierarchy of priests and bishops under the authority of the pope, a liturgy centered in the Mass, veneration of the Virgin Mary and saints, clerical celibacy, and a body of dogma including transubstantiation and papal infallibility. The Western Roman Catholic Church and the Eastern Orthodox Christian Church broke off from each other in 1054.

Relic – A part of a saint or blessed's mortal remains, or an object connected to a saint or blessed.

Reliquary – A container or shrine in which sacred relics are kept.

Sacristy – A room in a church where sacred vessels and vestments are kept and where the clergy dresses for Mass.

Saint – A deceased person officially recognized, through the rigorous process of canonization and final approval by the pope in the Roman Catholic Church, as the highest attainment of holiness.

Sanctuary – The most sacred part of a church, typically where the altar is located.

Saracens – The nomadic Arabic tribes that invaded the borders of the Roman Empire.

Second Order – The female branch of an already established male order.

Stations of the Cross – There are 14 Stations of the Cross that depict Christ's final journey to Calvary, and prayers are said at each one.

Stigmata – The wounds of Christ's passion recreated in a person desiring to imitate Christ and experience the pain of His wounds. There are the visible stigmata and the invisible stigmata. St. Francis of Assisi was the first known person to experience the stigmata. Since then, hundreds of men and women have manifested the wounds, typically in the hands, feet, side and head.

Tertiaries – Also called "Third Order," a branch of a religious order that is comprised of lay women and men, who live in the world instead of in convents and monasteries.

Third Order – Also called "Tertiary," a branch of a religious order that is comprised of lay women and men, who live in the world instead of in convents and monasteries.

Transept – The transverse or horizontal wings of a cross-shaped church.

Translation – The removal of a saint's remains from one place to another.

Transubstantiation – The belief that during the ritual of the Mass, the bread and wine are literally changed into the body and blood of Christ.

Pilgrims praying, Porziuncola

Acknowledgements

We could not have written this book without the loving help and assistance of many people. We depended on the kindness of strangers and friends to show us how to create a book from an idea to the form it eventually has taken. We thank God, Paramhansa Yogananda, and all the saints for guiding us every step of the way.

In the beginning, we talked to many people for information and leads on where to go: Michael Taylor, Jürgen Kramer, Mary Mintey, Mary Mieth, Mantradevi LoCicero, Vairagi Escobar, Lila Devi and Deborah Gregorelli. Dianna Smith created a questionnaire in Italian that helped us survive with very little knowledge of the language. During our travels, there were many priests, nuns, and staff at the shrines who cheerfully provided us with the information we needed, and who we couldn't have done without.

In the process of writing this book, we thank Sahaja Ellero for the Italian translations in the book and for communicating with the shrines, and Michael Taylor for coming to our aid in corresponding in Italian and editing our confused Italian. We appreciate the many people who gave us honest feedback that ultimately made a better book: Anandi Cornell, Sheila Rush, Jan Shapiro, Mary and Mark Perini, Julia Ross, John Gorsuch, Jyotish Novak and Suzanne Buckley. Expert advice was received from Carol Randall for the Travelers' with Disabilities resources, and John Matusiak straightened us out on Orthodox Christianity.

For teaching us to set style and the miraculous use of Control-Z, we thank Alan Heubert. Many thanks for technical help in areas unfamiliar to us: logo and letterhead, Sarah Brink; typesetting with spirit, Nirmala and Peter Schuppe; and creating our index, Theodore Timpson.

For proficient, thoughtful editing, we want to thank our neighbor, Cathy Parojinog. She was always there for us when we needed her for answers. And, Sara Cryer for her generous, expert guidance in designing our book and teaching us much along the way.

For being there when we needed her during this second edition, Stephanie Steyer, an expert graphic designer with the patience of a saint.

For providing us with a daily example of how to create with Divine inspiration, offering everything we do to our creator, we thank Swami Kriyananda.

And, to all our friends and family who encouraged and supported us through the years.

Bless all of you for helping us to share the light and love of these great saints with pilgrims everywhere.

Bibliography

The American Standard Version, *The Holy Bible*, 1901.

Appleton, Robert, *The Catholic Encyclopedia*, Volume IX, 1910, Online Edition 1999, Kevin Knight, www.newadvent.org.

Belford, Ros, & Martin Dunford, & Celia Woolfrey, *Italy: The Rough Guide*, Rough Guides, Ltd. London, 1999.

Cruz, Joan Carroll, *The Incorruptibles*, Tan Books and Publishers, Inc., Rockford, Illinois, 1977.

Gillman, Helen & Stefano Cavedoni, et al., *Lonely Planet: Italy*, Lonely Planet Publications, Victoria, Australia, 2000.

International Bible Society, *The Holy Bible, New International Version*, 1984.

Lintner, Valerio, *A Traveller's History of Italy*, Interlink Books, New York, 1998.

Macmitchell, Melanie, *Sacred Footsteps: A Traveler's Guide to Spiritual Places of Italy & France*, Opal Star Press, Encinitas, California, 1991.

Thurston, Herbert J. & Donald Attwater (eds.), *Butler's Lives of the Saints*, Christian Classics, Allen, Texas, 1996.

Wright, Kevin J., *Catholic Shrines of Western Europe: A Pilgrim's Travel Guide*, Liguori, Missouri, 1997

SAINTS

BLESSED ANGELA OF FOLIGNO
Lachance, Paul O.F.M., (trans.), *Angela of Foligno: Complete Works*, Paulist Press, Mahwah, New Jersey, 1993.

ST. ANTHONY OF PADUA
Jarmak, Claude M. OFM Conv., *If You Seek Miracles: Reflections of Saint Anthony of Padua*, Edizioni Messaggero, Padova, Italy, 1998.

BLESSED BONAVENTURE OF POTENZA
Vassalo, Francis Xavier, *Blessed Bonaventure of Potenza: Glorius Son of St. Francis of Assisi*, Monastery of St. Francis, Ravello, Italy, 1982.

St. Catherine of Bologna

Guigni, Guido, (rev.), *The Saint: A Short Life of St. Catherine of Bologna*, (Booklet), Corpus Domini Sanctuary, Bologna, Italy.

St. Catherine de' Ricci

Agresti, D.Di, & G. Zaninelli, *Catherine De' Ricci: A Profile, (Booklet)*, Prato, Italy.

Di Agresti, Domenico (ed.) &. Jennifer Petrie (Trans), *St. Catherine de' Ricci: Selected Letters*, Dominican Sources, Oxford, 1985.

St. Catherine of Siena

Ferretti, Lodovico, *Saint Catherine of Siena*, Edizioni Cantagalli, Siena, Italy, 1996.

O'Driscoll, O.P. Mary, (ed.), *Catherine of Siena: Passion for the Truth, Compassion for Humanity*, New City Press, Hyde Park, New York, 1995.

Curtayne, Alice, *Saint Catherine of Siena*, Tan Books and Publishers, Inc., Rockford, Illinois, 1980.

Noffke, O.P. Suzanne, (trans.), *Catherine of Siena: The Dialogue*, Paulist Press, New York, 1980.

St. Clare of Assisi

Miller, O.S.F., Ramona, *In the Footsteps of Saint Clare: A Pilgrim's Guide Book*, The Franciscan Institute, St. Bonaventure, New York, 1993.

Bartoli, Marco, & Sister Frances Teresa O.S.C., (trans.), *Clare of Assisi*, Franciscan Press, Quincy, Illinois, 1989.

St. Clare of the Cross

Sala, P. Stefano O.S.A., *St. Clare of the Cross of Montefalco Augustinian*, (booklet) Ediz. Monastero Agostiniano Santa Chiara, Terni, Italy,

St. Dominic of Bologna

Drane, Augusta Theodosia, *The Life of Saint Dominic*, Tan Books and Publishers, Inc., Rockford, Illinois, 1988.

St. Francis of Assisi

Goulet, O.F.M. Xavier, McInally, O.F.M. Ciaran, Wood, O.F.M. Joseph, *The Basilica of Saint Francis: A Spiritual Pilgrimage*, (booklet) Casa Editrice Francescana, Assisi, 1994.

Canonici, Luciano, *The Land of Saint Francis: Umbria and Surroundings*, Edizioni Plurigraf, Terni, Italy, 1987.

Desbonnets, P. Théophile, *Assisi in the Footsteps of Saint Francis*, Edizioni Porziuncola, Santa Maria degli Angeli, Italy,1993.

The Shrine of La Verna, (booklet), Shrine of La Verna, Italy.

Ricci, Teobaldo, *Historical Background and Spirituality of "Le Celle" of Cortona*, Editrice Grafica L'Etruria, Cortona, Italy, 1994.

ST. IGNATIUS OF LOYOLA

Purcell, Mary, *St. Ignatius Loyola: The First Jesuit*, Loyola University Press, 1981.

Forbes, F.A., *Saint Ignatius Loyola: Founder of the Jesuits*, Tan Books and Publishers, Inc., 1998.

Pollen, J.H., Marie Jutras (trans), *The Catholic Encyclopedia, Vol. VII*, Online Edition Kevin Knight, 1999.

O'Neal, Norman, S.J., Rev., *The Life of St. Ignatius of Loyola*, Le Moyne College, http://web.lemoyne.edu/~bucko/V_IGNAT.html.

ST. JOSEPH OF COPERTINO

Pastrovicchi, Angelo, O.M.C., Fr., *Saint Joseph of Copertino*, Tan Books and Publishers, Inc., 1980.

Parisciani, Gustavo, O.F.M., Nevin Hammon, O.F.M. (trans), *The Flying Saint: The Life of St. Joseph of Copertino*, 1968.

ST. LEOPOLD MANDIĆ

Bernardini, P.E., *Leopoldo Mandić Saint of Reconciliation*, Sanctuary of St. Leopoldo Mandić, 1989.

BLESSED MARGARET OF METOLA

Bonniwell, Father William R., O.P., *The Life of Blessed Margaret of Castello*, TAN Books and Publishers, Inc. and IDEA, Inc., Madison Wisconsin, 1983.

ST. PHILIP NERI

Matthews, Fr. V.J., *Saint Philip Neri: Apostle of Rome and Founder of the Congregation of the Oratory*, Tan Books and Publishers, Inc., 1984.

ST. PIO OF PIETRELCINA (PADRE PIO)

D'Apolito, Padre Alberto, *Padre Pio of Pietrelcina: Memories Experiences Testimonials*, Edizioni "*Padre Pio da Pietrelcina*" San Giovanni Rotondo, Italy, 1986.

Da Ripabottoni, Allessandro & Gerardo Di Flumeri, *Guide to the Shrine of Our Lady of Grace and Padre Pio's Friary*, (booklet), Editions "Padre Pio of Pietrelcina" Our Lady of Grace Capuchin Friary, San Giovanni Rotondo, Italy, 1987.

Da Ripabottoni, Allessandro, *Guide to Padre Pio's Pietrelcina*, (booklet), Editions "Padre Pio of Pietrelcina" Our Lady of Grace Capuchin Friary, San Giovanni Rotondo, Italy, 1987.

ST. RITA OF CASCIA

Sicardo, Fr. Joseph, O.S.A., *St. Rita of Cascia: Saint of the Impossible*, Tan Books and Publishers, Inc., Rockford, Illinois, 1990.

ST. VERONICA GIULIANI

Knox, Oliver, Dr. (trans.), *Saint Veronica Giuliani: The Purgatory of Love*, (Booklet), Centro Studi Veronichiano, Città di Castello, Italy, 1983.

Index

About the Authors

James and Colleen Heater have combined their interest in the lives of the saints and their love of travel to create a unique series of spiritual travel guides. As longtime practitioners of yoga, the Heaters teach classes on meditation and inspirational music as members of a spiritual community in Northern California. Their honeymoon to Italy in 1998 evolved into a journey of pilgrimage and sparked the idea for writing travel guides to sacred destinations. Since then they have written and published pilgrimage guides to Italy and France, with plans for adding Spain and India to the collection.

Colleen's professional background includes working as a licensed marriage and family therapist, specializing in addiction and codependency, while offering the opportunity for spiritual renewal to her clients. Colleen has lived and traveled throughout Europe for both pleasure and pilgrimage, and is currently devoting her time to writing and promotion for Inner Travel Books.

James, a licensed architect, practices in both religious and secular design, with projects in America, Europe and India. His background in meditation and music—including being an accomplished guitarist—has prepared him to understand the subtle energies of some of the holiest shrines in Europe and Asia. With this base of knowledge, he has led guided tours to sacred places in the United States and Italy.